MAPPING THE TERRAIN OF THE HEART

MAPPING THE TERRAIN OF THE HEART

The Six Capacities that Guide the Journey of Love

Stephen Goldbart, Ph.D.
David Wallin, Ph.D.

ADDISON-WESLEY PUBLISHING COMPANY

Reading, Massachusetts ▲ Menlo Park, California ▲ New York
Don Mills, Ontario ▲ Wokingham, England ▲ Amsterdam ▲ Bonn
Sydney ▲ Singapore ▲ Tokyo ▲ Madrid ▲ San Juan
Paris ▲ Seoul ▲ Milan ▲ Mexico City ▲ Taipei

Excerpt from "Little Gidding" in *Four Quartets*, copyright 1943 by T. S. Eliot and renewed 1971 by Esme Valerie Eliot, reprinted by permission of Harcourt Brace & Company.

Many of the designations used by manufacturers and sellers to distinguish their products are claimed as trademarks. Where those designations appear in this book and Addison-Wesley was aware of a trademark claim, the designations have been printed in initial capital letters (e.g., Day-Timer).

A preliminary version of Chapter 1 appeared in *Tikkun*, vol. 5, no. 2.

Library of Congress Cataloging-in-Publication Data

Goldbart, Stephen.
    Mapping the terrain of the heart : the six capacities that guide the journey of love / Stephen Goldbart, David Wallin.
       p.   cm.
    Includes bibliographical references (p.   ) and index.
    ISBN 0-201-60865-0
    1. Love. 2. Interpersonal relations. 3. Man-woman relationships.
    4. Intimacy (Psychology) I. Wallin, David. II. Title.
HQ801.G58   1994
306.7--dc20   94-8326
                                                  CIP

Jacket design by Suzanne Heiser
Text design by Diane Levy
Set in 11-point Goudy by CopyRight, Inc.

2 3 4 5 6 7 -DOH-9998979695
Second printing, January 1995

Dedicated to the memory of
Dr. Paul Wallin
and
Rachel Goldbart

CONTENTS

ACKNOWLEDGMENTS

We wish to thank the many colleagues and friends who contributed to the evolution of this book. For their thoughtful reading of the manuscript in whole or in part: Jeannette Gurevitch, Carolyn Miller, Deborah Osnowitz, Illana Schatz, and in particular, Maggie Rochlin and Dr. Lillian B. Rubin. We also are indebted to Michael Lerner, editor of *Tikkun*, who first published our article "Mapping the Terrain of the Heart"; Geri Thoma, our agent, who read that article and urged us to develop our ideas at book length; Nancy Miller, executive editor at Addison-Wesley, who saw the book's potential and nurtured it; Meg Fry, whose editorial assistance moved the manuscript along; Doris Ober, whose extraordinary contributions in the final stretch helped give the book its finished form; and Dr. Lloyd Kamins, Catherine Kamins, LCSW, Michael Sheiner, LCSW, and Dr. Laurance Kaplan, our colleagues at Marin Psychotherapy Institute, all of whom provided steadfast support and encouragement. Finally, we want to express our appreciation to our patients (and to some of our friends) from whose "love stories" we've learned so much—and whose words and histories we've enlisted to illustrate the ideas at the heart of this book.

Each of us also has separate debts of gratitude to acknowledge: I, David Wallin, have many to thank. Heading my list of those most deserving acknowledgment is my beloved Linda Lassman Beard. To me she gave unstinting love, sweet support, patience, and inspiration. To this book she gave her uncanny insight and an invaluably true and critical eye and ear.

Then there are old friends to thank: Dr. Michael Blumlein, physician, metaphysician, and novelist, whose reading of the book's first chapters was a specific help and whose enthusiastic encouragement was a boon from start to finish; Nina Wise, artist, teacher, writer, who also gave the early chapters a reading that proved helpful—and who predicted confidently that the *Tikkun* article would become a book; Laurie Cohen, psychotherapist, whose personal and editorial support to me during this project were an ongoing asset; Dan Goldensohn, close pal and leader of the band, whose love and intelligence could always be counted on; Dr. David Socholitszky and Sandy Niemann, for their kindness and lucidity; and Lloyd Kamins, Michael Sheiner, Dr. Kathryn Frank, Sandra Schindler, and Tina Chase, all of whom offered their experience.

My mother, Freda, and my brother, Michael, were advocates and occasional editors throughout the project. For that—and their lifelong love—I thank them.

I also wish to express special gratitude to Dr. Beate Lohser, Melinda Marmer, and Dr. Philip Spielman.

I, Stephen Goldbart, would first like to thank my wife, Estelle Frankel. Without her continual support and encouragement my participation in this book project would have been virtually impossible. She has been my muse, my critic, my editor. She has read and reread (ad nauseum) this manuscript and provided invaluable advice. She has put up with my reclusiveness and moodiness. Throughout it all she has been a compassionate and loving partner.

I would like to acknowledge the tolerance of my daughter, Miriam, and my son, Elan. Elan, whose first two years of life corresponded with the writing of this book, has been a joy and at times an inspiration to my work. My sister, Dr. Dorothy Clark, English professor and poet, has also been a source of moral and intellectual support. My father, Meyer Goldbart, has been an unconditional source of support and encouragement.

I would like to acknowledge the love and sustenance of my close friends and colleagues Dr. Adam Duhan, physician and satirist, and Dr. Andrew Condey, psychologist and wilderness guide. Like my family, they have encouraged me when I was troubled and enjoyed with me the triumphs along the way. Thanks also to Dr. Joel Crohn, psychologist and writer, whose friendship and help was much appreciated. And at the Solano Center, Dr. Nadine Payn and Dr. Michael Grey provided interest and encouragement.

Finally, I want to thank all of my consultees and colleagues, a wonderful, critical audience, who gave many of their own ideas for this project.

PREFACE

*P*assionate romantic love that lasts is both infinitely desirable
and infinitely problematic—a seductive promise, but an elusive
one. We hope for so much from love: happiness, fulfillment,
sometimes even salvation. Yet the complexities of an actual relationship can turn love into an emotional labyrinth. Attempting
to make our way, many of us grapple with questions like these:

▲ Is it realistic to expect sexuality to remain satisfying over
the course of a long-term relationship?

▲ To what extent, in an intimate relationship, can we expect
to satisfy our independent needs while also remaining close
to our partner?

▲ Is it wiser to settle for a love relationship that is merely
"good enough" or to search for one closer to our ideal?

▲ How much disappointment in or anger toward our partner is too much? How much should we tolerate before
deciding that a relationship is not worth preserving?

▲ What conclusions can we draw when our current relationship seems to repeat the past?

▲ How can we accept the changes in our individual identity—
and sometimes the sacrifices required—when we commit
ourselves to a long-term relationship?

Understandably, we're tempted to look for answers to these questions wherever we can find them. The culture offers a collection of contradictory clues, a collage of other people's prescriptions and impressions. To look outside ourselves is a natural impulse, but success in love may ultimately depend on doing just the opposite.

Although we may be only dimly aware of it, each of us is guided (or misguided) in our intimate relationships by an internal map. As uniquely personal as our signature, this inner map is composed of our deepest and most influential images of ourselves and others. It is the product and the record of our history in love from childhood onward, registered in the core of our being as a series of emotionally charged impressions and stories-with-a-moral.

Originating in the particulars of our past, the inner map shapes our present and future. It determines our desires and fears, our realistic and unrealistic expectations of a lover or mate—and it can lead us to fulfillment or doom us to failure. When we are puzzled about a current interaction in love and where to take it, we unconsciously turn inward, where our own idiosyncratic map provides an interpretation and a sense of direction. But this map of ours—created always from limited personal experience—is invariably incomplete and frequently downright misleading.

Ideally, the map within each of us would be a work-in-progress, capable of representing the terrain of the heart more and more accurately as our experiences in love accumulate. In reality, however, the images of the inner map register most tellingly—and with the most lasting consequences—in the early years of childhood. Thus the map we use to orient ourselves as adults is often outdated. But like a love story whose ending has yet to be written, the map's images *can* continue to evolve.

The key (without which we are lost) is to recognize that we have all been mapmakers—and that, for better or worse, we are also made by our map. This insight lies at the foundation of the most current, influential, and effective theory therapists now use to help individuals and couples with problems in love. This perspective on the internal mapping of interpersonal experience is called Object Relations theory.[1]

The power of this theory stems from its merging of two previous approaches to understanding love, each of which, on its own, was incomplete. The psychology of the individual helped therapists understand the lover. Systems theory, the psychology of individuals in interaction, helped them understand the couple. Object Relations gives them a bridge between the two: the individual's internal map of the interpersonal world. Our book is a synthesis of all these ideas applied to the puzzle of love and an attempt to answer the six questions posed above.

*I*t would be only a slight exaggeration to say that the two of us have carried on to this day a conversation about love that began shortly after we first met at a graduate school faculty meeting in 1978. Originally we talked about the complexities of our own relationships with women. But as we began to practice and teach together, the dialogue about our own lives in love expanded beyond the personal.

The great majority of the people who enlisted our help as therapists were troubled by difficulties in their love relationships. Many of these men and women were burdened with deep ambivalence or fear. Some had problems beginning any relationship; others could hardly enjoy the relationships they had begun. Some found themselves quickly disappointed, falling too easily out of love or fighting for control with their partner as if love were a deal and they were wary of yielding the upper hand. Others wondered why it was so hard to keep their sexual passion alive: Was there something frightening about the intimacy of a sustained involvement? Or did time and familiarity always rob a relation-

1. The term *object relations* arises from Freud's original use of the term *object*: any thing or person with which a human being is emotionally involved or invested. For example, the infant's first objects might include the mother, the mother's breast, and the teddy bear.

ship of its erotic excitement? Still others were repeatedly frustrated to find themselves with partners who seemed unable to return their love.

As therapists we were moved whenever the individuals and couples we had come to know and care for were able to make their way to the other side of these difficulties—from ambivalent withdrawal to closeness, from persistent conflict to reconciliation, from disappointment to renewed desire. We shared in their pleasure when they spoke with relief—and sometimes excitement—about finally being in a romantic relationship that they felt was really working.

Later the two of us would discuss what had led these individuals and couples to feel that their relationships "worked." Sometimes, resolving the problems that had brought them to therapy was enough to generate this feeling. Sometimes the feeling came from a couple's new confidence that together they could weather whatever future difficulties might confront them. These were couples who spoke, understandably, with relief.

But the couples who spoke with excitement helped us to see that the happiest, most complete partnerships in love all seemed to be characterized by the recurrence of two experiences: passion and tenderness. When a couple experienced both regularly, the partners usually felt that they had hit the romantic jackpot. These two aspects of romantic love were apparently central to the satisfaction a relationship could bring.

Passion is kin to desire, tenderness to affection. In passion we feel transported, in tenderness we are present. When we love with tenderness we are more aware of our partner; when we love with passion we are at least as aware of ourselves. The culmination of passion is ecstasy and/or orgasm, while tenderness may evoke tears, then security or contentment. Tenderness involves the impulse to nurture and protect—and to be nurtured and protected. Passion involves the impulse to possess and be possessed.

Of course, there can be tender passion and passionate tenderness. A tender desire to protect can turn passionate or even ferocious if our partner is threatened. Listening to the individuals and couples with whom we worked, we came to regard recurrent experiences of passion and tenderness as practically defining those love relationships that were the most fulfilling. But what made such relationships possible?

In part, our curiosity had to do with our desire to know more about "peak experiences" in love. But as therapists committed to helping people overcome their difficulties and inhibitions in love, our interest was also broader. If passion and tenderness were indeed the signature experiences of those relationships that worked best, then identifying the pathways to passion and tenderness might help many people navigate love's labyrinth.

Early in this century Freud scandalized the Western world by asserting that human beings are lovers—erotic beings—virtually from birth. Without using the words *passion* and *tenderness*, he nonetheless pointed to the splitting apart of these twin currents in love as the root of suffering in many "neurotic" personalities: "Where they love," he wrote, "they do not desire. Where they desire, they do not love." We owe a considerable debt to Freud, but our approach to understanding romantic love differs from his in that we are just as interested in identifying the opportunities to love as the obstacles. If we want to answer one question it is this: What makes it possible for people to love, in a lasting way, with passion and tenderness?

For more than a decade, we considered our own experiences and those of the individuals and couples who trusted us enough to disclose the intimate details of their lives in love: their wishes, fears, and fantasies, what they thought and felt and did. We also took advantage of the accumulated experience and reflection of many other therapists and researchers in the area of intimate relationships. And because the capacity to love originates in childhood—human beings are social animals—we studied the observational and clinical literature on early psychological development.

Finally, this is what we concluded: From the cradle onward, human beings have the potential to deepen their capacity to love.

But the emotional education that makes such deepening possible is unavoidably complex because loving is a many-faceted ability. To fall and remain in love, passionately and with tenderness, all of us must develop and make use of six distinct psychological capacities, each of which plays a different role in lasting romantic love:

▲ *Erotic involvement*, which enables us to experience our sexuality with others not only as a source of pleasure but also as a mode of emotional connection, communication, and self-knowledge.

▲ *Merging*, which enables us to be close to others without feeling endangered by the possibility of losing our sense of identity, control, or autonomy.

▲ *Idealization*, which enables us to find (that is, partly to discover and partly to imagine) our romantic ideal in the person we have come to love.

▲ *Integration*, which enables us to remain in touch with our loving feelings even while disappointed in or angry at those we love.

▲ *Refinding*, which enables us to experience in our current love relationship the inevitable echoes of earlier loves—and to enjoy what is positive in this partial revival of the past while tolerating or mastering what is negative.

▲ *Self-transcendence*, which enables us to enlarge our sense of personal identity to include the couple (or the family) of which we are now a part.

To understand these six capacities is to understand a great deal about love—for they give us a framework that answers more questions about love than any other theory we know. The six capacities are at the heart of this book; a separate chapter is devoted to each one.

Taken together, all six capacities can be seen as a sequence of pathways through love's labyrinth. Whether we choose to follow a particular pathway with easy confidence or avoid it out of fear is determined by the images that characterize our individual mapping of the heart's terrain.

The psychology of love has been explored by several generations of psychoanalysts and psychologists. Freud pioneered this work by investigating the area of human sexuality: the territory of the body in love. Indeed, he went much further, and what he learned shaped most of the exploration that followed. Margaret Mahler, Otto Kernberg, Martin S. Bergmann, Ethel Person, and others have also made crucially significant contributions to the way we understand love. Their discoveries are woven into our discussion of each of the six capacities.

Our thinking about love as a mapping of six capacities evolved in many contexts. The most important were weekly seminars for experienced psychotherapists that we've conducted in the San Francisco Bay area since 1982. The therapists who participated in these seminars were invaluable in helping us clarify our thinking. While their enthusiasm suggested the potential broad value of applying the map metaphor to love, these therapists also suggested some possible limitations.

Given the subject matter, it came as no surprise that our ideas evoked discussions with seminar members that were highly charged with personal feeling—theirs and ours. We were challenged, as two male, heterosexual therapists, to examine our perspective on the differing experiences of men and women in love. Especially when it came to sexuality, issues of masculinity and femininity, and the impact of gender on the capacity for intimacy, we found we needed to look very closely at the biases and assumptions woven invisibly into our particular viewpoints as men. We believe that what we (sometimes painfully) learned is reflected in what we've written.

Several therapists asked if our ideas about love were relevant only to heterosexual lovers. This was a difficult question to answer. Because our view of romantic love arose mainly out of our thinking about love between men and women, so our framework seemed most likely to fit the experience of heterosexuals. But while heterosexual and homosexual romance may differ, we're inclined to believe that they also overlap considerably—and, therefore, that the ideas in this book might well be of use to gay men and lesbians.

In a similar vein, we were asked if our framework for understanding love would be universally relevant to all lovers, regardless of ethnicity or socioeconomic class. While this book does not directly address such issues, we recognize the powerful impact of both factors: regardless of the inner capacities of the lover, there are real external influences that also shape the fate of love relationships. For the most part, however, we have left the discussion of such influences to other writers and researchers whose work is aimed specifically at understanding these important social realities.

This issue of relevance was raised repeatedly. To which lovers did our ideas apply? Were we speaking only about people currently living together in committed, long-term relationships? Or were we offering an account of love that might have meaning for others living on their own or moving from one relationship to another?

The conception of love as a sequence of capacities that can be developed and deepened is both useful and true to the facts—for most human beings with a desire to love. More specifically, the framework we present is relevant not only to individuals and couples trying to make their romantic relationships work but also to people living outside such relationships. For the same capacities that enable us to love others also allow us to accept ourselves and enjoy the range of human relationships that are *not* romantic.

Like the collaboration that resulted in this book, nearly every emotionally charged relationship can be seen as an ongoing journey. Without guaranteeing a happy ending, the book provides a guide for better understanding the journey and more consciously influencing its outcome.

A cautionary note: Books on intimacy risk confronting their readers with a romantic standard that is hard to live up to. It's all too easy to feel discouraged or inadequate when faced with visions of ideal love against which actual experience pales. In framing love as six capacities, we don't intend to set up Olympian standards of romantic performance. It is our hope, rather, to bring into view the full range of experiences that loving makes possible: the risks and difficulties, but also the challenges and opportunities.

MAPPING THE TERRAIN OF THE HEART

The Inner Map, the Six Capacities, and the Role of Defenses in Love

Consider the experience of a couple—call them Adam and Rachel—whose early "made-for-each-other" attraction had so declined into disillusionment and contention that their marriage of five years was threatened. Adam, a thirty-five-year-old health program director, and Rachel, an attorney of the same age, finally sought therapy when the tension and emotional distance between them spilled into the bedroom, turning sex into a battleground. Rachel's growing sexual frustration was causing her to doubt her feelings of love for Adam. She saw her recent difficulty in achieving orgasm as the frustrating result of what she euphemistically characterized as Adam's "lack of sexual stamina." Although Adam believed that his wife's frustration was a result of *her* inability to give up control, he found himself feeling increasingly inadequate and unmanly. He blamed Rachel for his feelings of self-doubt and accused her of "undermining his masculinity." Caught in a downward spiral that burdened sex with increasing anxiety, Adam and Rachel each felt helplessly angry, guilty, and disparaged by the other.

The difficulties this couple faced are by no means unique. Most of us who have fallen in love start with high hopes and wind up eventually confronting doubt and pain. Early in a relationship, the dream of passionate romantic love that lasts seems to be within reach. Far too often, however, this dream is displaced by frustrating patterns that prevent relationships like Adam and Rachel's from remaining *both* sexually and emotionally fulfilling.

How can these patterns be understood? Just as important, how can they be changed?

THE INNER MAP

The psychological mapmaking so crucial to love begins when we are very young. Psychoanalysts call this process "internalization" because it involves making experiences from the external world part of our internal reality. For example, when a baby is lovingly held and nurtured by her mother on many different occasions, her repeated experience of secure intimacy will be internalized. That is, it will be imprinted on her inner map as a highly evocative image: a powerful meshing of memory ("Mommy holds and feeds me"), sensation ("her body's so warm and cuddly"), and emotion ("I feel perfectly cared for, completely safe"). Along with the many other images that will become part of her personal mapping of the heart's terrain, this one will define for her what it means to love and be loved.

Our most compelling images of love are usually reflections of our very first relationships—primarily with our parents, but also with others who played a significant role in our childhood. These influential relationships include those we observe (our parents' relationship, most important) as well as those we participate in. The inner map can be modified by adult experience, but it is our early images of intimacy that initially shape our capacity to love.[1]

1. Our map is made through the internalization of our experiences in love. Three factors affect the extent to which these experiences register as images that continue to influence us: How early in our lives did the experiences occur? As a rule, the earlier the experiences, the more influential. How prolonged were they? Usually, the more prolonged, the more influential. And how traumatic? Some occurrences of physical or sexual abuse, for example, need only have happened once in order to register as profoundly influential images.

Imagine a little girl who repeatedly experiences her father as a source of support. His enthusiasm encourages her in school, his pleasure in her athletic ability helps her feel good about her body, and so on. These positive experiences all register as emotionally charged images and accumulate (along with many others), giving her inner map its personal stamp.

But later this little girl notices that when she idealizes her father he becomes uncomfortable. When she treats him like her hero, he teases her or becomes withdrawn. The images of these not-so-positive experiences also become part of her map—and they will influence her as an adult when it comes to her capacity to love.

The first set of images might incline her to regard a man she cares for as a source of appreciation and support. Consequently, she might yearn for closeness. The second set of images, however, could incline her to keep quiet rather than express her feelings of love or admiration and risk the teasing or withdrawal of a man she cares for.

The story of our own life in love is shaped significantly by our inner map. Briefly, the process unfolds as follows: First, our experiences in relationships that matter to us are "recorded" in the form of emotionally charged images. Second, these uniquely personal images collect to form the internal map that represents for each of us the external world of intimate relationships. Third, this inner map gives us our own idiosyncratic orientation in love. It tells us what love is and what it can be. It establishes our expectations of ourselves and others in love. It influences our reactions to and interpretations of current and past experiences in love. And most important, it determines how freely we make use of the six innate abilities that enable human beings to fall and remain in love.

But this summary leaves out a crucial piece of the picture. The inner map wields such power precisely because its influence is usually invisible and forgotten. The story of Adam and Rachel will help make this point more vivid.

The Invisible Map

When their romance was still new, a conflict developed between Adam and Rachel that nearly undid them as a couple. Adam was writing a high-stakes grant proposal whose success would ensure that the health program he administered would flourish; without it, the program might not survive. Adam confided to Rachel that writing the proposal was bringing him to the edge of panic. Full of emotion, he detailed his difficulties with the project. Rachel wanted to be sympathetic, but she couldn't help feeling uneasy and a little put-upon. Why was he telling her so much so soon about his vulnerability? What did he really want from her? When Adam picked up on this undertone, he was angry and baffled. These were the ingredients of their first fight.

Both Rachel and Adam felt that their reactions were entirely justified. Neither of them could see at the time that these reactions were virtually dictated by the imagery of the invisible map each brought—unknowingly—to their every intimate relationship.

When Adam spontaneously attempted to enlist Rachel as a kind of consultant, he was unconsciously repeating with her (or trying to repeat) the safest connection he'd found with his mother. A critical woman and successful professor, his mother had seemed most available to Adam when she could help him with his schoolwork. Thus, Adam's behavior was entirely in keeping with what his map suggested would work in a close relationship with a woman. No wonder he was dismayed by Rachel's reaction.

But when Rachel became uneasy with Adam's need, she too was responding according to the imagery of her inner map. From the time she was very young, Rachel had felt helpless and ashamed at her inability to soothe her conspicuously needy mother. At the same time, Rachel's father, a seductively powerful but aloof businessman, had repeatedly demonstrated his contempt for the needs of others. He saw neediness as an imposition and a sign of weakness. With this history, Rachel's discomfort with Adam's plea for help becomes more understandable.

Like Rachel and Adam, all of us are profoundly influenced by the images of our invisible map. Over and over again, we project these images onto those we love. Our eyes may be fixed on our partner, but what we see is often the projection of an internal image. Our projections, however, *feel* exactly like perceptions. This is why we so easily confuse internal images with external realities—and why we can mistake the past for the present. Past loves unavoidably impinge on present ones, so long as the influence of the inner map remains invisible or forgotten.

Making the Invisible Visible

There are various ways in which our invisible map may become visible to us. Psychotherapy is conducted in part with this aim in mind. But outside the structured context of therapy, in our individual love relationships, we also have the opportunity to become aware of aspects of our inner map that are usually invisible to us. Whenever our reactions to our partner don't fit the facts, we may wonder if these reactions don't have more to do with our internal world than our external reality.

Consider the experience of Emma, a twenty-six-year-old journalist struggling to make her new marriage work. She and her husband are out together on a Friday night, hoping for a respite from the tension at home. They've just left a movie theater and are crossing the street together, both relieved to be absorbed in conversation about the film. Facing her husband, Emma is blind to an onrushing car headed straight for them, but her husband sees the danger in time and pulls Emma out of harm's way. Suddenly aware of the peril from which he's just rescued her, she reacts to him with. . . rage. At the curb after their near-catastrophe she yells at her husband, "Can't you ever let me take care of myself?" She knows her reaction doesn't fit the facts.

This is what eventually came to light: Unaware of it, Emma had been responding to her husband in terms of her most disturbing images of her parents' marriage. She had seen her mother as controlled and infantilized by her oversolicitous father. In Emma's view, her father was responsible for her mother's bitterness over having never realized her own potential. With shock, Emma now realizes that she's been angrily acting out with her husband her fear of reliving her mother's life. The blatant inappropriateness of her reaction to her husband's help opened her eyes to her destructive conviction, based on her parents' example, that a man's help is always disabling.

Like Emma, we may become aware of the invisible map when our emotional response to our partner seems inappropriate. We may notice that we respond too intensely, or stubbornly, or contradictorily, from one moment to the next. Or, like Emma's, our response may simply be incompatible with the behavior that stimulated it.

One man reported feeling intruded upon whenever his girlfriend cooked dinner for him. He enjoyed the food, so his reaction baffled him until he realized that in his family, as he put it, "love was a weapon": if his parents loved him, he felt he had no choice but to do as they wished. Distorted by the projection of these images, his girlfriend's cooking (which he saw as an expression of her love) became a gun to his head, a demand that he submit to her will.

Sometimes the map becomes visible after its imagery has been played out in one relationship after another. When we travel the same road often enough, it starts to look familiar—especially if it always winds up in a dead end. Before Rachel met Adam, she had been involved with a series of men who proved to be less interested in her than she was in them. Only after repeating this pattern (more often than she was comfortable admitting) did she recognize it as a replay of her relationship with her emotionally unavailable father.

Usually we are better off when we have a clear view of the outdated images that we bring to our relationships. But even when our invisible map becomes visible, its influence can be hard to shake. When we're traveling through unfamiliar territory we can be hugely reluctant to give up our only map—even an old one that has sometimes proven unreliable.

Remaking the Map

Our inner map can be seen as a work-in-progress that is gradually remade by new experiences in love, but it sometimes resists revision.

What is new is unfamiliar. Human beings seem to be more comfortable with the known than the unknown. Consequently, even when we're aware that our views of love derive from old experience, we may be reluctant to update them. One woman, for example, found it very difficult to give up the unhappy conviction that no man could be trusted. Her father had abandoned her family when she was young, and her suspicion of men was his legacy. Although she had plenty of evidence to contradict her mistrust, she was inclined to discount it rather than risk venturing onto unfamiliar and potentially dangerous terrain.

There is a second, less intuitive reason why we are reluctant to alter the imagery of the internal map. For this map is more than a simple depiction of our experiences in love: in a very real psychological sense, it is an internal *reproduction* of the most important relationships we have had. Our allegiance to these inner images, with their full-blooded, emotionally three-dimensional quality, is virtually a matter of family loyalty. Giving up the old images of ourselves and others is very much like giving up the old relationships. When we make significant revisions in our inner map, we suffer a sense of loss that evokes pain and necessitates mourning. In order to love, therefore, we sometimes have to grieve.

But while our fears of change, disloyalty, and mourning tend to keep the old images in place, most of us have a strong urge to grow—and the old images can be very confining. Laid down early in our life, these images are like a shaky or cramped foundation that won't accommodate a house whose design is more expansive than the original.

We can't change the past relationships that gave our map its original form. But if we let others matter to us, if we let new experiences affect us, we can change our map. This opens the door to more new experience—and further transformations in our imagery of what love is and can be. And these revisions and transformations can deepen our capacity to love.

THE SIX CAPACITIES

What is called the capacity to love is actually a composite of six separate capacities that unfold sequentially in the course of our growing up (see box, page 10).

The Developmental Sequence

First to emerge is the capacity for *erotic involvement*. Virtually from birth, love relationships rest on the potential for pleasurable connection with others. This connection begins with the infant in the mother's arms and, years later, becomes the embrace of lovers—but the bedrock upon which it rests is this rudimentary capacity for bodily pleasure.

Next, there is the capacity for *merging* that enables lovers to feel safe while feeling close. Merging originates in the closest closeness we ever know: the oneness of mother and child in a communication that at times seems almost telepathic.

When the child becomes a toddler and wanders a little distance from the parent, the reassuring sense of oneness threatens to fracture. Now comes an early version of *idealization*. To rescue themselves from the helpless terror of separation, small children compensate with fantasies of perfection: they see themselves as invincible and their parents as their heroes. The child's fantasy of perfect parents is the first edition of the adult's fantasy of the perfect partner.

The capacity for *integration* is the hard-won reward of a "good enough" passage through the first few years of life.[2] With integration, the child's world is no longer either-or, good or bad: now it can be both. By making "mixed feelings" possible, integration enables the child to accept the painful reality that reality is never perfect. As adults, integration helps us accept our own imperfections and those of our partner.

---

2. D. W. Winnicott, the British pediatrician and psychoanalyst, wrote helpfully about the "good enough" mother. With this phrase he conveyed that parenting need not be perfect for children to thrive: it need only be "good enough."

Much later comes *refinding*, the capacity that determines how we cope in current relationships with the inevitable echoes of our past loves—including, most of all, the love we knew with our parents. Usually, adolescent love brings the first refinding, but all our subsequent love relationships also provoke a measure of refinding—or a reaction against it.

The last capacity, *self-transcendence*, is achieved only in adulthood and enables us to expand our sense of identity to include the couple or the family of which we're now a part. Self-transcendence can both heighten intimacy and lighten the sacrifices that a love relationship requires.

The six capacities compose the repertoire of abilities we bring to love. As we mature, the capacities we develop build one upon the other, like a pyramid with the capacity for erotic involvement at its base and the capacity for self-transcendence at its peak.

Every capacity has the potential to affect the others and, although the capacities have their earliest origins in the relationships of childhood, all six can continue to evolve throughout our life. The developmental sequence in which the capacities first appear is mirrored by the sequence in which they take center stage in an ongoing love relationship.

The Relationship Sequence: The Stages of Love

Love relationships unfold in three stages (see figure, page 13). Two partners fall in love, they become a couple, and their love deepens over time. To see how the six capacities emerge and affect the stages of an actual relationship, we'll return to the story of Adam and Rachel.

The First Stage: Falling in Love

No more than a few hours after they first met, both Rachel and Adam began to feel that they had found the perfect match. Weary of men unable to form deep or enduring relationships, Rachel was swept away by Adam's warmth and his comfort with physical and emotional closeness. He seemed soulful, strong, and caring. His compassionate commitment to helping others easily

THE SIX CAPACITIES

Capacity	Problems in Loving
Erotic Involvement	
To experience our sexuality with others not only as a source of pleasure but also as a mode of emotional connection and communication.	Sexual inhibition as reflected not only in behavior but also in restricted emotional contact, bodily pleasure, or fantasy.
Merging	
To be comfortably close to others without sacrificing our identity or autonomy.	Isolation from others, emotional withdrawal, or submerging oneself in compulsive involvements.
Idealization	
To find (that is, partly to discover and partly to imagine) our romantic ideal in the person we love.	Tendency to devalue those who might be loved. Envy and/or competitiveness undermine admiration. Feelings of unworthiness generate self-defeating involvements.
Integration	
To combine our positive and negative images of ourselves (and our positive and negative images of others) so that love is sustained in the face of frustration and disappointment.	Love relationships made unstable by oscillating all-good and all-bad images. Abandonment concerns complicate love.

Refinding

To experience in current love the echoes of past loves—enjoying what is positive while tolerating or mastering what is negative in this partial revival of the past.	Difficulty combining passion and tenderness in one relationship. Guilt and/or anxiety inhibit sexuality and assertiveness. Triangular involvements complicate love.

Self-Transcendence

To enlarge our sense of personal identity so that it includes the couple or family of which we are now a part—and to put the needs of our partner on a par with our own.	Relationship lacks a sense of fulfillment or meaning. Commitment without shared goals or lasting passion.

overshadowed her momentary concern that as a successful attorney she earned more than he did. In bed Adam's passion made Rachel feel desirable and secure. It freed her to experience her sexuality more fully than she ever had before. She felt that if she could make a life with him, she would be happy.

Adam was thrilled to have found in Rachel someone who was smart, sexy, and strong. He had been involved with and disappointed by a number of women whose sexual allure for him was eventually compromised by their emotional neediness. With these women he had felt called upon to play an unwanted parental or therapeutic role. He described his former partners as dependent, demanding, and intrusive. Inevitably, they reminded him of his mother, a university professor of psychology who treated him, he said, like a loved but uncontrollable research project.

Rachel was different. She was abundantly self-confident, independent, and successful. Here was a woman who wouldn't confront him with the criticism and struggles for control he had endured in previous relationships. Rachel's strength was a turn-on for him. She could take the lead in bed or she could be more passive. In either role she seemed to respond to his sexuality with the same unrestrained pleasure. Convinced that he had met his future wife, Adam moved with due speed to capture her heart.

It's an intoxicating trio of pleasures that enables us to fall in love: sexual passion, the feeling of oneness, and the hope that we've found the perfect partner. When the three capacities that make these experiences possible—erotic involvement, merging, and idealization—are strong enough, falling in love can be the blissful beginning of an ongoing involvement. But when one capacity or more are vulnerable, two partners who fall in love may never really become a couple.[3]

For Rachel and Adam, the excitement and comfort of their early passion made their sexuality feel like an unambiguous asset. Both of them had a capacity for erotic involvement that made sex a delicious pleasure, as well as a way to communicate and feel close. Sex, however, is not just sex: for better or worse, it is a magnet that draws to it the emotional conflicts that inevitably surface as a couple's intimacy deepens. As we'll see, the bedroom can also be a setting in which to resolve these same challenging conflicts. Unexpectedly, years after their first lovemaking, it was exactly this challenge that Adam and Rachel would face.

Yet falling in love was bliss. Both Adam and Rachel had well-developed capacities for merging and idealization. Both could enjoy

---

3. It's also true, however, that an especially strong development of some capacities can compensate for weakness in others. One partner, for example, may be sexually inhibited. But this same partner may be quite comfortable with merging and idealization. The rewards of a healthy exercise of these two capacities may tide him or her over—while the capacity for erotic involvement has time to develop. In the fairy tale "The Beauty and the Beast," we see a variation on this theme. It may have nothing to do with inhibition, but Beauty finds the Beast repulsive. We can read the gradual change in her feeling, from aversion to ardor, as the outcome of her idealization eventually kindling her capacity for erotic involvement.

feeling close and both could feel that in the other they had found the perfect mate: a dream come true.

But after falling in love with Rachel's strength and independence, Adam began to worry that she might be too cool and distant, not nurturing enough. While irresistibly drawn to Adam's warmth and openness, Rachel was suspicious that his rushing might signal weakness or a lack of self-confidence.

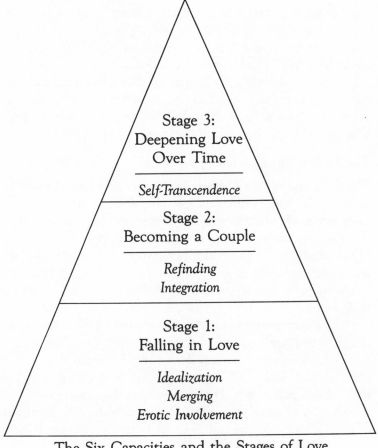

Stage 3:
Deepening Love
Over Time

Self-Transcendence

Stage 2:
Becoming a Couple

Refinding
Integration

Stage 1:
Falling in Love

Idealization
Merging
Erotic Involvement

The Six Capacities and the Stages of Love

Not uncommonly, men fear closeness and women fear separateness. Adam and Rachel (like many couples) reversed the gender stereotype: he was "merger hungry" and she was "merger wary." In nearly every other respect, however, the two of them felt uncannily alike: their sense of humor, their tastes, their values, all were comfortably shared. Each of them, moreover, experienced (and enjoyed) the admiration of the other, and both admired the other for qualities they felt they lacked in themselves.

These three advantages—the feelings of commonality, admiring the other, and being admired in turn—reflect exactly what many of us seek in our romantic ideal. Rachel and Adam might lose this feeling, might even feel they had fallen out of love, but when, early in the arc of a love affair, we feel we have found such a partner, idealization becomes a renewable resource. Adam and Rachel could later fall in love—again and again.

Not all partners are so fortunate. Idealization can not only get a relationship off the ground but also complicate it. For idealization entails the desire for a partner who is perfect roughly to the degree that we feel imperfect, and this can be a very problematic wish.

The Second Stage: Becoming a Couple

The more completely partners like Adam and Rachel know one another, the more difficult it becomes to maintain their initial idealization of each other. Integration becomes crucial now, for this capacity enables a couple's relationship to survive the waning of idealization. When the capacity for integration is poorly developed, partners may decide that a relationship that is no longer all good is really all bad—and they may be tempted to cut their losses.

Their respective capacities for integration enabled Rachel and Adam to weather the kinds of disappointment that always accompany long-term involvement. Both could be aware of the other's shortcomings without falling out of love. At the same time, both had enough patience and compassion for their own insecurities, jealousies, and unrealistic expectations to transform their fantasies of perfect love into the reality of an intimate, ongoing relationship. Having integrated a conception of the other's vulnerabilities, they were able to provide real support and nurturance.

A year after they met, Adam and Rachel married. Emotionally speaking, their honeymoon lasted for several years more. They even began to plan for a family. But outside their awareness, the ghosts of their pasts were gaining on them.

The capacity for refinding is key to understanding what occurred between Adam and Rachel and what occurs in many other couples. Because our inner map leads us unknowingly to superimpose the past on the present, refinding is nearly unavoidable. When what was most desirable in the intimacy of the past is refound in the present, our experience of love is enhanced. But when our past is laden with difficulty, refinding casts a long shadow over love.

In Rachel, Adam refound his strong and successful professor mother. What he hadn't bargained for was refinding his mother's critical, undercutting style and her difficulties in providing warmth and comfort. Adam felt that his mother identified him with his dad—a funny, likable, emotionally available man who had never found a career nor stood up to his wife. Initially, Adam saw Rachel as a "dream-come-true" solution to his plight with his mother. Rachel had his mother's strengths yet really believed in him and admired the person he had become. But as Rachel became more disillusioned, distant, and openly critical of Adam, many of his hidden insecurities emerged. It was as if he were reliving with Rachel his mother's coolness, her emotional withdrawal when he needed her, and worst of all, her depreciation of his masculinity.

For Rachel, Adam's warmth and generosity had seemed the perfect antidote to her experience with parents who were emotionally unavailable and self-absorbed. While openly critical of her father's cold dominance, however, Rachel secretly admired him and identified with his strength and competitiveness. Adam was nothing like him, for which she had been grateful. But now as she began to see Adam as needy, it was as though she found herself burdened again with her emotionally hungry mother.

Rachel began to see herself as superior to Adam—a view she justified, a little guiltily, on the basis of her higher salary and social status. Adopting the attitude of her admired father, she became progressively more distant and critical. She expected more "manliness" of Adam, more assertion, and less of his unbecoming wishes to "merge." So, she asked herself, why should it come as a surprise to him that I'm less turned-on, less orgasmic?

Conflicts and disillusionments like these can feel devastating. When our current relationship begins to feel like a rendezvous with the painful past, refinding is always in part the culprit. But the refinding of old difficulties, however painful, also gives us new opportunities to master them.

Adam and Rachel both realized their relationship was in trouble. Their present feelings of estrangement were an agonizing contrast to the love they had felt for one another not so very long ago. Until recently, it seemed, their sexual connection always enabled them to revive their feelings of closeness, even if temporarily. Now they were frightened at how far away from each other they felt—and how wary. Their earlier conversations about having a family seemed remote. Too guarded at first to confront the other directly, Adam and Rachel each found a safe place to talk about the crisis in their relationship.

Rachel began meeting with Liza, her younger sister. Liza had recently divorced a man who, she realized now, was very much like their father. The two sisters spoke about their parents in a way they never had before, and their views turned out to be sadly similar. Liza believed that she had married a man like their father for two reasons. She had been desperate to escape the suffocating dependency of their mother. Just as desperately, she had wanted to find, with a man as powerful as her father, the love and appreciation he had never been able to give her.

It was easy for Rachel to see herself in her sister. Although Liza's path out of their family was different from hers, Rachel became aware that she and her sister were driven by similar needs. Like Liza, Rachel had chosen a man to love in the hope that he would give her what her parents had not. Liza had always had a bit of a crush on Adam: she saw him as a nurturing man, strong but vulnerable. Now through her sister's eyes, Rachel was able to see Adam more clearly again for who he was, rather than as a stand-in for her mother or her father.

Meanwhile, Adam had spoken with his best friend, Nick, who happened to be a psychologist. It was Nick who had first introduced Adam to Rachel. Now Nick helped him see that while Rachel was definitely worth fighting for, she was also someone Adam needed to fight *with*. She wasn't his mother, he wasn't a kid. Adam wasn't entitled to demand payment from Rachel for his mother's unpaid IOUs from childhood—no matter how much hurt or unmet longing he still felt. But he also wasn't required to take Rachel's abuse. Nick's words did double duty: they enabled Adam both to begin to separate his image of Rachel from his image of his mother and to behave toward Rachel with more of the strength she had admired in her father.

Neither Rachel nor Adam understood all the details of their impasse. But both of them developed a healthy skepticism about what had previously been their own very entrenched positions. They were able to feel again that they wanted the relationship to work.

Sometimes only through the emotional emergencies brought on by refinding do we become aware of the influence of our inner map. Rachel and Adam began to acquire this awareness in the painful setting of a crisis that nearly drove them apart. Tentatively at first, both realized that they had been sleepwalking through old family dramas. But once they began to grapple with their internal ghosts, neither Adam nor Rachel needed to project them onto the other with such inflexible determination.

As the invisible barriers to their passion and tenderness dissolved, Adam and Rachel began to love, depend, and fight more freely than they had before. In this new atmosphere, their early idealization of one another was revived. They felt more committed, more "mated"—and they decided less than a year later to try to have a child.

The Third Stage: Deepening Love over Time

In love's third stage, we seem to want something more: a shared experience or project that can be realized only through the pooling of our own efforts with those of our partner. For many this desire can be met through starting a family; for others it may involve a collaborative venture like launching a business or remodeling a home. Sometimes the couple shares a commitment not to a project but to a practice, such as pursuing a spiritual path or ardently engaging in community activism. Ideally, the outcome of this joint effort is deeper love and involvement.

The third stage of a relationship is marked by a new awareness that broadening our sense of self requires sacrificing a measure of individuality. In the context of family or a comparable commitment, there is a re-ordering of the importance of "I" and of "we." Now we become capable of putting the needs of the relationship on a par with our own.

The capacity for self-transcendence enables us to meet the challenges of this stage of intimacy. Like Adam and Rachel, we may have struggled through hardships in love and achieved a shared sense of stability, acceptance, and mutual respect. There is now a deep appreciation for both our separate identities and the experiences we share as a couple. Ideally, we are able to use all five prior capacities as resources in love. We identify ourselves as a couple and are recognized as such (and hopefully supported) by our community.

Adam and Rachel's decision to have a child heralded their entry into this third stage of relationship. Both now had the desire to deepen their commitment and take on new risks to further what they hoped would be a lifetime of intimacy. They knew there would be challenges ahead. Their conscious struggle with the trials of refinding had strengthened their love. It had also alerted them to some of the emotional hazards that might complicate their experience of parenting. Would Adam find Rachel too cool and distant as a mother to their child? Would he experience Rachel's maternal preoccupation as a threat to their sexual relationship? Would Rachel's difficulties in temporarily relinquishing her career provoke her to resent their child? Could she let herself become more dependent upon Adam, as he assumed (at least for a time) the role of principal provider? Would they find ways of transcending the drudgery and routine of parenting to recapture their experience of passion as a couple?

The Stages of Love and the Fate of the Inner Map

Imagine a couple trying to find their way through a maze of streets in an unfamiliar city. The two of them are poring over their map—no, wait, they've got two maps, two different maps. For a time they seem to cooperate, comparing their maps to find some common ground between the two. As long as their progress through the city is reasonably pleasant, they can tolerate the contradictions between their maps, even finding some humor in their predicament. But after a few dead ends and too many circles that bring them to where they began, their good humor is exhausted. The conflict over whose map should prevail heats up. When it starts to rain, the battle is joined in earnest. There's even the risk that the two will decide to go their separate ways, both trusting their own map and rejecting the map of the other.

While we don't wish to trivialize the difficulties involved, this scenario represents roughly the situation partners confront in a love relationship. Usually, partners with maps that are wildly disparate don't join forces. When they do, their alliance is often stormy and/or short-lived. More commonly, the maps of two partners who fall in love have some overlap, which presages harmony in certain areas and the potential for conflict in others.

As partners move from one phase of relationship to the next, different areas of their maps are compared. Are their images of sexuality compatible? Does each partner have an equivalent capacity for erotic involvement? What about their images of closeness and boundaries? Does each partner have a similar capacity for merging? And so on.

For a couple's relationship to progress, their two maps (and the capacities they facilitate) need not be identical. But when two partners' maps in a particular area contain contradictory images, there is likely to be friction. This friction may be very productive or it may stall love's progress. For love to grow, there must be · some accommodation between the two differing maps. Over time, relationships that last usually revise the map of each partner, so that the couple's disparate imagery of love gradually becomes more similar.

Our original map is the uneven legacy of our prior experience in love, but later relationships can update and upgrade it, making new experiences possible, which register as fresh images and deepen our capacity to love. Unfortunately, there may be complications.

Foremost among these is our need to protect ourselves from the dangers represented in the cautionary imagery of our inner map. Perhaps these dangers have more to do with the past than the present. No matter—we usually react (consciously or otherwise) as though the threats were very real. Our self-protective reactions are called defenses; they inhibit our exercise of the six capacities and block new experience. Defenses can freeze the evolution of our inner map, keeping its imagery forever faithful to the past.

LOVE AND DEFENSES

Talking to her sister, Rachel was reminded of the summer camp story that had become a part of family lore. She was ten, her sister seven. The weeks at Camp Tawonga were their first ever away from their parents. Like many children, Rachel initially experienced camp as a nightmare: dark cabins, scary new kids, hikes that blistered her feet. In a panic she wrote to her parents about the plight she and her sister faced. When her counselor called her to the phone to speak to her father, Rachel's spirits soared: rescue was imminent. With relief she poured out the details of their misery, concluding, "Dad, it's just too hard!" Now, years later, she still remembers the long silence and the sting of his response: "You don't want to be a little crybaby, do you, Rachel? No one likes a crybaby."

It was as though the ground had dropped out from under her, but only at first. She suppressed what might have been a flood of tears, then turned herself inside out and became the little girl she thought her father wanted her to be—someone without needs, someone more like him.

Our defenses serve us well. When the alternative is to feel over-whelmed, our defenses may represent the best possible solution under what feel like impossible circumstances. Rachel's defenses kept her pain within manageable limits and enabled her to continue loving her father. But the same defenses that got her through this episode and others as a child became part of her style of self-protection as an adult. In certain settings these defenses were still useful. In others (we saw their impact on Rachel's marriage) they were more of an obstacle than a resource.

Self-Protection in Love: Price and Payoff

The individual defenses we use in love take many forms. A partial catalog: we may blame our partner, forget what distresses us, grow distant from uncomfortable feelings, deceive ourselves and/or change our sense of reality with drugs or alcohol. But whatever the form our defenses take in love, they usually have both a price and a hidden payoff.

The Price of Protection

Defenses generally enhance our sense of personal safety, but sometimes our defenses distort our perceptions of ourselves and others. Sometimes they blind us to certain aspects of reality. In love, the cost of self-protection is specific: defenses inhibit a healthy use of the capacities crucial to loving.

Suppose we've been hurt in love before and now we're fearful that our love won't be reciprocated. To deal with this fear in relation to a new partner, we may defensively mobilize an attitude of mistrust or depreciation. Our defenses inhibit our capacity for idealization: it's very difficult to idealize a partner we put down and mistrust. The price we pay for safety may be an inability to fall in love.

Rachel's example is another that illustrates the self-defeating consequences of self-protection. Rachel's denial of her dependent needs eventually interfered with her capacity to merge with Adam. Being close might evoke these needs that had proven dangerous in the past. The same denial of dependency also made it more difficult for her to idealize Adam—since he was tainted with the very neediness she found contemptible.

How heavy a price we pay for self-protection depends on the nature of the defenses we use and the level of flexibility associated with those defenses. Defenses that severely inhibit merging and idealization make it difficult for us to fall in love. Defenses that limit integration make it difficult to remain in love. As a rule, the more inflexible the defense, the higher the cost in love. Ideally, our defenses allow us to respond with flexibility, meaning we have them at our disposal but are not wed to them. We can protect ourselves in moments of perceived danger but lay down our arms, so to speak, when we feel secure again.

How do we decide whether the emotional danger in a relationship is "real" or "perceived"? Sometimes knowingly, but more often not, we compare our current experience with the relevant imagery of the inner map. When the old images are reassuring, it's easier to assess a current situation on its own merits—and to feel less threatened. But when the old images provoke anxiety, it's a signal (appropriate or not) to keep our defenses mobilized.

Hidden Payoffs

Defenses come up mainly to protect us from feelings of vulnerability. But they may also make possible the covert expression of deep-seated needs or fantasies of an aggressive or sexual nature.

Jordan, a twenty-nine-year-old building contractor, couldn't make up his mind about a woman. He'd fall in love, then become consumed with doubt and ambivalence. Over and over again, he backed out, just when he seemed on the verge of proposing. He wouldn't deny that he was afraid of commitment, but he would also rationalize his behavior. After all, there was nothing wrong with wanting to make sure his choice in marriage was the right one.

On the surface he seemed genuinely troubled by this pattern of interrupted involvement. What he could not admit to himself was his pleasure in leading a parade of women toward the altar and then abruptly withdrawing. In therapy Jordan eventually became aware that bringing women to the brink of marriage made him feel like a conqueror. Marriage, by contrast, filled him with fears of feeling weak, victimized, and controlled.

Jordan's defensive pattern was certainly self-protective, but it was covertly angry as well. Without being aware of it, he was "fighting back" against women who he feared would control and emasculate him if he ever married. The origins of this fear lay in Jordan's internal imagery of his parents' marriage and his mother's domination of his father.

Jordan paid a price for his defenses: he was frustrated, guilty, and ultimately lonely. But the hidden payoff—the intoxicating feeling of power—made it difficult for Jordan to relinquish his pattern of seduction and withdrawal, because it not only protected but also gratified him.

To the extent that these three influences—the need for protection, the price paid for it, and the hidden payoff—are unconscious, they are very difficult to master. The more we can recognize and understand the forms of self-protection that play a role in our relationships, the more we may begin to gain control of our defenses and defensiveness.

Individual Defenses and Interpersonal Knots

Just as each of us brings our inner map to a relationship, so we bring our own styles of self-protection. Invariably our defenses interact with those of our partner. This interplay generates complex *collusions* and *collisions* of defense.

Collusions

A "marriage" of defenses can both protect partners from their own individual fears and conceal the conflicts they may experience as a couple. Collusions of defense are useful when partners are falling in love, but they can be problematic later in a relationship. When a couple colludes, the individual defenses of one partner either mirror or mesh conveniently with those of the other.

Two partners, for example, may each habitually avoid their own problems rather than confront them. The collusion that results may keep the peace, at least in the short run. By enabling partners to steer clear of their conflicts and differences, a couple's collusion can stabilize their relationship,

A less stable collusion results when two partners have differing defenses that nonetheless mesh. For example, one partner may deal with anxiety by taking charge while the other may cope by yielding control. This lets partners temporarily avoid a power struggle. But defenses tend to polarize, and polarizations are inherently unstable.

Collisions

Each partner's defenses may provoke and intensify the other's, as Rachel and Adam's experience illustrates. As their defenses collided, however, Adam and Rachel could also see more clearly the nature of the differences with which they had to grapple as a couple. Collisions of defense thus may reveal the very conflicts (both internal and interpersonal) that collusions have kept concealed. To resolve these conflicts, it is necessary for partners to collaborate.

Collaboration

Two key questions must be addressed if a couple's intimacy is to survive. Can each partner live with the defenses of the other? Can each partner empathize with, and find tolerance for, the conflicts in the other that have motivated these defenses?

Doing so requires modifying our old defenses in the setting of a new interdependence—a kind of mutual defense pact with our partner that enables us both to feel safe. Collaboration makes use of both partners' best intentions and strongest abilities. Collaborating effectively requires self-understanding, the effort to empathize, and the commitment to try to work things out together. Our past intimacies may not have prepared us for this kind of relationship. Not infrequently, collaboration feels like swimming upstream.

Self-Protection, Revenge, and Mastery

The tide that goes against us is the unconscious tendency for partners to enlist one another in a re-creation of the past. Rather than confront inconsistency, we're inclined to interpret present experience in such a way that it matches the outdated imagery of our inner map. Of course, this may be more difficult when our partner's behavior challenges that imagery.

Suppose a young woman has internalized the image of her father's treating her mother with disrespect. This, then, is how she expects her boyfriend to treat her. But he doesn't. He admires her, supports her strengths, and often defers to her needs. For a while she might convince herself that his support hides a patronizing attitude—that *his* disrespect is covert, unlike her father's. But this belief may be harder and harder to sustain. To maintain allegiance to the past, something more must be done.

Often, to continue to believe in our own projections, we must campaign on their behalf. We do this by (unconsciously) treating our partner in such a way that he or she comes to identify with the image we've projected. To the extent that the woman with the disrespectful father is committed to that particular image, she will gradually induce her boyfriend to treat her with disrespect. Without being aware of it, she will try to provoke in him exactly the behavior she'd say she likes the least.

When in this way we enlist our partner in a re-creation of the past, we satisfy a variety of needs, including those for self-protection, revenge, and mastery. We re-create a version of the past in the present in order to protect ourselves from the risk of experiencing something unfamiliar and potentially threatening.

We re-create the past to satisfy grudges against our parents (and others) by playing them out with our current lovers. Most important and most hopeful, perhaps, we re-create the past in order to master it. Refinding can thus be used as an opportunity to confront old problems and generate new solutions. Eventually, these new solutions have the potential to modify our inner map, thus deepening our capacity to love.

USING THIS BOOK

This is a self-knowledge book more than a self-help book. It can be used to recognize the images of your own inner map and to understand the impact of these images on your experience in love.

Each of the next six chapters explores in detail one of the six capacities crucial to loving. Every chapter is devoted to a different area of experience in love, a different sector of the inner map. Every chapter closes with three vignettes that illustrate how, for different individuals, each capacity may be experienced as a resource, a compromise, or a struggle. In all probability you will recognize aspects of yourself in parts of these narratives. Looking across the narratives in all six chapters, you may come up with a profile of your overall capacity to love. Pay particular attention to the section in each chapter on the defenses. You may recognize some of your own defenses and how they have interacted with the defenses of past or present partners.

If you are currently in a relationship and your partner is also reading this book, it may be helpful for the two of you to compare your self-evaluations in terms of the capacities and the defenses that affect them. Partners may also find it useful to explore whether their views of themselves match their partner's views of them. This kind of discussion can be difficult but very beneficial.

CHAPTER ONE

The Capacity for Erotic Involvement: The Role of the Body in Love

Sex is composed of friction and fantasies.
—Helen Singer Kaplan, M.D.

Sex is a sacred rite in the religion of mutual love, and
like all sacred rites is an encounter with the mysteries.
—Ethel S. Person, M.D.

*J*ust how central is sex to love?

When sex is good, it can mean the difference between a relationship that is satisfactory and one that feels unquestionably right. When sex is a problem, it can turn a relationship that might otherwise be workable into one that becomes hard to bear.

Sex occupies such a central role in love because, paradoxically, *sex is not just sex*. The capacity for erotic involvement makes possible a lot more than pleasurable sensation, orgasm, and the ability to procreate. Fully developed and explored, the capacity for erotic involvement ensures that one can be comfortable experiencing and expressing the entire range of emotions, urges, and fantasies that surface in a sexual relationship.

This means that sexuality has the potential to become not only a continuing source of intense pleasure but also a way to communicate intimately with one's partner and to know more about oneself. At its best, the sexual relationship of a couple in love provides them with an enduring, nonverbal medium for strengthening their emotional connection and working through the psychological issues that usually arise as intimacy deepens. For such a couple, passion can be a permanent resource in love and sexuality the vehicle for exploring an extraordinarily rich and complex inner geography. This is the golden promise of the "territory of the body" in love. To explain how that promise can be realized, we will answer a series of questions as this chapter unfolds:

▲ What aspects of sexuality make it so central a factor in love?

▲ Beyond the obvious—pleasure and procreation—what motives drive (or inhibit) our erotic desires and shape our capacity for erotic involvement? What turns us on and why?

▲ What are the roles of sexuality during love's successive stages? What rewards can we reasonably expect from sexuality at the different stages of a relationship? And what are the pitfalls we can anticipate along the way?

▲ How does the capacity for erotic involvement develop as we grow up? And as adults how can we nurture it?

▲ Generated by personal experience, what specific expectations, desires, and fears shape our capacity to be physically, emotionally, and imaginatively passionate in love?

HAVING SEX AND MAKING LOVE, OR, WHAT'S SO IMPORTANT ABOUT EROTIC INVOLVEMENT?

Our emphasis on the centrality of sex to love will probably seem misplaced unless one understands that what we mean by sexuality is really *psycho*sexuality.

The capacity for erotic involvement makes possible something very special, namely, an integrated expression of body and psyche in the context of an intimate relationship. When sexuality is at its peak, three separate aspects of our experience converge: simultaneously we are immersed in the sensations of our body; tuned in to the inner promptings of fantasy; and deeply, emotionally engaged with a loved partner. If we are lucky, what we experience in making love is that the psychological—the mesh of feeling/fantasy/desire—is inseparable from the physical. And the personal merges with the interpersonal.

The ability to enjoy fully all three elements of lovemaking—the pleasures of the body, of fantasy, and of intimacy—defines the upper limit of our potential for erotic involvement. By way of illustration, listen to a man rhapsodize:

> Making love with my wife is like a symphony—like listening to it, responding to it, writing it, and playing the instruments, and *being* the instruments all at the same time. The touch, taste, smell, sight, sound of her when we're in bed—it's like each of my senses is one of the different instruments playing in harmony. And any one of them—the soft feel of her nipple against my lips or the smell of her warm skin or the sweet taste of her mouth—can trigger a feeling in me, or an image or a memory or a new desire. And it's as though the music between us keeps changing—I change it or she does or we do—and the themes keep moving: I might be feeling very manly and strong, or very close and loving, and then maybe kind of babyish and wanting to be passive or I'm feeling like an innocent boy being seduced or maybe then like I imagine a woman might feel. And my wife's responses to my impulses fit in—or they don't—and I go along with her or she goes along with me. It all feels intensely physical, but very emotional, too. Very primitive, but somehow also refined at times. What a mixture for the two of us! Body and spirit. Love and energy and power and surrender.

This man would have no trouble understanding the psychoanalyst Otto Kernberg's poetic insight that the body of the beloved becomes a geography of personal meanings. To use a different metaphor, there are stories sleeping in the body that may be aroused and played out in the unspoken conversation of making love to one's partner.

These are "love stories," to be sure, but many other kinds of stories as well. The more we learn about the private lives of people the more clearly we understand that, along with love and the delights of the body, fantasy energizes sexuality—and that fantasy, usually with roots in childhood, takes many forms and involves us in many roles: passive and aggressive, maturely parental and babyish, masculine and feminine. To a significant degree, the depth and longevity of our passion depend on how much of this erotic inner life we can admit into our relationship.

What makes all this even more important is that the intimate arena of sexual love is often the only one we have in which to know and express these aspects of our personality. Partly this is because cultural expectations limit the social roles with which most women and men are comfortable. But the inflexibility of public roles need not translate into an inflexibility of sexual roles. The bedroom can be a kind of private playground for grown-ups. In fact, the sexual play of adults seems to share a lot with what psychologists refer to as the symbolic play of little children: both sorts of play are fun but also, ideally, full of feeling and meaning. Through symbolic play (like that of the little girl who plays house with her dolls—and later with her friends), children get to know themselves and work through what is challenging or troubling them. Through sexual play, adults get to know themselves in very much the same way and work through what is challenging or troubling *them*.

One may object that we are being unrealistic or even utopian when we place such emphasis on the centrality of sex to love— valuing it not only as a continuing source of pleasure but also as a means of communication and a route to knowing some of the deepest aspects of ourselves and our partner.

Certainly our view contradicts the conventional expectation that the importance and pleasure of sex will always wane as partners become more familiar, hence less exciting, to each other. And granted, like many other therapists, we have commonly found that fading sexuality figures in the experience of the couples we see in treatment. The question of course is, what accounts for it?

Not, we would answer, sexual boredom—as if, in a variation on the "familiarity breeds contempt" theme, a languishing desire for our partner were simply an inescapable consequence of monogamous sexuality itself. The real explanation, both more complex and more hopeful, is this: As intimacy deepens, we often come upon unanticipated, hitherto unrecognized limitations in the development of our capacity for erotic involvement. Sometimes such limitations are already in evidence when a couple's romance begins. More commonly, they emerge only later, as the couple confronts the predictable challenges to passion that are part of the later phases of every relationship.

WHEN SEXUALITY IS COMPROMISED

If there are limitations in our capacity for erotic involvement, we will have trouble with one or more of the three dimensions of sexuality: it will be difficult for us to delight in the pleasures of the body; to know, construct, or play out our fantasies; or to be emotionally intimate with the partner we love.

When the passion of early romance diminishes, it is usually because previously *covert* limitations of this kind have been brought to the surface by a deepening of the couple's relationship. Sexual conflicts, concerns, or inhibitions can often seem to be nonexistent while a relationship is still young. In reality they may well exist but remain outside awareness, at least for the moment. Even when it becomes more difficult to feel turned on, one can mislabel the problem in a variety of ways: "The excitement has worn off with time" or "My wife has put on weight" or "My boyfriend has gotten out of shape."

Contrast these mislabelings with the insight of a patient in psychotherapy whose once-passionate desire for her boyfriend had all but disappeared six months into their relationship:

It's as though the more intimate we get, the more he seems like family. And the more he seems like family the more difficult it becomes not to see him as like my dad. And then I feel disgusted and sort of panicky: I just don't want him to touch me. His touch begins to remind me of the way my father was always touching me, much too intimately, when I was a little girl.

Limits on our capacity for erotic involvement take many distressing forms—not only inhibition or loss of desire but also variations on these themes, including premature ejaculation or impotence in men, problems achieving orgasm in women, a rigidity or narrowing of the focus of sexual satisfaction (sometimes called perversion), a compulsive need to create romantic triangles, and so on.

These examples are dramatic and painful, but they don't tell the whole story. A couple's capacity for erotic involvement can be restricted not only in very obvious and debilitating ways but also subtly, in which case the development of their sexuality may seem to have stalled, albeit at an "acceptable" level.

Such limitations can emerge out of various circumstances, running the gamut from traumas as profoundly disturbing as incest to the subtle guilt that results when a child interprets the parent's silence about sex as an unspoken prohibition. At times, a simple lack of awareness about sexuality's potential—which may lead us to confuse orgasm with fulfillment—can be enough to put the brakes on our erotic development.

Whatever the source or circumstances of our limitations, they make it more difficult for us to take full advantage of the multiplicity of ways in which sex serves love. Fortunately, these limitations are never insurmountable, though sometimes that is exactly how they feel. The more we know about the capacity for erotic involvement—in general and in ourselves as individuals—the more we can use it as a resource.

The key is to be aware of the tremendous rewards sexuality can bring us in a relationship. Recognizing this, we need to understand first what drives sexuality and second what inhibits it.

WHAT DRIVES THE SEXUAL DRIVE?

Freud believed that anatomy was destiny and that at the most basic level, human behavior was motivated by the sexual drive. In our view the sexual drive itself is energized by three motives that have as much to do with psychology as with anatomy, and these motives—namely, pleasure, self-esteem, and mastery—shape every one of the six capacities crucial to loving. Listen to a woman whose experience illustrates how the interplay of the three motives shapes sexuality. Louise, a thirty-three-year-old nurse and mother, is describing to her therapist a new development in her sexual relationship:

> I feel a little embarrassed talking about this, but I'm so excited about what's happening. You know I've always wanted to get into some different fantasies with my husband—fantasies more like my masturbatory fantasies, either where I'm really teasing him or he's teasing me. We'd talked about this before but never done anything about it. So the other night he was touching my thigh and he felt something under my skirt and said, What's this? I'd put on a garter belt and some sexy lingerie. He got really turned on—I think partly because he thought my wearing this sexy underwear was a kind of signal to him that I might be open to some new things. Which was true.
>
> We were sitting on the couch and he reached out to undo the buttons on my blouse, like he wanted to get my clothes off really quick. But I wouldn't let him. I wanted him to know this was going to go slow, that I was going to be in charge and he was going to have to sort of be my slave—totally adoring me and doing what I wanted. And then *maybe* I'd satisfy him. This is embarrassing, I sound like such a tease, but I guess that's the whole point. Another part of my fantasy has always been that he's naked while I'm dressed—so that's what we did. I just felt totally desirable and powerful. I'd get him excited by touching him or licking him so he was kind of straining toward me, then I'd back off.

And then somehow I let the whole thing reverse, I kind of gave myself to him, let him get on top—and it switched: I really wanted *him* but he was teasing *me* now, moving real slow and letting me know he was in charge and I'd have to submit to him...you know, he'd start moving inside me... and then he'd stop. I felt like, I'll just surrender, I'll do whatever he wants me to do...After we both came, we were holding each other and I felt like I was really accepted for who I was, including this part of me that seems slightly kinky. It was like we reached this new level of trust and intimacy: like we were *really* naked now.

How can we understand Louise's sexuality in terms of the three central motives we've mentioned? Clearly one motive for acting out her fantasy is the wish for pleasure. But what exactly is the *pleasure* in being teased—or in teasing? And where in this fantasy can we see the satisfaction of her wish for *self-esteem* or her desire for *mastery* in relation to an earlier, unresolved experience?

The "Pleasure Principle"

Let's start with the question about Louise's pleasure in teasing and in being teased. The wish for pleasure always has the potential to involve various elements, three of which we'll discuss here. First, there are physical (and psychological) pleasures of the kind conventionally associated with the erotic and with affection, including active and/or passive experiences of kissing, caressing, stroking, licking, gently biting in areas of the body sensitive to touch, and intercourse.

Second, there are pleasures associated with aggression or self-assertion. Exactly why pleasure should be linked to aggression is a matter of controversy.[1] That there *is* such a link between

---

1. The debate centers on whether aggression is an intrinsic part of sexuality, a biological given, an aspect of our human genetic inheritance, or whether it emerges only as a response to the frustration that intermittently accompanies the physically nurturing childhood experiences within which our sexuality develops.

aggression and sexuality is something that most of us know from experience, but many of us are uneasy admitting it. It must be emphasized strongly that we are *not* talking about abuse or coercion but about a variety of consensual sexual activities that can bring enjoyment to both partners: taking charge or being taken charge of, biting or being bitten, spanking or being spanked, teasing or being teased, aggressively penetrating or being penetrated, and so on. Here we're edging into the arena of sadomasochism, which used to be regarded as "perversion," but which is coming more and more to be regarded only as one aspect among many of healthy sexual expressiveness.

Third, there are pleasures that might be called dependent: experiences of being held, hugged, or cuddled that are associated with feeling taken care of, comforted, or simply loved. Often, such experiences contain the echoes of real or wished-for interactions with our parents.

All three kinds of pleasure played a part in motivating Louise's excitement in teasing and being teased: affectionately erotic pleasure in the touching, licking, and in various aspects of her experience in which she feels adored or adoring; aggressive pleasure in the teasing itself, but also in taking charge—as she becomes the director of a play in which her masturbatory fantasy is the script; and dependent pleasure both in taking the role of the adoring child who wants to please and in being held and feeling accepted.

Once we understand that our sexuality has the potential to involve these three kinds of pleasure, we each can ask: How much of myself am I actually allowing into my sexual relationship? How much am I allowing myself to experiment? What am I allowing myself to know about what I like sexually? And how much of that am I communicating to my partner—so that perhaps my sexual wishes might be fulfilled in reality rather than remain permanently confined to private fantasy?

Self-Esteem in Sexuality

The second motive that drives sexuality—the wish for self-esteem—can be inferred from the satisfaction with which Louise recounted her erotic experience to her therapist. In addition, she seemed to derive self-esteem from identifying and giving voice to her (potentially embarrassing) desire—and making sure she satisfied it with her husband. The courage and freedom expressed in this behavior, not to mention the experience of being adored and having a partner worthy of her adoration, led her to feel good about herself.

The Mastery Motive

Mastering the Past

The third motive involves the desire to feel control or competence in relation to an earlier situation in which one felt neither. For Louise, mastery involved taking charge in fantasy of what in her childhood had been a painfully out-of-control experience. Her father, she felt, had repeatedly made himself available to her in very inviting ways, but had then unpredictably withdrawn, leaving her full of hurt, longing, and confusion. In effect, he had teased her. In her erotic fantasy, Louise takes control: choosing to tease when she wants to and alternately choosing to be teased. This leads to an important generalization about the relationship between sexual fantasies and the impulse toward mastery.

It regularly turns out that what most turns us on is a disguised reflection of early difficulties—even traumas—that we are trying to master. This sort of mastery through fantasy takes two main forms. In the first situation, which psychoanalysts have called reversal or "turning passive into active," one turns the tables, and what was passively experienced earlier is now actively reversed. So a woman who felt teased as a child now finds it erotically exciting to tease others. In the second situation, called "the sexualization of trauma," what one once experienced unwillingly as the victim, one now initiates and experiences with pleasure. Louise's excitement in setting up a situation in which she is teased can be understood from this angle.

More broadly, there may be an explanation here for the thread of aggression that runs through much of our sexuality. It is nearly universal for children to experience frustration or anger growing up with parents who seem to have all the power. Aggression in sexual fantasy (as in Louise's fantasies of teasing) may reflect early efforts to cope with these difficult childhood feelings.

Notice too that Louise—like most of us—can take pleasure in acting out both sides of her fantasy. Reversals can be reversed. At least initially, one role (active or passive) may be more appealing than the other. But as a rule, opposite roles are just two sides of the same coin. If we enjoy one (say, teasing), we can usually enjoy the other (being teased).

Discussion of fantasies that involve aggression demands a crucial distinction between the healthy acting out of fantasy in the service of mastery and the abusive acting out of fantasy in the service of revenge. Distinguishing whether fantasy is driven by the impulse toward mastery or the wish for revenge is complex. But distinguishing between healthy and abusive acting out is not. Here the question is, Do both partners want to act out the fantasy or don't they? It's a matter of mutual informed consent. When overt or covert coercion is involved in matters of sexuality, the acting out can only be judged abusive.

Thus far we have seen how the impulse toward mastery works in adults trying to take psychological control of disturbing childhood experiences. But the capacity for erotic involvement can also be energized by a wish to master present problems.

Mastering the Present

Consider a marriage, not atypical, in which an uneven distribution of power and responsibility had left both partners feeling discontent. Allen was troubled by his need always to feel in charge, while Dorothy felt she was being treated like a little girl. This uncomfortable pattern was in part worked through in their lovemaking where Dorothy felt more active and powerful. In one fantasy that excited them both, Allen took on the role of the innocent, naive boy whom Dorothy seduced and initiated into sexual love. Allen discovered that he could actually take pleasure in giving up some control, and Dorothy found out more about her pleasure in taking initiative.

The mastery motive can also shape sexuality when lovers deal with the anger that can be generated by a quarrel. When a couple express anger through unusually aggressive lovemaking, they can feel considerable relief. Because the anger is channeled into a context that is basically loving, it can be detoxified, so to speak.

Plainly, the terrain of the erotic beckons with considerable promise. To feel pleasure, to heighten self-esteem, and to master troubling experience is an alluring combination of motives. If this were all that shaped our capacity for erotic involvement, however, there would be no such thing as the familiar guilt, shame, or embarrassment with which sexuality is also associated. Nor would we find the sexual inhibition and diminished desire so commonly experienced by long-term couples.

WHAT INHIBITS THE SEXUAL DRIVE?

Most commonly, sexual inhibition reflects the self-defeating impact of psychological defenses. Unfortunately, many of us have drawn conclusions from our own experience that lead us to regard sexual involvement itself as threatening. Consequently we protect ourselves with psychological defenses. The drawback is that these defenses accomplish their purpose by inhibiting or restricting our capacity for erotic involvement, which in turn undermines love by taking a key resource out of our hands. What starts as the solution becomes the problem.[2]

One or both partners may explain either that they have lost their desire for sex or that their sex drive has always been very low. Other partners who enjoy sex may feel inhibited about one aspect or another of sexuality: a man doesn't like to kiss, a woman

2. While the causes of sexual inhibition are far more often emotional than physical, there are also medical conditions (such as diabetes) and medications (including anti-hypertensives, beta blockers, and others) that may also decrease sexual desire and/or activity.

finds intercourse unappealing but enjoys foreplay. There are couples for whom the sexual disinterest of one partner is experienced as a problem by the other, who feels frustrated or rejected. And there are situations—like male impotence—in which the desire of both partners may be achingly present but the ability to satisfy it, at least through intercourse, is not.

The greatest difficulty in overcoming such sexual inhibitions is that, paradoxically, they almost never feel like sexual inhibitions. Their real nature is hidden and hard to recognize. For example, a patient trying to understand his impotence may tell his therapist with complete candor, "I *have* no sexual fantasies. It's not that I'm afraid or guilty or defensive about them. I just don't have any."

But what this patient doesn't know *will* hurt him. When, unconsciously, he inhibits his awareness of sexual fantasies, he may succeed in shielding himself from some troubling aspect of these fantasies. In the process, however, he inadvertently disconnects from a major wellspring of sexual energy. And now he wonders about his impotence.

The psychological reality is this: Our sexual inhibitions—though often unrecognized as such—nearly always reflect self-defeating reactions to situations we regard as dangerous. We may have a hard time specifying the nature of the sexual danger (is it fear of feeling guilty? or inadequate? or provoked to re-experience some old trauma?), but we will usually try to protect ourselves from it.

To overcome these kinds of limitations in our capacity for erotic involvement, it is necessary for us to *recognize* the defense, *describe* it in detail, and *interpret* its meaning or motive. We also need to assess the price we pay for this kind of self-protection and to identify the hidden payoffs, if any.

By way of illustration, listen to Joel, a married thirty-year-old radio engineer who could hardly stand to be kissed:

For years kissing disgusted me. I didn't even ask why, it was just a bodily reflex. But eventually it began to seem like something I had to think about. At first because the various women I'd been with all liked to kiss and the fact that I didn't got to be a problem. Then on top of that I began to feel a little weird, also like maybe I was missing something—because what everyone else seemed to like so much I just found a turn-off.

Now finally, it's changing...gradually...in my relationship with my wife, Adrienne. I've realized that the whole thing with me is much more complicated than I originally thought. To begin with I got clear that I really *did* want to kiss Adrienne, but that it just made me very uncomfortable for some reason. So, to avoid feeling uncomfortable, I avoided kissing. But it was really like I had fooled myself: I was saying, I don't want this—when the reality was there was something about what I wanted that scared me. Like somebody kissing me was imposing something on me.

But it's changing. Partly because I'm understanding more about where my disgust with kissing comes from and partly because I don't feel I always *have* to kiss my wife, which is what I always felt with my mother. I think my mother was so lonely and depressed that she sort of turned me into a substitute for my father, who was never there for her. Into my teens, even after that, I felt she was all over me. I didn't know anyone else whose mother made a habit of kissing them on the mouth.

RECOGNITION.   Joel began grappling with the limitation in his capacity for erotic involvement when, rather than take his reaction entirely at face value ("...kissing disgusted me. I didn't even think about why, it was just a bodily reflex"), he recognized his defensive inhibition for what it was—a form of self-protection: "I got clear that I really *did* want to kiss Adrienne, but that it just made me very uncomfortable...."

DESCRIPTION.   How, specifically, did Joel's defensive inhibition work? He tells us he "fooled himself": "I was saying, I don't want this—when the reality was there was something about what I wanted that scared me."

INTERPRETATION. This involves identifying the unconscious threat or danger that seems to make the defensive inhibition necessary. Joel's dislike of kissing protected him from all the feelings associated with his mother's intrusive expressions of affection and need.

PRICE AND PAYOFF. Once we recognize, describe, and interpret our defensive inhibitions, we need to assess whether or not it's worth our while to try to give them up. Is the protection they afford worth their price? And what hidden payoffs, if any, do we need to factor into our appraisal?

Joel was motivated to struggle with his inhibition about kissing. He understood what the inhibition protected him from, and considered the price for protection too high: not only had his inhibition generated problems in his relationships, but he had begun to suspect that it also deprived him of a potential pleasure. After all, he couldn't easily believe that everyone else was faking it when they acted as though they enjoyed kissing.

Nevertheless, Joel was aware of a nagging reluctance to surrender his inhibition. It was hard for him to admit it, but there was a rather unsavory payoff concealed in his perfectly reasonable wish to protect himself—even with his wife—from the sort of intrusion he'd experienced much earlier with his mother. The hidden payoff here was revenge. It was too dangerous for Joel when he was young and dependent to be angry or to assert control. But now, as a married adult, he'd be damned if he was going to submit to the same kind of treatment he'd received as a child from his oppressively affectionate mother! Joel's capacity for erotic involvement was inhibited in part by his guilty desire for revenge—itself triggered by *refinding* his mother in his relationship with his wife.

To sum up: Limitations in our capacity for erotic involvement are best understood as psychological defenses. These forms of self-protection must be recognized, described, and interpreted, and their costs must be assessed. Then the hidden payoffs that help keep our limitations in place must be identified. But one other factor plays a key role in keeping these limitations in place or helping us relinquish them: that factor, not surprisingly, is our partner.

THE ROLE OF THE PARTNER,
FOR BETTER OR WORSE

Psychotherapists often talk about the "identified patient," by which they mean the partner in a couple whose difficulties are currently taking center stage. Even though one partner's problems have become the focus of attention, the "identified patient" bears no more or less responsibility for the couple's discontent than the other partner, whose role may be harder to identify. Regardless of how it may appear or even *feel*, when it comes to limitations in the capacity for erotic involvement, both members of the couple invariably play a part.

The Interpersonal Alternatives:
Collusion, Collision, or Collaboration

Ideally, two partners' loving collaboration permits a flowering of their sexual potential as a couple. Frequently, however, partners are involved in collusions or collisions of defense that undermine their shared capacity for erotic involvement. Collusions conceal—and collisions reveal—the conflicts between two partners. Collaboration is the means, hopefully, by which the conflicts are resolved.

The Couple in Collusion

The colluding couple has made a deal—usually unrecognized as such—that serves the self-protective needs of both partners, though it may also diminish their pleasure, self-esteem, or opportunities for mastery. In such a deal, the individual defenses of one partner either mirror or mesh with the defenses of the other.

For example, a husband and wife, both inhibited by guilt, may "decide" together that sexuality is not a significant part of a love relationship. Psychologists would probably see in their decision a rationalization—that is, a defense in which a "good" reason is substituted for the real reason. Conveniently, the husband's rationalization of his sexual withdrawal is mirrored by his wife's rationalization of hers. Such shared defenses can make for collusions that are quite stable. Peace is maintained, but sexuality as a potential resource for psychological development is sacrificed.

Less stable collusions involve partners whose individual defenses differ—but mesh, at least for the time being. Nadine and Kevin were this kind of couple. She was a young woman whose strict fundamentalist background had led her to feel guilty about her sexual desires. He was an apparently confident but secretly shy man with his own burden of sexual inhibition. Kevin blamed Nadine for throwing cold water on their passion, thereby protecting himself from shame about his own awkwardness. Nadine meanwhile blamed *herself* for being such an out-of-date prude. In so doing, she preserved a sexless status quo that protected her from the guilty desire a less-inhibited partner could have sparked.

A collusion like this, in which the partners' defenses are different, always has the potential to become a collision. Originally, Kevin's defensive blaming meshed with Nadine's tendency to blame herself. But eventually this arrangement led her to feel *too* bad about herself—and then the stage was set for conflict. Turning the tables, she began to blame Kevin, at first for being too sexual, and later for being too inhibited. Now the fight was on.

This wasn't necessarily such a bad thing. So long as partners collude, their real fears and desires may remain hidden. As long as Kevin's concerns about his own sexual inhibitions were never directly confronted, they would be very hard to resolve. By the same token, Nadine's sexual desire might have remained a stranger to her had she continued to collude with the idea that Kevin was the only partner in the relationship with sexual feelings. When a collusion like this one breaks down and a collision results, some painful but potentially liberating realities can come into focus for the first time.

Couples usually pay a price for their collusions. But collusions are also a normal and useful feature of the first phase of a love relationship, in which partners often unconsciously conspire to ignore the difficulties, sexual or otherwise, that threaten to short-circuit romantic bliss.

The Couple in Collision

Sex therapists use the term *desire discrepancy* to refer to the disparity between two partners in the frequency with which they desire sex. At the unhappiest extreme, one wants and the other doesn't. Our experience with couples in trouble has shown us that desire discrepancy is the single most common outcome when the individual defenses of two partners collide.

Joel (who didn't like to kiss) felt safe so long as he could maintain a little distance. Adrienne, his wife, was reassured when she could feel close. Yearning for physical closeness, Adrienne would become seductive. Anxious at the prospect of physical intrusion, Joel would pull back. As this uncomfortable scenario was repeated, Adrienne felt increasingly hurt and sexually hungry, while Joel felt more and more nervously inadequate and remote from his desire. The collision of their defenses had provoked a discrepancy in their levels of desire.

The same kind of collision can occur when partners use projection as a defense. In projection, uncomfortable aspects of ourselves are disavowed and "relocated." Uneasy with our own anger, for example, we may deny feeling it, but we begin to suspect that our partner is angry.

Consider a couple like Jeff and Sharon, who each experience an internal conflict between sexual desire and sexual guilt. To make an internal conflict an interpersonal one requires projection. Jeff (the "high-desire" partner) projects his guilt about sex onto Sharon—and then experiences her as uptight and moralistic. Meanwhile, Sharon (the "low-desire" partner) projects her sexuality onto Jeff—and begins to see him as sexually obsessed and demanding. Once again, the outcome of a collision of defenses is discrepant desire, and a couple's journey across the territory of the erotic is stalled.

The way out of the impasse is through collaboration. Partners can think and feel and talk together in the effort to *understand* their dissatisfaction, rather than see it as an inevitable fact of life that places them on opposite sides of the fence. They also can agree to take some risks in bed—but this leap into the realm of actual *doing* is almost always easier after a few things have been understood.

The Couple in Collaboration: Understanding the Impasse

Collaborative understanding originates with the challenging realization that the responsibility for a couple's sexual discontent is almost invariably shared. It may be tempting to blame our partner: "She's too aggressive" or "He's too absorbed in satisfying his own needs." But the reality is we do *choose* our partner. And our choice, informed by a wisdom we are often unaware of, has a great deal to do with our *own* psychological wishes and fears.

Unfortunately, the same fears that draw us to our partner in the hope of mastering unfinished psychological business may also provoke the defenses that inhibit our sexuality. Collaborating with our partner to understand (rather than to blame) becomes much easier once we see that the "dangers" we experience in a relationship usually have this kind of double significance. On the surface, they seem to be nothing more than threats from which we need to protect ourselves. On a deeper level, they present us with the opportunity to successfully confront our demons—whether of sexual insecurity or sexual guilt.

A couple may choose—out of fear that seems overwhelming, or a lack of self-awareness, or a simple preference for the security of the familiar—to let inhibition stall, perhaps permanently, the development of their capacity for erotic involvement. Or they may summon the courage and humility to collaborate in understanding the obstacles that keep them from making the fullest possible use of sex as a resource in love. The latter alternative is a little like choosing high-adventure travel. Whether white-water rafting, trekking across exotic mountain terrain, or scuba diving along a barrier reef, the dangers and difficulties are unavoidable, and the potential rewards exhilarating.

The most valuable equipment with which to begin the journey of understanding is a couple's knowledge *that* they are protecting themselves, *how* they are protecting themselves, and *what* they are protecting themselves from. The couple must, in other words, recognize, describe, and interpret the defenses that have derailed their sexuality. This approach should sound familiar: it duplicates what we have recommended to the individual trying to come to terms with his or her erotic limitations. The additional challenge for a couple is to appreciate that the individual defenses of each partner are interacting with those of the other to generate collusions and/or collisions.

Once we have begun to grasp the means by which we stop ourselves and the motives that drive us to do so, we face another point of choice.

We can accept our own forms of self-protection (and those of our partner) as limitations that can be lived with, out of respect for our fears. When this acceptance is the product of real understanding it usually brings a modicum of change: what was feared is no longer quite so inhibiting. Or as a couple, we can decide to gamble that the rewards in challenging our limitations, and learning to tolerate more of our fears, outweigh the hazards. We can agree, in other words, to collaborate in taking some risks.

Collaboration Elaborated: "One Leads, One Follows"

Positive reframing refers to a technique therapists use to help their patients see difficult experiences in new and empowering ways. For instance, what feels to partners like a discrepancy in their level of sexual desire can be reframed as an occasion to explore new erotic territory by taking a risk. In this reframing, "one wants, the other doesn't" becomes "one leads, the other follows."

Now the high-desire partner may learn more about seduction, the low-desire partner about allowing himself (or herself) to be seduced. This same reframing makes sense when partners find themselves confronting different preferences in sex: one partner, say, loves oral sex, while the other shies away from it. Here one lover can take the lead in exploring new erotic territory and the other may choose to be led.

This brings us to an absolutely crucial distinction: We are talking explicitly about collaboration, *not* coercion. "One leads, one follows" is always an agreement about roles. "One threateningly demands, the other fearfully submits" is never anything but abuse.

The easiest, most familiar model for leader-and-follower as a form of collaboration may be dancing. Conventionally, at least in old-fashioned ballroom dancing, men led. In sex and in other relationship matters, however, there is no reason at all why the roles of leader and follower should ever be rigidly tied to gender. Not uncommonly, one partner in a couple is more at home than the other with one (or more) of the three key dimensions of sexual experience: bodily sensation, fantasy, and emotional connection. A husband may have had more "practice" getting to know and enjoy his fantasies, while his wife may be more comfortable with a wider range of physical stimulation (oral and anal, perhaps, as well as genital). Whichever partner is more relaxed about or familiar with a particular aspect of sexuality (say, emotional connection) has the ability to lead the couple in exploring this terrain—while the other partner is lucky enough to have found a guide.

Erica, a social worker in her mid-thirties, explains how she took the lead with her husband:

> Matt is a very loving guy but I always used to have the feeling that he couldn't quite express it sexually. In a way, he's a traditional male with all the Madonna/whore stuff that a lot of men seem to be saddled with. So he loved seeing me in sexy lingerie and doing all this fantasy stuff—which I like too—but I began to feel like he couldn't quite be there in bed with *me*. And I realized that a piece of this was that he almost never looked me in the eye when we were making love. Either he'd be getting off on looking at my body or he'd have his eyes closed.

I remembered being with the first guy I ever lived with and how we'd be kissing passionately and looking into each other's eyes. And how intimate it felt.

So I talked about this with Matt—not so much in terms of, I had this great experience with my first boyfriend and how come you're such a schmuck? More like, hey, there's this thing I'd like to try, this way of making love together which I think would be really interesting, where we might feel even more connected and turned on. And then I suggested, amazingly enough, *looking into each other's eyes* while we were having sex.

He was willing to try it—first when we were kissing. It was kind of scary for him...he said he felt sort of shy and exposed. And I actually felt that too. But we've been getting into it more and more. Looking at each other, even sometimes when we're coming, and it's pretty amazing. It's a completely different kind of intimacy.

This kind of collaboration—"one leads, one follows"—is so important and intrinsic a feature of the way couples grow for one very simple reason: Though we might wish it were otherwise, partners in love don't regularly develop in tandem or in synch. Psychologically we grow at different paces, in different directions, at different times.

In fact, although we may be unaware of it at the time, these kinds of differences between partners are a big part of why we choose to love those whom we love. Our unconscious wisdom moves us to join forces with others from whom we can learn. And having chosen a partner with the potential to take the lead, we may feel grateful or as though we're reluctantly being dragged along. We may also unconsciously choose partners whose inadequacies help us avoid confronting our own. When we seem to have chosen someone less developed in a particular area, it is often because we actually have unfinished business in the very same area.

Recall the relationship between Kevin, who was secretly shy, and Nadine, whose shyness was no secret. When she refused to be cast as the only inhibited partner in the relationship, the collision that resulted led to a more collaborative partnership between them. Here is Kevin's account of one aspect of their collaboration:

> Nadine always wanted the lights out. I mean, she would only make love with me in the dark. She grew up in a family where sex was a big secret. You always had to hide it. On top of that she felt self-conscious about her body after her pregnancy. For myself I feel like I've been growing out of this repressive kind of attitude about sex. What's more, I wanted to look at her body, which I think is beautiful, and also have her look at me and not feel like everything had to be covered up.
>
> Of course this led to some conflict. Nadine felt that I was demanding something of her that she couldn't be comfortable giving me. I felt it was absurd that she was still dominated by her parents' attitudes about sex and nudity.
>
> Then I realized I was fighting against the same kind of background myself, the same fundamentalist thing. That I was sort of worried myself about having sex with the lights on. But then I thought, No! I'm not going to let us be overcome by this stuff about sex is guilty and so on. So I pushed it.
>
> Not really pushed it. More finessed it. I wasn't real heavy about it, because I could see her uptightness, I could understand it. So I talked about candlelight, one little candle, not a spotlight. Could we try it just once and see? Something about my approach, the romantic stuff, candlelight and so on, made it more comfortable to her. Now it's part of what we do. But it wouldn't have been if I'd just given up on the thing.

Kevin led and Nadine followed. She risked enduring some anxiety in allowing their sexuality to be "illuminated." He risked encountering her disapproval and anger in pressing for his satisfaction. But what if she had said no?

The story might still have had a happy ending, but a different one. The very process of going after what we want can be useful—

even if our desire is frustrated. Kevin would still have found himself taking a look not only at his wife's feelings about sex but also at his own: he would still have given himself the opportunity, in other words, to confront, perhaps to resolve, some of his own sexual guilt and inhibition.

Collaboration and risk-taking are by no means always conflict free. But conflict in love is not a problem per se. Conflict can clarify two partners' differences. And often, as we've seen, it is in their differences that lovers can identify the new erotic territory that they may wind up exploring together.

But to accept, and eventually even value, our differences, it is necessary to understand more about how such differences arise.

THE PATHWAYS OF SEXUAL DEVELOPMENT: HOW DID WE GET TO BE THE WAY WE ARE?

Each of us has a personal inner map of the terrain of the erotic— the internal representation or summing up of the experiences that have shaped our sexuality. These experiences, especially early in life, register as a series of images of ourselves and of others that are key in determining the particulars of our capacity for erotic involvement.

Some images of ourselves and others reflect (more or less accurately) what we feel is real, other images are of the ideal or "wished-for," and there are those images that reflect our fears. In the happiest case, we are comfortable with our actual images of ourselves and of our partner: pleased with the reality, we can plunge into a range of erotic experiences without worrying about being confronted with strong feelings of inferiority, guilt, or shame.

By contrast, when we are dominated by how we *wish* we were, we may hesitate to venture very far into sex, for fear of confronting the disappointing reality of who we actually are. And if we are overly preoccupied with our *feared* images of ourselves or our partner, we may be very inhibited indeed—for sexuality then threatens to confirm our "worst-case scenarios" of dismal inadequacy or hurt.

So what determines the balance among the real, ideal, and feared images in the area of sexuality? Certainly, in part, it is the quality of our sexual experience as adults. But what generally exerts more influence, at least in the psychoanalytic view of development, are the experiences we have growing up. These experiences shape our *gender identity*, that is, how we have come to feel about our masculinity or femininity; and they shape what might be called our *sexual flexibility*: how confident and comfortable we are in knowing and expressing the full range of our sexual desires.

Masculine or Feminine—Or Both?

The place of gender identity[3] in sexuality is both emotionally difficult and crucially important to address. The categories of "masculine" and "feminine" have been burdened by our history and culture with meanings that are not only stereotyped but oppressive. The challenge now is to talk about gender identity in a way that neither perpetuates its oppressive implications nor ignores its profound psychological significance. For the way in which men and women in this culture grapple with the feelings they have about their "masculinity" and "femininity" has a deep and abiding influence on their sexuality.

To understand this we have only to think about how some women inhibit their sexual initiative out of the fear that being too forward isn't "feminine"—or about some men who can't enjoy being seduced or "pleasured" because it feels too passive or "feminine." In each of these cases, feared sexual images, associated with vulnerabilities of gender role identity, are dominant.

---

3. The term *gender identity* refers to the individual's broad sense of his or her own combination of masculinity and femininity. Gender identity has three main components. The first, sometimes called "core gender identity," has to do with knowing that one is a member of one sex and not of the other. The second, usually referred to as "gender role identity" (or "sex role identity") has to do with how one acts and how one feels he or she is seen in terms of sex roles. The third has to do with "sexual identity" or "sexual partner orientation" and refers to the preferred gender of the love object.

Half of the story, then, is that men are fearful about not being masculine enough and women are fearful about not being feminine enough. (Men tend to be much more worried about all this than women—men seem vulnerable to a kind of "femininity phobia.") But the other half of the story is that men want to be feminine. They want to experience those aspects of themselves (the desire to be passive, to be taken care of, and so on) that our culture conventionally associates with femininity. By the same token, women want to experience parts of themselves (such as their power, their desire to protect and control, and so on) that our culture has linked to masculinity. These are the universalities of what might be called "cross-gender" impulses—sexual desires that our culture has made the property of the opposite sex. The whole truth—an uncomfortable truth for many—is that all of us not only fear but also wish for the satisfaction in sexuality of our "cross-gender" impulses.

Bart, a fifty-year-old medical statistician, was articulate about these impulses:

When I was first married I felt one hundred percent male-oriented in my fantasies. I was raised on images of John Wayne and Burt Lancaster. Whether I was playing it out with my wife or just experiencing it as part of my fantasies, I liked to be on top sexually. What appealed to me were all the usual, conventionally masculine roles and attitudes. . . .

Then at a certain point, my wife started to get more aggressive sexually, initiating more, taking control more. All of which was unfamiliar to me. . .the fact was I didn't like it, at least to start with. It didn't feel like me, like what usually aroused me. But before long, I found myself almost *preferring* that she take on this role at times. Which was fine with her, she obviously enjoyed it, the power she felt or whatever. I mean, she initiated it, which was part of the appeal for me. . . .

But I think the crux of it, the deep appeal, it was in just giving in to her. . .giving myself to her, opening myself to her. These are the words that come to mind. It was as though I was expressing my love for her in a way that I always associated with women. You know, the classic screen image of the woman melting in the arms of the heroic man. Well, I now felt this delicious, vaguely taboo pleasure in melting in the arms of my wife. It felt like an expression of my admiration for her, of my looking up to her. She's a formidable person. But also it just felt good, it felt like, aha! so this is part of the whole thing, too.

These kinds of cross-gender impulses have long been recognized in Jungian psychology (where the terms *animus* and *anima* represent, respectively, the masculine aspect in women and the feminine aspect in men) and in psychoanalytic theory (which assumes the existence in all of us of "psychological bisexuality"). It is the process called "identification" that explains the reality—disturbing to many of us—that men and women are not just masculine or feminine, but in some sense both.

Identification: Becoming Like Those We Love

In earliest childhood, our images of ourselves begin to evolve as we "identify" with those we love. If we could interview a baby girl on the subject of identification and gender identity, she might say: "I figure out who *I* am by looking at my mother and seeing who *she* is."

This tiny vignette may suggest that developing a sense of gender identity will be different for the girl and the boy. If the baby girl above were to elaborate, she might say: "I see myself reflected in the mirror of my experience with my mother. *She* is feminine and so it is easy to see *myself* as feminine." And if she were a little older she might add: "Because I love Mommy, *I* want to be exactly like *her*." The key here is that for a girl, the first identification is with mother. Therefore, her sense of herself as feminine has deep roots in the very first important relationship of her childhood. All of which gives the gender identity of women a very solid foundation.

In stark contrast, the boy—whose first love and first identification is *also* with mother—secures a sense of his masculinity only when he can *dis*identify with his mother. He can feel masculine, in other words, only to the extent that he remains out of touch with his earliest image of himself. For this image is a reflection of his mother's image.

Being taken care of passively without having to *do* anything is a big part of every child's healthy experience of being a baby with mother. The problem for the little boy in our culture (with its binary division of gender identity) is that this very desirable experience promotes an identification with the feminine. Therefore, in order to feel masculine, the little boy has to put behind him his first intimate experience with his mother and all the feelings and wishes that were part of it.

In light of these facts of early development, masculinity looks like a house built on a foundation that must always remain hidden—for the foundation of the house is feminine. This helps explain why men can be so worried about becoming aware of their "feminine" impulses to be taken care of or to be passive. To do so threatens their sense of masculinity.

Of course, the images we have of ourselves—men and women alike, at least in traditional intact families[4]—derive not only from our relationship with mother but also from the next love relationship of our childhood, which is with father. It is through not only disidentifying with his mother but later identifying with his father that a little boy develops his sense of masculinity. But the little girl, too, sees herself in her father's image, and she also identifies with him.

Boys and girls *each* identify with *both* parents; masculinity/ femininity is never an either-or matter. All of us, men and women

---

4. Less and less is the intact family the norm. On the other hand, there is evidence that children are surprisingly resourceful when it comes to finding substitute role models outside the home. Unfortunately, other evidence suggests that the role models available to children may offer only the most superficial and/or confusing versions of masculinity or femininity. Increasingly these surrogates are media figures (Rambo or Madonna) rather than the relatives or neighbors who might actually be on the scene to participate in a relationship with the child.

alike, have feelings and wishes of our own that we nonetheless associate with the opposite sex. All of us, then, are masculine *and* feminine: individually, the question is how we feel about these parts of ourselves.

Masculinity/Femininity and Our Real, Ideal, and Feared Self-Images

The nature of our particular cross-gender wishes and fears is the outcome of our own unique experience, especially our identifications with each of our parents. When we have difficulties here—when, for example, a man's desire to be taken care of in bed undermines his ability to be sexual because he no longer feels "masculine"—it is usually because these parental identifications have somehow been problematic.

For men, this usually means that there has been too little separation from mother and not enough closeness to, or admiration of, father. When this is the case, a man's identification with his mother will be stronger than that with his father—and his sense of his own masculinity will be vulnerable. His sexual image of himself as he actually is may be unrealistically modest or inadequate. Awareness of his feminine impulses may be very frightening because they can trigger his feared image of himself as pathetically weak or even emasculated. A final complication: To compensate for his fear of inadequacy, his ideal image—his fantasy about himself as he would like to be—may be inflated to grandiose proportions. Both burdened and buoyed up by such images of himself, a man with this psychological profile might come on very "cocky" but actually be terrified of failing to meet his own impossible standards of masculine performance.

As for women, too little intimacy with or admiration for mother and/or too much seductiveness from father can tilt the balance in troublesome ways. These kinds of experiences in a woman's history can undermine her identification with her mother and amplify her identification with her father, with the result that her confidence in her femininity will be shaky. Her fear of inadequacy in this area may provoke either withdrawal or an exaggerated, Scarlet O'Hara kind of sexuality as compensation. The problem with the latter solution for a woman is twofold: On the one hand, it may be hard for her to sustain the conventional feminine image in bed. On the other hand, the fear of *not* doing so can inhibit the natural expression of the sort of aggressive sexual impulses that are traditionally linked to masculinity.

When we are fortunate enough to feel at home with our own particular balance of masculine and feminine, it is easier to be sexually confident. It is also easier to satisfy the full range of erotic desires that can emerge in a love relationship—easier, in other words, to be sexually flexible.

Sexual Flexibility

We're talking here about sexual variety, not acrobatics. At the heart of our capacity for erotic involvement is the ability to experience and express the wide but idiosyncratic variety of impulses, fantasies, and feelings that make sexuality such a rich resource in love. Variety, unfortunately, is what many sexual relationships lack. One result is that sexual boredom is mistakenly regarded as an inevitable development in the life of every love that lasts.

When sexual flexibility is limited and erotic variety is minimal, it is usually the outcome of strong and rigid sexual preferences (wishes) and/or strong sexual inhibitions (fears), both of which have their earliest origins in our experiences growing up. But before we say more about how sexual flexibility develops, let's take a look at how it is—or is not—manifest in our relationships.

Sexual Inflexibility

One or more of the three dimensions of sexuality we've described—physicality, fantasy, and emotional involvement—may regularly be downplayed. This kind of inhibition will obviously narrow the sexual repertoire of a couple or an individual. Inhibition combined with rigid preferences leads to a "routinization" of sex that more or less quickly brings lovers to a point of diminishing returns. Preferred (or merely familiar) positions and behaviors may be repeated month after month—their pleasure gradually growing flat without the spice of novelty or experiment. The same is true of fantasy. Roles and scripts that were once exciting (whether privately experienced or explicitly acted out) may lose their power to stimulate if repeated too long without variation. Finally, the nature and intensity of a couple's emotional intimacy can be restricted when only certain preferred kinds of feeling (say, loving affection) are allowed expression in bed.

Of course, we all have sexual preferences and, to one degree or another, sexual inhibitions. When it comes to our own capacity for sexual flexibility, the question is whether these preferences and/or inhibitions are so unyielding that they curtail our erotic pleasure or freeze pursuit of our sexual potential. At one extreme are preferences so strong and exclusive that without their satisfaction no sexual satisfaction is possible at all. Here we are referring to "perversion," in the most contemporary sense of the term— that is, the inability to be orgasmic without the use of one specific, restricted activity or fantasy. (By this definition a person wed exclusively to intercourse in the missionary position might be called perverted.) At another extreme are inhibitions so intense that they make sexual involvement itself nearly impossible.

The Erotic Map: Childhood Origins

Such extremes of wish and fear usually originate in profoundly disturbing childhood experiences, such as incest or severe physical abuse. But less extreme preferences and inhibitions can also rein in sexual flexibility, and these too have their roots in early experience.

Our own preferred erotic fantasies can be understood as disguised versions of the difficulties with which we needed to cope as children. Some of these difficulties are nearly universal, and they generate fantasies that many of us share. For example, as children we all had moments in which we felt powerless in relation to our parents. In the genesis of erotic fantasy, such difficult experiences are either sexualized (in which case it might turn us on to imagine ourselves powerless in relation to our lover) or reversed (in which case we might be stimulated by feeling powerful in relation to a lover we imagine is powerless).

To understand how the circumstances of childhood can limit sexual flexibility, consider the example of a forty-year-old married man whose mother's frustration with her brood of eight built at times to an unpredictably volcanic and terrifying rage. In this man's masturbatory fantasies, he always preferred to imagine himself with adoring, powerless women whom he seduced, dominated, and demeaned. Here we can see his effort to psychologically master—through reversal—the trauma of being hurt by the mother he loved and depended on. His problem now, however, is his unhappy sexual relationship with a wife whom he adores. Their life in bed together has grown so empty of excitement that he finds himself longing for the "sexual freedom" he imagines he might enjoy with a woman he cared nothing about. In a way, this man's sexual flexibility is cramped by love. The guilt provoked by his aggressive sexual preferences ("sexual anger" he calls it) leaves him terrified that these impulses might spill into the relationship with his beloved wife. And so with her, all but the "purest" of his desires are inhibited. Unfortunately, this means leaving most of his eroticism outside the bedroom door.

In contrast, a woman whose previous romances had been derailed by an erotic wanderlust that led her from one affair to the next explained the success of her present marriage in this way: "Now I act out my fantasies *in* my relationship."

Sexual flexibility of this kind grows out of an acceptance of our sexual preferences and an openness to knowing more about our own desires. It involves a willingness to explore and to be surprised by what turns us on. Inhibition, on the other hand, results from guilt, shame, or fear in relation to our desires. Put differently, inhibition occurs when our feared sexual images of ourselves—as too angry or too passive or too masculine or too feminine—take up too much psychological space.

Identifying the Imagery of the Erotic Map

All of us see ourselves in the mirror of our parents' response to our childhood sexuality and our body. Were they comfortable holding and nurturing us physically? Did they enable us to feel good about our body? Were they relaxed about our flirtation, with them or with others? How did they react when they became aware that we were masturbating? What was their response to our curiosity about sex, and to our first actual forays into the sexual world of our peers?

We also learn from observing our parents' relationship to their own sexuality. Did they seem comfortable with their body? Did we see them openly show their attraction for each other? Were they relaxed expressing physical affection for each other, or was such behavior hidden nervously or denied? What was their attitude toward sex, as expressed in words and body language?

And finally, we make interpretations of whatever occurs around us sexually that is ambiguous. If nothing was said to us about sex, did we attribute this silence to the danger or "badness" of the subject matter? Or did we wind up concluding that sex was a great, alluring, and very adult mystery? If we felt we shared a special "romance" with the parent of the opposite sex, did we worry that the other parent might feel excluded? As "Daddy's little girl," for example, were we concerned about mother's jealous anger or hurt? Or did we assume that she was happily impressed by how grown-up and "sexy" we were becoming?

The Erotic Map: Past and Present

Our capacity for erotic involvement is shaped by the past, but it can continue to evolve in the present. Our real, ideal, and feared sexual images of ourselves and others, our masculinity/femininity, our sexual flexibility—all these emerge from personal history. But our map of the erotic is never fixed or immutable, unless we regard our own current sexual expectations, wishes, and fears as the very last words on the subject.

Every developing love relationship is like a journey into new terrain that may demand changes or revisions in the old map. Each stage of the journey presents sexual opportunities and challenges that can alter and deepen our capacity for erotic involvement.

THE SEXUAL JOURNEY: WHAT CAN WE EXPECT ALONG THE WAY?

In the model outlined in this book, love relationships evolve through three successive stages: falling in love, becoming a couple, and deepening love over time. In each stage the rewards of sexuality and the risks that threaten it are different.

When we are falling in love, sexuality is "chemistry." It is part of the magnetism that draws us to our partner and helps us weather the fears and overcome the reservations that can stall intimacy. Lovers may feel a little awkward or hesitant at the start. There is room, therefore, for sex to improve, and often it does throughout the first phase of a relationship.

The erotic risks in early love are of two kinds. On the one hand, the sexual attraction between partners may be at a low ebb from the outset—in which case they may lack a resource that enables others to get through hard emotional times more easily. On the other hand, an initially potent sexual chemistry may be undermined by deficits in other capacities crucial to loving. For instance, when one or both partners have fears of *merging*—that is, they worry that their autonomy or identity is threatened when they get close—sexuality may be the first casualty. When one or both partners have trouble with *idealization*—that is, they are fearful of deeply admiring someone or uncomfortable being deeply admired—they may find it difficult to remain sexually excited. Faultfinding or self-consciousness may get in the way. If sexuality is not to be derailed, these defenses must be understood.

In the second stage of love, sexuality has the potential to be an arena in which intimacy, pleasure, communication, and understanding can flourish. If lovers share a capacity for sexual flexibility, they can permit more and more of themselves to be known and expressed in bed. To the extent that this is possible, monogamy becomes an arrangement in which more is gained than lost. In particular, because deepening familiarity with one another during the second stage of love means disappointment and frustration (as well as appreciation), sex can be a context for safely expressing aggression, in a defused way. By taking the "edge" off it, sex can help integrate the anger that is an inevitable (if unwelcome) part of love.

The predictable risk during this second stage of the journey is that sexuality will be stalled—not by familiarity but by inhibition. Inhibition can result when one partner or both have difficulties with the capacities for integration or refinding. Without integration, disappointment can be overwhelming when the perfection of early love yields to the mundane realities of daily life as a couple. As for refinding, when the past rears its head in the present and we see in our partner reflections of a parent, our sexual interest may diminish, because sexuality now has "incestuous" overtones; or inhibition may spring from anger or fear.

The challenge is to resist the temptation to take our inhibition at face value, as though it were the only sensible response to the shortcomings of our partner. The more promising course is to see it as a personal, or interpersonal, development that must be generously understood and resolved. By enlisting our partner to play a role in an old family drama we have guaranteed that there are more than two people in bed when we make love. Once we discover the identities of these bedside intruders, we can begin to exorcise their destructive influence.

The third phase of the sexual journey is in some ways the most difficult (though potentially the most rewarding) because it confronts many of us with the realities of parenting and aging that can give refinding a *plausibility* that makes it hard to overcome. Giving voice to a common experience, one woman said:

> I see my husband playing with the kids. He's graying, he's put on weight, and the combination of his being a daddy and

the way he looks as he gets older...it makes it impossible for me not to see my father when I look at him. And that's hardly a turn-on.

The other side of the coin is that knowledge of ourselves and our partner, coupled with the security of a time-tested relationship, provides a rich and safe context within which to pursue and create a fulfilling, passionate, and varied sex life.

SELF-APPRAISAL: THREE SEXUAL PROFILES

Assessing our own capacity for erotic involvement is both useful and difficult. To the extent that we understand our own strengths, as well as the defenses we use to shield ourselves when we are vulnerable, we will have less need to blame our partner. But because objectivity about ourselves is hard to come by, this kind of self-understanding may be difficult to achieve. Sometimes, however, in looking at the personalities of other people, we can recognize hard-to-identify aspects of ourselves.

The three sketches that follow embody many of the characteristics that differentiate among high, mid-range, and low capacities for erotic involvement. We won't, of course, find a perfect fit between our own traits and those portrayed in the three profiles. We may see areas of overlap, however, between ourselves and the personalities sketched below—in terms of the degree of sexual flexibility vs. inhibition, the resolution of conflicts of gender identity, and the form and consequences of the defenses we use to contend with dangers on the erotic front.

Bettina: Sexuality as a Resource

Married for a second time, with children, this thirty-nine-year-old interior designer has come a great distance on her erotic journey. She was not blessed with a perfect childhood, but she made exceptionally good use of the opportunities her adult relationships afforded her, with the result that she is now very comfortable with her own sexuality.

Bettina and her husband enjoy what seems to be an expansive erotic life together. There is room to both express love and play with fantasy. She allows herself to be very aggressive and very submissive, very much the parent and very much the child, very feminine and very masculine. In fact she feels she has become acquainted with many of these aspects of her personality expressly in the context of her sexual relationships.

Bettina's mother was a somewhat self-effacing woman who seemed to enjoy the role of the long-suffering martyr. She was a bright, energetic, and nurturing woman, but apparently ill at ease with her sexuality. Her father was an active participant in raising his children, but he was also a firm disciplinarian who believed in corporal punishment. Bettina's parents slept in separate beds. Apart from the children they produced, Bettina never saw the slightest evidence of a physical relationship between the two of them.

In her first marriage, to a man in whom she plainly refound her father, Bettina had the good fortune to encounter someone who, for all his shortcomings, was nonetheless sexually relaxed and in fact quite adventurous. In bed, at least to begin with, he led and she followed. She found herself discovering and enjoying aspects of her sexuality she had hardly imagined. In her second marriage, to a man who was emotionally open but somewhat sexually inhibited, she has led erotically and he has followed. The consequence is a sexual relationship in which husband and wife experience their shared sexuality as a resource—which enables them not only to grow closer as a couple but also to feel stronger and more self-knowledgeable as individuals.

Jonathan: Sexuality That Is Compromised

A twenty-eight-year-old video editor, Jonathan has a difficult time being himself sexually with his wife. He is troubled by two kinds of fears: that he is sexually inadequate and that he is sexually perverse.

The first fear arises from experiences he has had with premature ejaculation. The second fear has to do with his masturbatory fantasies. In this private sphere, he is either very dominating or very submissive. He worries that this reveals a side of his erotic persona that is deeply unsavory and would inevitably alienate his wife.

He had a brief affair some years ago that left him nearly crushed by guilt. The woman was not someone toward whom he felt great affection, yet he can't stop thinking about the pleasure he enjoyed enacting his fantasies with a partner for the first time.

A Catholic upbringing left him, he says, with a Madonna/whore complex. By this he means that he can enjoy sex only with someone for whom he has little feeling. To be sexual with his wife would be to soil her with his very undesirable desires and, in fact, to risk losing her. Complicating this picture is a mother he experienced as overly possessive ("she could never stand any of my girlfriends, nor my wife") and a distant father he saw as ineffectual.

He copes with the conflict between his wishes and fears, his sexual preferences and his sexual guilt, by losing touch with much of his sexuality when he is with his wife. Only in private or, briefly, with a woman he devalued, could he be himself sexually. But this alienation from his own aggressive sexuality leaves him vulnerable to fears that he is not a "real man," and his submissive fantasies, also hidden, exacerbate these fears.

The compromise for Jonathan is to deeply love his wife, while at the cost of repressing his sexuality. He has the capacity to love with tenderness, but with little passion.

Carol: Sexuality as a Struggle

A high school teacher in her mid-forties, Carol had been involved in a long but nearly sexless marriage to a very handsome man who turned out to be a transvestite. Having divorced and begun another relationship, Carol sought therapy to try and ensure that her sexual experience with her new partner would be happier than previous ones.

Carol's sexuality was complicated. First, though she felt very sexual, she could at times be uneasy about intercourse, irrationally associating penetration with the threat of damage to her genitals. Second, she was aroused mainly by sadistic and/or masochistic fantasies that she was fearful of revealing to her partners. And third, she felt very alienated from her own femininity: somehow her intense sexual desires, tinged as they were with aggression, left her feeling uncomfortably "masculine." These feelings about her sexuality derived from two kinds of experiences—the first involved her mother, the second her father.

Her mother, a coolly charismatic woman, had been relatively unavailable to her: she had suffered from a number of illnesses, had been involved in several extra-marital affairs, and had died in childbirth when Carol was ten. Carol's ambivalence about her mother undermined her ability to identify with her. Moreover, the nature of her mother's death (which Carol in a very childlike way interpreted as a result of her affairs) generated the association between sex and genital damage.

As for Carol's father, he had been alternately seductive with her and brutally rejecting. He would hold her comfortingly in his lap, caress her, tell her that she was his "girlfriend"—and in fact introduce her to others using the same word. But he could be unpredictably critical and angry. When at sixteen she became pregnant, he sent her to a home for unwed mothers, telling her that she was a "whore," unfit to live under the same roof as decent people.

As a reflection of this history, Carol's erotic map was defensively "split." She experienced sexuality either as extremely magnetic (as a source of comfort) or as extremely threatening (as a source of potential damage and guilt). First, she had lived out one side of this split by being sexual with many men—which to her meant being sexually in control. In so doing, she angrily "sexualized" her father's accusation that she was a "whore" and lived out an identification with her mother who had affairs. Then, in marrying a transvestite with whom she had virtually no sex, she protected herself from the threats of sexuality through extreme inhibition. Now with a new partner, she is finally beginning to integrate the various aspects of her extremely conflicted sexuality.

CHAPTER TWO

The Capacity for Merging:
The Role of Boundaries in Love

You can't worship love and individuality
in the same breath.
—D. H. Lawrence

If passion is the emotional hallmark of sexuality, it is tenderness that suffuses that closest closeness we call merging.

To merge our life with the life of someone we love promises release from the lonely prison of our own separateness. Having fallen in love, we feel that we are home at last. We have found a family (at least, the beginning of one) and the wished-for feelings that go with it: warmth, belonging, and tenderness.

Yet this experience of merging also has a problematic side. Losing oneself in the tender thrill of loving another means to feel in danger at times of losing one's *self*—or at least one's most comforting ideas about oneself. Perhaps more disturbing, there is the possibility of being found lacking by the lover we reveal ourselves to and the fear of being abandoned. These kinds of worries explain why falling in love is nearly universally experienced as both blissful *and* difficult.

Only a few of us lead our lives in love as though merging were exclusively one or the other, either irresistibly desirable or overwhelmingly threatening. Most of us are caught somewhere in the middle: We don't want to be alone, we want to be part of a larger whole—a couple or a family; but we are anxious about the risks and sacrifices that seem to be asked of us as the price of admission.

A young woman on the threshold of marriage describes the dilemma poignantly:

> I'm torn not about what I'm going to do but about what I feel. I know how much I want to be with Eric, how committed I am to having kids together. I adore him and admire him. I want to take care of him and have him take care of me. He's just about the perfect person for me. But after a few days of feeling close, I always want to push him away. He'll ask me a harmless question like, How's your work going? and I'm ready to snap at him, What business is that of yours? I'm worried he's going to want to know *everything.* Or he gives me something special and I feel like, Uh-oh, there goes my control. I feel I've got to be super-protective of my individuality or else I'll just give up somehow and my life will start to revolve around his.

In resolving this basic tension between the desire to be one with another and the fear of losing our individuality, the capacity for merging is absolutely central. To begin with, this capacity is instrumental in determining whether or not we can fall in love. Once we have fallen in love, it determines the extent to which we enjoy and deepen intimacy—or run from it. Finally, our ability to merge influences the degree to which *tenderness* can be at the heart of our experience of loving. Are we able to feel gentle and soft, protective toward and protected by someone we care for who cares deeply for us?

To appreciate just how this capacity affects our relationships, we must begin with a paradox: Healthy merging involves the ability to *merge without merging.* It involves the ability, in other words, to stretch our boundaries to include someone we love without giving up our boundaries altogether. To better understand how merging, boundaries, and love are connected, it is helpful to return to the metaphor of the map.

BORDERS AND BOUNDARIES: MAINTAINING IDENTITY AND SOVEREIGNTY IN LOVE

The term *boundaries* frequently crops up in conversation about relationships, but what does it really mean? Personal boundaries can best be understood here as the psychological equivalent of the borders that surround the territories depicted on a map. In the same way that geographic borders define national (or local) identity, our personal boundaries define, and protect, our individual identity. Within geographic borders people usually share a sense of collective identity, a feeling of "us" and "them," that defines those inside the borders as separate from those outside. Our personal boundaries draw a similar line: inside is "self"— that is, our own understanding and feeling about who we are— and outside is "other." Boundaries protect us by keeping our definition of ourselves separate from the ideas others have about us.

This self-definition, this "understanding and feeling about who we are," is experienced internally as a sense of identity. To the extent that we are comfortable revealing who we are, however, our sense of identity will not only be experienced internally and privately; it will also be actively and "publicly" expressed in our relationships with other people.

Suppose, for example, that our sense of identity includes a view of ourselves as shy. Our comfort making public this private view of ourselves will largely depend upon the state of our boundaries. With good boundaries, we won't feel overly threatened by our partner's reactions. Then, paradoxically perhaps, we'll be able to express our shyness quite openly, by letting our partner know that intimacy will deepen only slowly, at our own cautious pace. Thus, boundaries (like borders) do more than define and protect our sense of identity: they also affect our relationships with other people and, in particular, our sense of *sovereignty*.

In international law (if not always international relations), a country's borders guarantee its sovereignty, that is, its right to make its own choices and to negotiate when these choices conflict with those of other sovereign states. The same is true of our psychological boundaries: they not only establish identity but also make possible our sovereignty—that is, the conviction that the choices that affect our lives are ours to make.

When we merge in love, we "redraw" the map of self and other in two ways: we open our boundaries to let our partner in and we let ourselves be included within our partner's boundaries. This means allowing our partner to become important enough to us to influence our sense of our own identity and sovereignty.

But there is more, and here we must return to the paradox. Ideally, when we join our life to that of someone we love, we merge without merging—merge, that is, without permitting ourselves to be submerged. Our boundaries, in the best case, are selectively permeable. They can open, but they can also close when necessary to protect us, in the same way that national borders may close when a country is threatened. Flexible boundaries of this kind are possible to the extent that we know and accept who we really are.

Consider the experience of a woman, Helen, married for nearly thirty years, now happily surprised to find herself feeling more and more intimate with her husband:

A combination of things—therapy, some professional and personal successes, my connection to my kids, both of whom have finished college now—has led me to feel clearer and better about myself. The result is that I'm able to be much less reactive to my husband. Leonard has always been a very smart, very powerful, rather emotional guy who can easily get others embroiled in dramas that are really his own. I used to get upset or angry or defensive with him when he'd get me involved in one of these high-tension scenes. But now I'm more inclined *not* to get involved, to see instead that the tension is really his—it's not mine. And his reaction to this "new" me has been to be more revealing about what's really going on with him. I maintain my boundaries more; his stuff is then more clearly his—he knows it and I know it—and that lets us get more intimate.

Helen's example shows how self-knowledge and self-acceptance can affect our ability to use our boundaries flexibly—to merge without merging. It also highlights the crucial fact that our understanding and feeling about who we are can evolve in adulthood. With flexible boundaries and a healthy capacity for merging, joining our life to that of a partner we love means our sense of ourselves can grow larger at any stage of our development. When merging is problematic, by contrast, we can feel submerged or suffocated by our closeness to another, as if the space we occupied together had grown confining, airless, too small for two.

The challenge for each of us is to strike a workable balance between love and individuality, between merging and self-definition. When states or territories link their fates and form a nation, they work out the degree of autonomy and identity they will retain. Usually, they try to respect individual identities while sacrificing some autonomy to reap the rewards of merging into the larger whole. And sometimes countries—like marriages—break apart when the rewards of merging are overshadowed by the sacrifice of identity or autonomy. When the sacrifice is too great, the union is unstable, whether it's the merger of partners in a couple or territories in a nation.

More than two thousand years ago, the philosopher Plato specifically defined love as merging: love meant, in his words, "becoming one instead of two." Now that we appreciate the apparent contradiction that healthy merging involves merging without merging, a more realistic aim comes into focus: to "become one *as well as* two."

MOTIVES FOR MERGING

Carl and Ellen chose to see a therapist to help them resolve their dilemma about having a child. Tall and striking, Carl was a graphic artist with aspirations to be a serious painter. Ellen was a dark, attractive woman who was just beginning to earn a living as a writer of mystery novels. They were ambivalent about the new level of merging involved in becoming parents. And they were eloquent about the rewards of the merging they had already experienced.

Carl:

My last birthday somebody asked me to make a wish before blowing out the candles. I said I already got my wish when I met Ellen. There's this feeling finally of completeness, of warmth, like I've got somebody to play with now, permanently, somebody to grow old with. I no longer see myself floating from woman to woman. I've got a partner on this island. In the morning, sometimes I'll see her asleep, looking vulnerable. . . and I'll feel protective. . . and grateful to be there with her. It's like I've opened a door and she's walked in and the fit is pretty amazing. In bed, it's like we sort of melt together at times, the fit of our bodies is so right, my skin against hers. Maybe we were born on the same street in the same town, it feels that easy to be on the same wavelength. The other side of it is Ellen's strong enough to deal with me when I'm acting impossible. . . angry or babyish. . .which means I don't always have to edit myself, I can trust she's not gonna let me roll over her. . . . We can fight and it's safe. . . . It's funny but that's one of the ways I feel taken care of by her. And I see all this could change once we have a baby. I'm not sure I'm ready to give it up yet.

Ellen:

I remember once lying on our bed and looking into each other's eyes and his asking me, Why do we love each other so much? And I said, Because we're so much alike. . . . Even though I know we're really not. What I meant was just that emotionally we can be in the same place at the same time. There's this great easy feeling of overlapping we have. But I also feel what Carl said a second ago, that we give each other room to move, room to be a little weird or difficult or angry, room to be ourselves.... It's like Carl is a mirror and I get to see things about myself there that otherwise I might not see...really might not want to see. I reveal aspects of myself that I've hidden before, even from me. And being part of Carl's life makes me feel good about myself because I feel good about him. We both want a child at some point, but we have feelings now with each other that we don't want to let go of...I mean now, it's like we each get taken care of by the other and with a baby it could all become something else. God forbid, there might not be that experience of constant mushiness.

These sound like songs of love. Merging (in Ellen's words, "this great easy feeling of overlapping") is deeply satisfying for this couple. Ellen and Carl each emphasize slightly different aspects of the experience, but together they catalog nearly completely the motivations for merging. And these, it turns out, are the same three motivations that energize all the capacities crucial to loving: the wish for pleasure, the need for self-esteem, and the desire for mastery.

The pleasure they describe, even in bed, has more to do with tenderness than with passion. It is the pleasure of gazing into each other's eyes, of melting together, of caressing and being caressed. Besides the tenderly erotic pleasure of merging, there is pleasure in their closeness that is aggressively tinged ("we can fight and it's safe") and pleasure that is healthily dependent ("we each get taken care of by the other").

For Carl and Ellen alike, to feel a part of each other's world enables them to feel more complete, more comfortable with themselves. To feel loved by, and also similar to, the other enables both of them to feel good about themselves. In Ellen's words, "It's the ultimate to love someone who you know loves you."

Then, there is the opportunity to master uncompleted psycho-logical business. To one degree or another, all of us are motivated to grow, to mature, to develop as people. This means confronting the unmastered fears with which our experience has left us burdened. But where is the mastery in merging? How does merging enable us to confront and master our hidden and sometimes disabling fears?

The metaphor of clothing, as a *visual* boundary, helps to clarify how merging can be a context for psychological development. Clothing covers and conceals our body. Depending on how we feel about our body, we may be uncomfortable shedding our clothes and letting ourselves be seen—even by those we love. We may be particularly reluctant to expose those parts of our body that are "private" or cause us feelings of shame or inferiority.

Personal boundaries are the emotional equivalent of clothing: depending on how we feel about who we are *inside*, either we will feel free to open our boundaries and let ourselves be seen, or out of fear and shame, we will feel the need to hide.

In regard to merging, these are the questions: Can we be emotionally naked when we choose to? Can we open our boundaries and expose our inner reality to someone we love? Or are we inhibited, like a person who is reluctant to undress with a lover unless the lights are out? What parts of ourselves are we comfortable or courageous enough to reveal? And what must be kept walled-off, boundaried within ourselves?

Just as clothes conceal what we can't accept about our body, personal boundaries protect our secret selves from the real or imagined dangers of exposure. Just as ceasing to hide our body from those we love can initiate a process of self-acceptance, self-disclosure has the potential to begin diminishing our secret shame and fear. Healthy merging involves precisely this kind of healing self-disclosure.

Ellen recalled an episode at a party just weeks after she and Carl had met. She found herself angry and distressed at Carl's flirtation with another woman:

I'd already begun to care a lot for Carl. Seeing him practically coming on to someone at this party just blew my mind. My first impulse was to do the familiar thing, to try and be cool rather than getting into a fight with a man I was trying to get close to. . . . But then I thought, No, if Carl and I were going to have a chance at a real relationship then I was going to have to be real. That meant letting him know what I felt and what I needed, what I would and wouldn't tolerate. I was sure I was taking a huge risk with him. Plus I was taking a stand with a man in a way that was very difficult and out-of-character for me at that time. Anyway, I got him into the hallway and talked to him: I was strong and direct, I felt totally committed to what I was saying. I told him that he could flirt all he wanted. But if he wanted to be with me then he was going to have to cut it out. Right now. He seemed taken aback. But he seemed to like it, too.

Ellen's experience here shows how merging can be a context for mastering uncompleted psychological business. In her previous relationships with men, she had made all the compromises. For Ellen, the fear that she couldn't take care of herself had made losing her partner's affection a terrifying prospect. So she had been chameleon-like—not merging, but allowing herself to be submerged. She played up qualities she thought would please, hid her resentments, and wound up depressed. Early on with Carl, by contrast, she felt secure enough to let him see what she had hidden from men in the past: her strength, her jealous desire, and her anger. In so doing, she opened her boundaries to Carl and let him in. The double reward for her was the beginning of a relationship grounded in reality and the opportunity to rework an old pattern in which she sacrificed her identity in exchange for love.

This episode also exemplifies what we mean by merging without merging, joining with another without losing one's self. Ellen opened herself to Carl and revealed her caring and commitment—

by setting a limit with him. While stretching her own boundaries, she proposed to Carl that they draw a new boundary that would surround their relationship and protect it from the intrusions his flirtation invited. This sort of boundary makes two people a couple, enables them to become "one as well as two."

Carl's view of the same episode shows how one partner's self-disclosure can affect the other:

> When Ellen got in my face about what I was doing at that party I knew that I was dealing with someone substantial. It brought me up short. I don't think I was aware of what I was up to until she confronted me with it. I saw that I was doing something really funky that would more or less guarantee that Ellen and I wouldn't get too close. Also I think I was trying to get her to feel insecure and trying to avoid any of that myself.

Carl experienced Ellen's limit setting as a challenge to him to be both more intimate and more real. It was as though she had said to him, "I don't want to play games: I'd like to have a relationship that is secure enough to make each of us feel safe enough to be real."

We have been explaining how merging provides opportunities for mastering unfinished psychological business. Here is Carl's version:

> Getting women interested in me has always been a way to reassure myself and avoid feeling insecure. When Ellen put her foot down it was like she was saying, Can't you come out from behind the Don Juan stuff and just be yourself? I think what made it possible for me to do that finally, to risk being more exposed, was seeing how passionately involved with me she was willing to be. That kind of thing is very reassuring, all by itself. But also I have to say, having taken some risks being more transparent, it's shown me there's less to be scared of than I thought....

Upward Spirals, Downward Spirals, and a Catch-22

As Ellen and Carl's experience suggests, the motivations for merging—pleasure, heightened self-esteem, and psychological mastery—can reinforce each other and generate an upward spiral in love. The warmth and tenderness we feel when we're close to someone we love heightens our confidence and sense of well-being. In turn, this can make it easier for us to risk exposing and confronting difficult realities that heretofore we may have avoided. Eventually, not always without pain, letting our secret shame and fear see the light of day brings partners closer to one another—thus promoting tenderness, self-esteem, and the willingness to take further risks.

By contrast, when our capacity for merging is limited, we tend to hide from our partner (and sometimes from ourselves) aspects of our personality that disturb us or that we fear others might find disturbing. Ellen was tempted to hide her assertiveness, Carl his insecurity. Had either partner kept the boundaries sealed around these troubling feelings, the couple's opportunities for pleasure, heightened self-esteem, and mastery through merging would have been very much diminished. Instead they might have found themselves caught in the kind of downward spiral that doomed Ellen's earlier relationships and kept Carl forever playing the unfulfilled Don Juan.

The dynamics of merging in love seem to have something of a "rich get richer, poor get poorer" quality to them. Only when we *already* possess flexible boundaries and the ability to reveal who we really are is it possible to merge and reap the rewards of merging, which include the potential for deeper merging and greater rewards. The apparent Catch-22 arises because the motives that drive our desire to merge—pleasure, self-esteem, and mastery—are very often in painful conflict with one another.

For example, our wishes for pleasure can conflict with our needs for self-esteem. To enjoy feeling taken care of, we may want very much to be close to someone we love. But the very wish to be taken care of is linked (by many men and some women) to feeling weak or babyish. Simply becoming aware of such a desire can be enough for some of us to feel that our self-esteem is threatened. As a consequence, we may hide our wish to feel taken care of—or in the worst case, we may be so dominated by our fear of dependency and closeness that it will be impossible for us to fall in love at all.

Or, there can be a conflict between our self-esteem needs and our need to master uncompleted psychological business. If we have learned (as many men have) that being in control is a way to feel good about ourselves, then it may be difficult for us to master the necessary challenge of yielding control at times. If we have learned (as many women have) that pleasing men is a way to feel good about ourselves, then we may have a hard time mastering the necessary challenge of asserting ourselves when self-assertion means displeasing a man.

Our own particular motivations—and their conflicts—will inevitably affect our ability to merge and our experience of intimacy. We may enjoy closeness and seek it out. Or we may fear closeness and so avoid it.

TO MERGE OR NOT TO MERGE: ONENESS AND SEPARATENESS, DEPENDENCY AND ASSERTION

Each of us makes our choices in love with the help of a map of self and other, the initial outlines of which were laid down early in our life. Freud was the first to explore how in childhood we each develop an internal map of the erotic that shapes our adult sexuality. In comparably pioneering fashion, Margaret Mahler, a brilliant psychoanalyst of children, explored how in childhood we develop the maps that tell us what it means to merge.

In 1975 Mahler published her landmark study, *The Psychological Birth of the Human Infant*. Through observing infants and young children with their mothers, Mahler discovered that our capacity for merging develops out of the early struggle to balance what may be our two most basic psychological needs: the need for oneness and the need for separateness. Neither is more or less important than the other; both are equally vital to the experience of being human. The difficulty at times is that we may feel compelled to choose between the two.

On the one hand, as infants we must be close to mother to be fed and nurtured in order, quite literally, to survive. On the other hand, healthy development also requires independent activity, like the baby's first steps away from mother or the toddler's autonomy that begins with the word "no."

Balancing our needs for oneness and separateness is difficult because early in our life the one person we are most dependent on is the same person we are learning how to be independent from. So we are torn. And because our childhood love relationships are models for those that follow, we may still struggle with the tension between oneness and separateness when we fall in love as adults. We may feel that it is an uncomfortable matter of either-or, rather than both.

The polarity of "oneness" and "separateness" may sound abstract. But two features of this polarity—namely, dependency[1] (an aspect of oneness) and self-assertion (an aspect of separateness)—involve experiences in love that are tangible and familiar to all of us.

By dependency we mean the desire or need for the caring of others. The prototypical image is the infant cradled in its mother's arms. But dependency is also reflected in our wish for the comfort of a hug when we are down or the sympathy of an interested listener when we feel troubled.

---

1. *Dependency* is a psychological term that has come to carry excess emotional baggage, most of it negative. Few of us would happily be characterized as dependent. Moreover, dependency can be confused with *co-dependency* (which has many meanings, some obscure, all bad). The difficulty we have unhooking this term from its conventional negative connotations in part reflects the intensely conflicted reaction many of us have to our own very human dependency.

By self-assertion we mean the forceful expression of our own will. Among the earliest versions of self-assertion is the tantrum of the toddler in the throes of the "terrible twos." But self-assertion is also reflected in our ability to say no, to express our anger and set limits when necessary, or to press for the satisfaction of our own wishes, even when they conflict with the wishes of others.

Just as we all have desires for oneness *and* separateness, all of us have impulses to be dependent and assertive. It is never a matter of either-or: it is always both. When it comes to merging in love, the question is: Can we be aware of wishes to be cared for and wishes to assert our own will, or must our wishes remain unknown to us? And if we are aware of such wishes, can we express them to someone we love, or must their expression be inhibited?

Dependency and Merging

When we are comfortable with our needs to be cared for, the prospect of being dependent on someone we love is no barrier to intimacy. On the contrary, it is part of what makes us yearn to be close. But if we regard our needs as shameful or threatening, or if we assume that others will be intolerant of our needs, then in various ways we may have to cut ourselves off from those we love.

Ben, a social worker of forty, recounts the powerful shifts that have occurred in his marriage after seeing how deep his fears of dependency run and how strong are his longings:

I'm finally understanding that I have *needs*—and it feels like I've just cracked a safe, like I've heard that sound, that little click, and I know I've got the combination now. I look back and I see what's happened between me and Maggie in the past: the way I've always felt crushed by *her* needs. But now I realize that I was fooling myself, deciding that I was the big daddy who didn't need a thing and she was just this big baby—when the reality is I've been terrified of that part of myself. It's like I've had these two images of myself: one's the guy who doesn't need anything 'cause everything comes to me without even trying, but then there's the guy who's just totally crushed and helpless and really needs a lot but feels too humiliated to reveal any of that. So I would just get withdrawn. Or I'd feel burdened 'cause Maggie needed to be rescued. Or I'd decide she couldn't stand to see men cry. Now I've begun to see that my having needs or her having needs is natural, the most natural thing in the world, and it's like, whew, I can breathe. God, it makes it so much easier to feel close to her. . . .

Ben describes his ability to be dependent and consequently to be close as having been shaped by two images. There is the ideal image of himself in relation to others—The Man with No Needs, or at least none that have to be articulated. There is also a feared image of himself as dependent ("totally crushed. . .helpless. . . humiliated") that makes it easy to understand why he's had a hard time acknowledging what he now calls "the most natural thing in the world." Trapped between the pressure of his ideal and the threat of his fear, he has had enormous difficulty in allowing himself to be "real," that is, a human being with needs.

Like Ben, we have all developed images of ourselves that tell us what it means to be dependent. In general, we try to live up to our ideal self-images (no matter how incomplete, grandiose, and unattainable they may be). At the same time, we try to protect ourselves from experiences that threaten to leave us feeling identified with the self-images we fear. We have also developed internal images of others. These images influence both *our* attitude toward the dependency of those we love (to Ben, Maggie's needs meant that she was "a big baby") and *their* presumed attitude toward our dependency (Ben told himself that Maggie "couldn't stand to see men cry").

The images that compose our personal map of dependency are acquired in different ways. In part they are the record of actual experiences with our parents at times when we needed to feel cared for or taken care of by them. The most influential experiences of all were probably those in early infancy—in Margaret Mahler's words, that "unrememberable and unforgettable" time when we were quite literally and helplessly dependent. What sort of reception did our needs for physical and emotional nurturing receive then? Usually we can only make inferences about this by recalling, for example, how our parents dealt with us later in our life when we were ill or unhappy. But the nature of our first experience of dependency is crucial. It is responsible, in large part, for determining whether or not we possess "basic trust": the confidence that other human beings are likelier than not to be safe and gratifying. Our earliest experiences of dependency determine, too, our fundamental sense of the "goodness" or "badness" of our own needs and desires in relation to others.

Our images of dependency were also shaped by observing how our parents dealt with their own needs to feel cared for. Did they seem comfortable revealing to us or to each other the pain or difficulty they experienced in their life? Did they seem capable of giving and receiving comfort from one another during these times? Or did their needs seem exaggerated, their demands for support or care disturbingly desperate? What we saw our parents feeling and doing in relation to their own needs becomes part of our personal imagery of dependency.

One more point must be made about how our map of merging and dependency evolved: We always do more than passively witness and take in the events that mold us. From the time we are very young, we also *respond* to what we experience and *interpret* what we observe in very individual and particular ways. Ben's story helps make this clear:

> Rather than learning that it was the most natural thing in the world to have needs, I learned that it was inappropriate. I've heard from my older brother that after I was born my mother got very depressed and couldn't really take care of me. For a while my grandma came and stayed with us. . . . But I know I always felt I had to be good, you know, not too demanding—and I think I also felt that my mother was sort of pathetic in her helplessness. Meanwhile my dad was this war hero who jumped into an icy river in the dead of winter

to rescue a guy who was drowning. That was the way you were supposed to be, not a big baby. Let my mother be the baby or let my wife be the baby. Just so long as it's not me.

In relation to a mother who was absorbed with her own pain, Ben learned that he shouldn't need too much. By observing a father who was portrayed as a heroic rescuer, he learned to feel good about himself by rescuing others. Ben's response to his mother's unavailability was to withdraw into an illusory self-sufficiency (a very different response from that of his angrily demanding older brother or his dramatically helpless younger sister). Ben interpreted his father's heroic stance in a way that added another dimension to his imagery of dependency: to be a man, it appeared, he should have no needs, but should attend to the needs of others.

Ben's experience helps brings into focus the relationship between dependency and gender. To be dependent as an adult not only threatens to leave a man feeling babyish but also threatens his confidence in his masculinity. This threat has its earliest roots in the little boy's dependency on and identification with his mother, but it is amplified by a society that still teaches that "big boys don't cry."

Society doesn't stigmatize women's dependency in the same way. In fact, culturally, femininity and dependency have been yoked together. And yet, for women as well as men, the wish to be cared for can be a most ambivalent wish. As one woman put it, "I don't *want* my boyfriend to know I have needs—it gives him too much power over me, power to say no or to take advantage of my vulnerability. It's just like it was with my mother. Of course she'd take care of me, but there were always strings attached." Men and women alike may have had early experiences that lead them to fear that once they reveal their dependency, they will be misused by those they love.

But self-revelation is at the heart of merging in love. Being intimate is best defined as being real with someone who matters to us. And intimacy almost invariably arouses the desire to be cared for and taken care of at times.

Whether or not we emerge from behind our boundaries and let ourselves be known for who we really are has to do with both our self-images and our images of others. If revealing our dependency triggers a feared and painful image of ourselves as weak, greedy, pathetic, or emasculated, then self-revelation will be avoided and intimacy undercut. If our feared images of others lead us to worry that revealing our needs will evoke contempt, abuse, or disappointment, then our needs may have to remain closeted. We may also have a wary reaction to our own dependency (and sometimes that of others) if our ideal images—like Ben's image of his heroic father—place an exaggerated value on self-sufficiency.

The key is balance and moderation, in terms of our relationship to our own dependency and in terms of the dependency expressed by two partners in a couple. Ideally, we can tolerate and sometimes satisfy our own needs to be cared for, rather than suppress them. Ideally, our needs are neither so intense nor so peremptory that they overwhelm the beloved's capacity to respond to them.

Balance is also desirable between caring and being cared for. The ability to switch roles is as important in the area of dependency as it is in sexuality. When one partner feels capable only of giving and the other can only be taken care of, there is an imbalance that will inevitably take its toll—both on the relationship and on the individuals.

Of course, dependency and oneness are only half of the story. Merging without merging requires, in addition, asserting our separateness.

Self-Assertion and Merging

All of us are driven by contradictory desires: our yearnings for closeness vie with our wishes to be independent. We begin our life in a relationship of profound dependency, yet from the start we are also forcefully asserting our own will. The universal human conflict between the desire for oneness and the necessity for separateness and self-definition reaches peak intensity during the "terrible twos." But it is a lifelong conflict.

Yet this conflict can also be a partnership. With the ability to say no, it is easier to say yes. When we are at home with our assertiveness, we usually feel safer letting ourselves be dependent.

Carol is a forty-six-year-old high school teacher, recently divorced, whose experience with a new boyfriend helps make this connection clear:

Pablo came over the other night and I was feeling distant because he'd been acting unavailable the last few times we'd gotten together. But now all of a sudden he was being very affectionate, physically. Then when I wasn't responsive, he started to be some combination of hurt and angry and I just said to him, "Pablo, I'm not feeling close to you right now 'cause you haven't been making yourself available to me. I don't know if you've been preoccupied with work or what, and in any case, the explanation doesn't really matter. The truth is, I'm just not feeling intimate with you and I'm not going to try to force it." The weird thing, maybe not so weird, is that after being very straight with him about all this in the way I was, I actually felt very close to him. I guess letting him know that I didn't feel intimate was actually a very intimate thing to do.

Indeed, self-assertion helps make merging possible. Carol believed quite rightly that she was "rejecting" her boyfriend—or more specifically, her boyfriend's bid for an intimacy she could not feel. She was asserting her will and making a boundary that defined her experience (she felt distant) as separate from his (he felt the desire for physical closeness). Carol was asserting herself, but in the process she felt that she was also letting her boyfriend in:

There've been other times that Pablo's been unavailable and then suddenly he's there again, expecting me to be close. What was different this time was my response: I just opened up and told him honestly where I was at. In the past, I'd either just go along with him and pretend to be involved and turned on when I didn't feel it—or else I'd just be totally overwhelmed with feelings of abandonment and then I'd blast him. But neither of those responses felt like I was being myself, just honestly expressing my reaction to what was going on. When I'd comply or when I'd blast Pablo it was as if I was too scared or too overwhelmed to just be myself and say what was going on like I did the other night.

I think it's been Pablo's behavior with me that's made it possible for me to do something new. He's very confrontative, wanting me to be strong enough to say what I really think and feel. . . . And also he's got a way of containing my anger: he doesn't just *take* it and he doesn't take it too personally either.

Self-assertion plays at least two roles in merging. First, a comfortable capacity to assert our will means we can define ourselves *within* a relationship—rather than feel that we must be alone to be ourselves. Second, with a tolerance for assertiveness (our own and that of others), we can freely use our boundaries, instead of guiltily fearing that revealing their existence is tantamount to withholding love.

The freedom with which we assert our will (whether saying no, getting angry, or expressing our differences) is directly related to our internal imagery. So also is the control and appropriateness with which our will is exercised. Assertiveness that is unrestrained or destructive can be at least as significant a problem as assertiveness that is inhibited.

Sometimes the inhibition of assertion and its destructive overintensity are two sides of the same coin. Listen to Carol's description of the hurt and angry child within her, which inspires both her fear of being angry and her violent rage when her anger is finally released:

I feel like I've got this scared, incredibly angry little girl inside who I'm always trying to keep at bay 'cause she's gonna get me in trouble with her paranoia and her temper. All the memories of being criticized by my father and abandoned by my mother are wrapped up in this image. All the hurt and anger I had to keep to myself 'cause it was too dangerous to let it out—and all the fear. Now it all seems to be part of this image of myself as a little girl. And I'm afraid of her, like she's gonna sabotage me with this pent-up rage. So most of the time I just go along with the program. I get close-mouthed. I don't get angry at all. Then I blow up.

Like Carol, we all have images that tell us what it means both to be assertive and to be the target of the assertiveness of others. These images—like the internal images that make up our map of dependency and sexuality—have their origins in our early experience and in our interpretations of that experience.

How safe is it to feel angry at those we love—or to be separate from them, or to see things differently than they do? And what are the acceptable ways to express our anger, our autonomy, our difference? Without being aware of it, we answer these kinds of questions by referring to a map made up of images of assertiveness that may well be outdated, and therefore misleading.

Stretching far into the past—but still dominating our view of the present—there is usually a consistent pattern of parental response to our self-assertion. If we recall what went on when we were older (during adolescence or even beyond), we can often make inferences about what occurred when we were very young, and most profoundly subject to our parents' influence.

Most of us have forgotten our parents' reactions to us during those halcyon days known as the "terrible twos." This is the period (actually beginning in most cases before age two) during which children typically make their debut as assertive beings. Their favorite word is usually *no*, and anything that can be fought over with the parents will be.

But the child's "negativism" is the earliest version of healthy self-assertion, and the parents' reactions to it are enormously influential. When parents respond to our rudimentary assertiveness with understanding, they lay the foundations for us to accept and express the adult versions of healthy self-assertion. When they set limits in a loving way, they make it possible for us to control our aggression as adults. When, in contrast, they respond punitively or fail to set limits, they may inadvertently set the stage for adult difficulties with self-assertion—difficulties involving either inhibition or destructive lack of control. Our images of assertiveness also develop through observing our parents. Could they effectively communicate their anger (or difference or separateness)? Or, when asserting themselves, did they seem inhibited or destructively out of control?

Finally, we bring our own interpretations to bear when the evidence is ambiguous. Suppose we grew up in a family in which one parent tended to explosive anger while the other responded to conflict with determined reasonableness. We would have to decipher for ourselves the meaning of their contradictory examples. We could decide that the only effective way to assert ourselves is through rage—or that rage represents a pathetic loss of control. We could conclude that real power is expressed through being steadily reasonable and controlled—or that reasonableness and control are only disguises for weakness. Our own mapping of assertiveness will be very different depending on how we interpret what we have experienced and observed.

If our individual map leads us toward self-assertion and dependency as safe and desirable features of a love relationship, then we will be able to merge without merging. But if our wish to be taken care of and/or our desire to forcefully assert our will threatens to take us into dangerous territory, then our journey with our partner may be stalled by our needs for self-protection. Our capacity for healthy merging will be challenged by the defenses we use to keep our fears at bay.

MERGER HUNGER AND MERGER WARINESS: STYLES OF SELF-PROTECTION IN LOVE

We can often vaguely articulate a fear of intimacy without being able to say exactly what it is about intimacy that frightens us. It's as though, once upon a time, we built a wall to protect ourselves from danger, but now that wall has grown so high and impenetrable that we can't see past it to assess the real nature of the threat. Healthy merging in love is frightening for many of us, but the defenses we use make it hard to know exactly why. Are we afraid to be close? Are we afraid to assert ourselves with our partner once we are close? Sometimes our defenses can make it difficult for us to know that we have any fear of merging at all.

The fears that inhibit our desires to merge differ depending on personal history. If we have grown up with very controlling or intrusive parents, we may fear losing our autonomy in a close relationship. If our parents gave us less attention than we needed, we may be overly willing to lose ourselves to our partner in order to be loved. If our parents were unpredictable or rejecting, we may worry that closeness will lead to hurt or loss. If our early experiences with dependency or aggression have been painful, then we may fear the reemergence of these impulses in our closest relationship. But whatever the fears that shape our conflicts about being close, their true nature can be glimpsed only when we identify the defenses that simultaneously protect us and cloud our view of what frightens us.

The fundamental reality is invariably two-sided: we all want to merge and we all fear merging. But our defenses obscure the complexity of this reality by keeping us in the dark about one side of our ambivalence or the other. When our fear of merging is hidden, we appear "merger hungry." When our desire for merging is in shadow, we appear "merger wary." But appearances can be misleading.

Merger hungry and *merger wary* are terms that describe common styles of self-protection in love. But these defensive styles are never absolutely stable. For example, a man might appear merger hungry until he finds a relationship, at which point he may begin to appear wary. Nor do these defenses always reflect at a deeper level what they seem to embody on the surface. Merger wariness, for example, might turn out to be a reaction against a frighteningly strong hunger for love.

There is also the question of gender and its relation to defensive style. We've discussed dependency in terms of gender, and it's probably obvious that the merger-hungry style is seen more frequently in women, while the merger-wary style is more common in men. Certainly, this isn't an either-or matter: there are plenty of merger-hungry men and merger-wary women. And yet there does seem to be a tilt in the distribution of each of these defensive styles. The question is, Why should defenses be distributed according to gender?

Men Fear Closeness and Women Fear Separateness: A Speculation on Gender and Defense

Men and women follow different developmental pathways while growing up. The key divergence is that for a man, his mother is both the object of dependent longing in the first years of life and the object of romantic/erotic longing during what Freud called the Oedipal period (approximately ages three to six).

Contrast this with the female's experience in childhood: Her mother, too, is initially the object of her dependent wishes. But when the little girl turns to her father for the fulfillment of her first romantic wishes, her mother to some extent is lost to her— or so she may worry.

What are the implications of this developmental contrast between women and men? The fears that they bring to adult love will differ. And the defenses they most commonly employ to cope with their fears will also be different.

For a man, a woman can be the focus of frighteningly intense desire, or rather desires—for she has the potential to satisfy all the dependent, romantic, and erotic desires that were first directed toward his mother. The very possibility that these desires might be fulfilled threatens to render the male slavishly reliant on the female, who has the potential, like the seductive Sirens of Greek mythology, to be dangerously irresistible. Perhaps more threatening still, a man who loves a woman is vulnerable to having his childhood wishes for closeness restimulated. This may revive his original identification with his mother, thus challenging his feeling of masculinity. And what might be the protection from these "dangers"? Like Odysseus, who heard the Sirens' song but kept his distance, many men adopt a merger-wary style of defense.

For a woman, there are fears to be dealt with in adult love that result from her first turning away from mother toward father. This redirecting of her childhood desire, this realignment of her early loyalties, often leaves the little girl with fears of loss and sometimes guilt. The need to cope with these feelings only amplifies the intensity of her wish to be loved by her father. For now his attention compensates her for whatever she may have lost in relation to her mother. As an adult, a woman's vulnerability to fears of loss is often the enduring legacy of this childhood triangle. And what might be her protection from this fear? Modeled on the original turning to her father, a merger-hungry style of defense.

The Defensive Style of the Merger Hungry

Those who are merger hungry seem primarily to act on their *desire* for merging. Separateness appears to frighten them more than oneness. Because the greatest threats are loss, separation, and being alone, closeness is experienced as the greatest good: it is the solution, never the problem. The merger hungry are often emotionally vibrant and available, quick to engage, capable of easy rapport. They seem better at relinquishing boundaries than maintaining them. Instead of merging without merging, they may find themselves submerged. Accommodating to someone they love, they may feel they are losing themselves.

There is a continuum of the merger hungry. At one end lie those whose emotional needs are extremely intense and whose anger or fear can nearly overwhelm them when their needs go unmet. They can feel such an urgency about merging that they become angrily demanding, threatening, or manipulative to avoid the terror of being alone. Unfortunately, this often jeopardizes the very intimacy they so desperately seek.

At the other end of the continuum are individuals whose dependency is less extreme and whose reactions to frustration are more moderate. Because they are less apt to feel as if their lives are one long emergency, their approach to satisfying their relationship needs can be more seductive, more appealing, and more successful. To make sure they are taken care of, they inhibit the assertion of their own will. But this leaves them worried that their development as separate individuals is in jeopardy.

The hunger for merging—whether expressed in a desperate demand or a seductive appeal—seems the legacy of a childhood in which the experience of closeness to or nurturing by the parents was never quite enough. It's as though the incompleteness of the original merging left the child either furious and frustrated to the point of despair or else simply yearning helplessly for more.

The Merger Hungry Who Angrily Demand Love

In this, the more extreme situation, the parents' neglect, abuse, or unpredictability prevented the child from developing anything but the most tenuous capacity for basic trust.[2] When this is the story of our early years, we can't comfortably assume that we'll be loved and cared for by others in adulthood. Instead, we'll feel the need to control, manipulate, or angrily threaten in order to satisfy our desperate hunger for love. Of course, the love we receive in this way may not be freely given, and so we're always in doubt about its genuineness. Moreover, the slightest disappointment can intensify such doubt, which in turn can make us angry and desperate for proof that we are loved. Our mistrust and the means by which we elicit reassurance, however, make it very hard for us to feel reassured.

2. Two more situations may undermine the bond of mother and child and interfere with the development of basic trust. First, Mahler's observations indicate that there can be a "communicative mismatch" or poor fit between mother and child. For example, the mother (a warm, "touchy-feely" sort) might be inclined to express her loving connection to the baby through an abundance of physical affection, while the baby (with a "look-and-listen" style) might experience this as intrusive—provoking a situation in which mother feels baffled and rejected and baby feels threatened and rejecting. Second, the baby is never a blank slate. From birth, infants have their own particular strengths and liabilities. Heredity loads the dice for better or worse. Just as there are mothers whose own problems interfere with their capacity to be nurturing, there are infants whose constitutions make it hard for them to be nurtured.

Unhappily, the absence of basic trust provokes a vicious circle that, if not well understood, leads us either to push the beloved away with our demands or else to seek a new partner. Usually the mistaken assumption is that the desire for love through merging is impossible to satisfy in the present relationship—not because of our own mistrust but because we have picked the wrong partner.

The Merger Hungry Who Please

In the less extreme situation, the child's early experience with mother was good enough to develop basic trust, but the difficulties in that relationship also left the child with unsatisfied longings to be nurtured. If this is the story of our past, we will be hungry for merging and as adults will turn to love in the hope of satisfying unmet dependency needs from childhood. But there will be problems.

Because we can never really be babies again, the old longings can never be completely fulfilled. Yet this reality doesn't stop us from experiencing an aching desire to satisfy them. When our longings become impossible to resist, the unsuccessful effort to gratify them can have some unwelcome consequences. We may feel frustrated and angry (but unentitled to these reactions because we *know* it's irrational to hope to be taken care of like a baby), and we may feel humiliated (it's mortifying to reveal these wishes to someone we love). Probably most common of all, we may be reluctant to be completely real for fear of exposing ourselves as hungry children. And this fear of exposure may lead us to run from relationships that might otherwise have enormous potential.

In each of these two variations on the merger-hungry theme, we can see how our solutions become problems, that is, how defenses can perpetuate the very difficulties they are meant to deal with. The hungriest of the merger hungry are convinced they won't be loved for who they are, so they demand love, sometimes angrily, as if it were their due. But they can never derive real esteem or comfort from the love they receive—and their demands may drive love away. The merger hungry who still yearn for the nurturing they missed as children pursue adult love as solace and compensation. But this pursuit is undertaken at a high price: it undercuts adult esteem, can inhibit ambition, and if never recognized for what it is, can be a perpetual disappointment.

The Defensive Style of the Merger Wary

Acting primarily on their *fear* of merging, the merger wary appear to be everything the merger hungry are not. They behave as if merging were dangerous. They worry about being trapped, about giving up their autonomy. The greatest threat to them is to lose control or be controlled. They may say they want to love, but they are wary of intimacy. At least superficially, they maintain boundaries more easily than they relinquish them. Cautious about emotional expression, they often seem aloof. Anxious about emotional involvement, they spend much of their time single, or in relationships in which they remain uncommitted.

At the extreme end of the merger-wary continuum lie those who protect themselves by sabotaging love. Their fear of merging is so intense that they are motivated, without being aware of it, to find such faults with potential partners that a decision to merge would seem unwise. As a rule, these highly wary individuals appear to think too well of themselves and too badly of others. Before long, lovers (or those who *might* be loved) are seen as either flawed beyond redemption or too self-interested to be trusted.

Lying at the other end of the continuum are those merger-wary individuals whose watchword is control. Their fears, though less intense, are still strong. To protect themselves, they try to control their own needs and feelings. To make sure they are not controlled by others, they may control others too much.

The Merger Wary Who Sabotage Love

The more extreme version of the merger-wary style seems to emerge out of an unhappy combination of two childhood experiences. The child's dependency needs were incompletely satisfied by overtly self-absorbed and covertly insecure parents and, as a result, basic trust was achieved only in the shakiest fashion. In addition, the child came to realize that the parents' needs to feel good about themselves would always come first—but that through satisfying these needs, he or she could connect with the parents. Through helping them to feel special, the child could also feel special. Then, in the emotional desert, an oasis could be found.

If we have such a history, we face a painful dilemma in adult love. On the one hand, we have our illusions of specialness as a comfort, even when we are alone. On the other hand, we are deeply needy, and because we feel deprived, we are also likely to be angry. We've learned, however, that to gain entry to the oasis that love represents, we must put a lid on our less savory qualities—especially our neediness, but also our anger. So a relationship can feel like a sacrifice or a vise: to love is to be constricted.

One alternative is, nonetheless, to love. But in doing so we risk exposing the dependent and angry feelings for which our parents had so little tolerance. The other alternative is to be alone. But it's very hard to live in the desert, so even when we become aware of our fears, we may well look for love. The tragedy is that our fear can lead us to sabotage love, mainly through finding fault with those who might be loved. It's difficult to resist the self-generated propaganda about our own perfection and the imperfections of others. But until all of this is understood, we will continue to live like a starving man at a banquet who tells himself the food just isn't good enough and therefore refuses to eat.

The Merger Wary Who Protect Themselves through Control

The less extreme version of merger wariness reflects the child's response to parents who were made uneasy by challenges to their control. These parents were probably quite relaxed taking care of a dependent baby. But when this baby became a willful two-year-old screaming "no," making a mess, or throwing a temper tantrum, the same parents became uncomfortable. Their own inability to tolerate what seemed aggressively out of control in their child led them to exert control too aggressively themselves. As a result, the "negativistic" child, the future merger-wary adult, learned both to overcontrol himself or herself and to fear the control of others. This child also learned that to be loved he or she had to be good. Unfortunately, being loved in this way felt like a humiliating submission.

There were two solutions: First, to be as unaware of feelings as possible—not only angry feelings but also feelings of love. And second, to resist the parents' control—but mostly covertly, so the pretense of innocence might still keep the child in the parents' good graces.

When this is the story of our childhood, adult love risks becoming a power struggle—or a test to see if even now we must always be good to be loved. And if love is a struggle or a test, then understandably we will do our best to stay in control—keeping dangerous feelings at a distance, keeping our boundaries in place, and keeping merging to a minimum.

Each of the two versions of the merger-wary style is a self-protective response to painful childhood experience. But the defenses we enlist to protect ourselves—whether making a fetish of control or finding fault with those we might love—have some unintended and unwelcome consequences.

If we protect ourselves by diminishing others and withdrawing from them, then either we end up completely alone or, perhaps no less lonely, we keep our distance while pretending to be involved. Our desperate, often unconscious effort is to avoid feeling again what we felt when we were small: needy, helpless, and angry. But to avoid our needs by deciding that no one has anything worth wanting means that our needs will never be fulfilled.

If we protect ourselves by denying our feelings and reducing love to a contest for control, then we may wind up lonely, though not necessarily alone. It's as if we won't let go of the struggle with parents who demanded that we always be on our best behavior. Now as adults in love, we carry on the old war—internally, where we crush our dangerous feelings, and in our relationship, where we carry on a covert guerrilla action in which the battle cry is, "I won't yield!"

WHAT IS TO BE DONE?

In the preceding chapter, we discussed an approach to understanding the defenses that inhibit our sexuality. We can use the same approach—which involves recognizing, describing, and interpreting our defenses—to deal with the forms of self-protection that inhibit our capacity for healthy merging.

Recognition

To recognize that we are indeed using defenses comes more easily if our choice to protect ourselves has been a conscious one—if, for example, we've deliberately pulled back from our partner to protect ourselves from the threat of feeling hurt. What is more common and more problematic, however, is for us to use our defenses without being aware of it. For example, we might be flirting with someone new, without realizing that we are trying to make our partner feel insecure as a shield against our own insecurity.

We can recognize such unconscious defenses through self-observation and inference. When we inexplicably feel less comfortable with our partner, when we notice that our feelings or ideas about him or her have shifted rather suddenly, when we become aware that aspects of our relationship have become rigid, stereotyped, or lifeless—then one possible inference is that we have felt threatened and have unwittingly taken measures to protect ourselves. (An alternative possibility, of course, is that we are responding to our partner's defenses. Both could be true.)

Description

We need to be able to describe in as much detail as possible exactly *how* we are protecting ourselves. It's not enough to be aware in a vague or intellectual way that our fears have triggered defenses. Because our defenses are woven so seamlessly into our ordinary ways of experiencing ourselves and others, they can remain practically invisible. If we are to make the invisible visible, we have to look at ourselves searchingly and continually. It can also be useful to consider the points of view of others who can see us more clearly at times than we can see ourselves. In these ways we may each come to know our own individual style of self-protection. Once the details of this style come into focus, our defenses are less likely to take a toll on our relationship.

Interpretation

The next step is to understand what we are protecting ourselves from. Here's an example: A man stands in his kitchen, cooking dinner for his new girlfriend. Like a flash, the painful thought crosses his mind that she might not find him sufficiently attractive. Then the thought is gone. Moments later he finds himself worrying that maybe his new girlfriend isn't attractive enough for him. Let's stop the action here for a moment. If this man now looked at the sequence of his thoughts and feelings, he might come up with this interpretation: To protect himself from his worry about the adequacy of his physical appeal, he has begun to worry about her physical appeal. Such interpretations begin to answer the question, What dangers make it necessary for us to protect ourselves in the first place?

In addition to recognizing, describing, and interpreting the motives for our defenses, we must assess the price we pay for the protection they afford. Finally, we need to identify the hidden payoffs, if any, that play a role in keeping our defenses in place.

To illustrate, consider the experience of a woman who fell in love with a much older man, and a dream she told her therapist that enabled her to become clearer about her pattern of emotional self-protection:

> I dreamed that you came to my bedroom early in the morning just when we'd usually be having our therapy hour. And I thought, How great, I won't have to go to your office...I felt like I was really being taken care of, getting this special attention from you. But then I thought, Wait a minute, isn't this pretty intrusive? But I didn't want to say anything... 'cause maybe you'd leave. Then you turned into my boyfriend Jake.

Which makes me more aware of something about myself that's just sort of been on the tip of my tongue. I've been vaguely aware that the way Jake comes over here and just strides into my bedroom, flinging his clothes all over the place, turning on the TV or the stereo, grabbing a magazine or whatever—that it bothers me. He doesn't just make himself at home, it's sort of like he owns the place. And it's not his place. It's mine! At first I didn't realize it bothered me. But when I began to I still didn't say anything. Just like in the dream with you. I have the same feeling about the way Jake planned our vacation. It's great to have him take responsibility for everything, but then I feel like it's totally his thing, not mine at all. Which I don't say either. Then I also have some feelings I've kept to myself about giving up my community theater stuff so we'd have nights together. . . .

I wasn't really aware how much these things bothered me. None taken separately are a big deal but now the way it adds up sort of scares me: the pattern of keeping all my objections to myself. I think I could actually lose track of myself, the way I've felt so tempted to give things up for Jake. But I really love the way he loves me and takes care of me. What would the alternative be? Maybe to get pissed off—but wouldn't that put everything in jeopardy? But pretending everything's cool when it isn't is really going to screw things up with Jake, bigtime.

This woman's dream enabled her to recognize for the first time what was previously "on the tip of her tongue," namely, the influence on her relationships of a particular style of self-protection. She is also able to describe her defenses as having two aspects: she remains only dimly aware of what bothers her, and when she's clear about what bothers her, she keeps it to herself. She also interprets the motive for her defenses: she is worried that the alternative to her denial and reticence is "to get pissed off. . . and put everything in jeopardy." It's "just like in the dream," in which she fears that if she tells her therapist he's being intrusive, he may leave her.

Her defenses are of the merger-hungry variety, and so is her motivation: she wishes to be taken care of (by an older man), and thus she feels she must keep her self-assertion in check. Worrying that she could "actually lose track of myself," she is aware that the price is high. As for the payoff—being loved and taken care of—it is barely hidden at all. To be dependent, she's been ready to relinquish her boundaries. Yet she seems to realize that her defenses put in jeopardy not only her identity but also her relationship: "Pretending everything's cool when it isn't is really going to screw things up with Jake, bigtime."

This vignette raises a number of questions. What would be the alternatives to self-protective denial and reticence? What if she were to confront her boyfriend with what she sees as his intrusiveness? More broadly, what is the role of our partner, either in reinforcing the defenses that interfere with healthy merging or in enabling us to relinquish them?

THE INTERPERSONAL ALTERNATIVES, REVISITED: COLLUSION, COLLISION, AND COLLABORATION IN MERGING

Imagine watching a video of two partners in love relating to one another with unaccustomed awkwardness. The couple is on a couch; no one else is present. She reaches out, apparently affectionately, to touch his cheek, and he shies nervously from her touch. Beneath the surface of their interaction lie emotional realities we can't see. She is frightened and insecure, while he is fearful of feeling needy like a child. What we *can* see are their defenses: Her defensive style is merger hungry, while his is merger wary. Her gesture is affectionate, but it is also a bid for his reassurance, to help protect her from her own insecurities. His withdrawal may reflect some nervousness about being intruded upon, but it also involves a defense, namely, projection. In his mind *she* is the dependent one, while he is self-sufficient, choosing to withdraw only in order to avoid being smothered by her need.

If this couple is typical, they too may confuse the surface with the reality that lies beneath it. They may confuse defenses with what their defenses protect them from: her insecurity and his fears of dependency. To make matters worse, they may act on this confusion and wind up blaming each other. She might decide he's an uptight, unsupportive, withdrawn man, rather than someone terrified of his own needs. He might decide she's a needy, demanding, intrusive woman, rather than someone frightened by her insecurity.

In so deciding, each would not only be misunderstanding the other, and potentially jeopardizing the relationship, they would also be missing an opportunity to know and perhaps master a crucial aspect of themselves, albeit a painful one. This kind of opportunity is part of what merging in love has to offer us; it is one of the reasons we merge. The question is whether or not we can recognize, through the veil of defense, the existence of such opportunities.

Let's stay with our merger-hungry/merger-wary couple a little longer. Like all couples, their love will be profoundly affected by the way they deal with the impact of their defenses (her reaching out, his pulling away) upon their relationship. Probably without being aware of it, they will drift toward one of three kinds of responses: they will collude with each other, collide, or collaborate.

Suppose they collude, making an unspoken deal as a couple to stay away from what threatens them as individuals. In this case, each partner will remain discontented but safe, supported by the conviction that the problem in the relationship originates with the other. Paradoxically, each will behave with the other in ways that provoke exactly the behavior that each complains about: her pitch for reassurance will drive him away, while his coldness will intensify her need for contact, which will push him further away, and so on. But there will also be small adjustments—she'll pull back a little, he'll thaw out—to maintain the acceptably unhappy equilibrium of their love.

On the other hand, they may collide: one partner or both will become so discontented with the pattern of her pursuit and his distance that conflict will break out. In the confrontation, something new may be learned about the painful emotional reality that underlies her pursuit or his withdrawal.

Finally, they may collaborate. Through trust, gentle confrontation, empathy, and dialogue, both partners may recognize in the love of the other a safe opportunity to come to terms with what in the past has undermined their own ability to be close.

The Couple in Collusion

Couples collude to avoid merging for different reasons. Most commonly, they are motivated by fear: both partners' needs for self-protection are satisfied by the unspoken or unconscious deal that is struck between them. But partners may collude out of love for each other, as well as fear. Sensing the other's vulnerability, one partner (or both) may act protectively—fostering a collusion, say, to inhibit the expression of anger or dependency in the relationship.

Unfortunately, such protectiveness is always a double-edged sword. Deciding that a partner's vulnerabilities require protection takes the decision out of the partner's hands. It also leaves him or her in the dark as regards the real nature of what is now going on. Whether collusions are motivated by love or fear, however, the consequence is the same: a modicum of security (though it may be false), attained by limiting the couple's exercise of their capacity for healthy merging.

Like our individual defenses, our collusions as partners in a couple can be difficult to recognize—and without being recognized, they can be neither actively chosen nor modified. But just as we often see smoke before we spot the fire, we can usually see evidence of collusion before realizing that we are colluding. We may experience a sense of discontent with the relationship that is hard to explain. Or we may notice that a superficial or repetitive quality has crept into our interactions with our partner. Or we may become aware that we are censoring ourselves when we communicate with our partner (or our partner may seem to be censoring).

It is also helpful to know that our defensive collusions ordinarily take one of three forms.

The Merger-Wary Collusion

Both partners deal with their discomfort through withdrawal. Defensive withdrawal may be motivated by different experiences (fear, depression, anger), but it always takes the same form. Rather than turn to others when we feel uncomfortable, we turn away from them—as if they represented a danger.

When both partners find security (or at least relief) in withdrawal, they will collude to create distance. They may find reasons to spend nearly all their time apart, and to share little of themselves. They may be bored or discontented with each other. At best, they may feel a wholly unromantic "togetherness" of the sort suggested by one woman who confided to her therapist with some ambivalence that her husband "fit like an old shoe."

But couples purchase even this kind of security at a high price. Because their boundaries are closed, their merging is minimal and so the rewards of merging (the tender pleasures, opportunities for heightened self-esteem and mastery) will also be minimal. Merger-wary partners may be alone together, but they are more alone than together. And for some this may be enough. When it is not, two such partners may well find reasons to go their separate ways or, usually because one of the two becomes unbearably lonely, they will collide.

The Merger-Hungry Collusion

Both partners fear being alone and being unable to take care of themselves emotionally. The second part of the "merging without merging" equation is the one they have yet to master. They will collude, therefore, to avoid the anxieties that arise with experiences of independence, separateness, or self-assertion. They may spend little time apart and will try to minimize conflict and difference.

And the costs of this form of collusion? The overdependence of merger-hungry partners upon one another usually limits their individual development. Moreover, their partnership can be vulnerable in periods of shared stress: because each partner looks to the other for a kind of belated parenting, there will be trouble when both partners feel the need to be taken care of at the same time. In any case, because the longing to have childhood IOUs redeemed can never be completely satisfied, the consequence is disappointment and anger—emotions for which a merger-hungry collusion allows no room.

But for better or worse, what the merger-hungry couple represses often returns to haunt them. When feelings of anger or disappointment become impossible to contain, they may emerge with a vengeance. Then, once more, two partners in collusion may find themselves on a collision course.

The Merger-Hungry/Merger-Wary Collusion

This may be the most common collusion of all. Gender stereotypes cast the woman in the merger-hungry role, while the man plays the role of the merger wary—and indeed there are aspects of early psychological development that contribute to this assignment of roles.[3] But each of us, regardless of gender, is capable of playing either role. And in the less rigid versions of the merger-hungry/merger-wary collusion, partners switch roles. The key here is that, appearances to the contrary, both partners—the one who reaches out and the other who pulls back—may be equally fearful of healthy merging.

Consider, for example, the decades-long marriage of an insecure, apparently merger-hungry man who pursues the affection and sexual interest of his beautiful, apparently merger-wary wife. Whenever she briefly and intermittently yields, his successful pursuit allows him to feel temporarily confident of his masculinity.

---

3. A not uncommon contemporary pattern is the following: over the course of a lengthy involvement, the male partner who began by occupying the merger-wary role finds himself after a number of years in the uncomfortable and unaccustomed position of hungering for his newly merger-wary female partner.

Meanwhile, as the object of his pursuit, his wife also feels reassured. But their collusion, as stable, even comfortable, as it may be, involves a shared avoidance of deeper intimacy—an intimacy that is no less threatening for the husband who seems to pursue it than for his wife who mainly resists. If they were to modify their collusion, he might be faced more directly with his insecurity and his fear of dependency. And if she weren't always fending off his pursuit (and feeling reassured by it) she might have the opportunity to become acquainted with herself as something more than the object of his desire.

On the face of it, the frustrated merger-hungry partner would appear to have the tougher row to hoe. Often, however, the merger-wary partner feels painfully guilty about his or her withdrawal, because it seems so rejecting and so hurtful. It may be useful to recognize that both partners suffer here—and both are protected. Each avoids the particular threats associated with closeness, but in so doing each forgoes many of the rewards that closeness has to offer.

The Couple in Collision

Every collusion has the potential to become a collision when one or another partner decides that his or her loneliness has become intolerable, and that the other partner is to blame, or when the partners come to feel so stifled or angry in their mutual dependency that they collide, or when the equilibrium of frustrated pursuit and guilty withdrawal breaks down. In the best case, the resulting confrontation unearths emotional realities that their collusion has kept buried.

Collisions disrupt the familiar stability couples achieve through their collusion of defenses. Collisions are always anxiety-provoking, but because they shake up a couple's status quo and turn a static situation fluid, they create the potential for something new to emerge. If partners have the ability to collaborate, then the crisis of collision can be transformed into an opportunity.

The Couple in Collaboration

Merging in love can sometimes feel like being caught in an emotional storm. When we're being buffeted about by our feelings, acting effectively—unless we have the benefit of understanding—is difficult, if not impossible.

Necessary Assumptions

When we become absorbed in blaming our partner—for wanting too much from us or giving us too little, for being too close or too distant—we are nearly always betraying some ignorance about our own conflicted motivations for merging in love. Of course, it is tempting to blame. Just as nations have shown a preference for locating enemies outside their borders rather than facing problems at home, most of us are more comfortable when we can turn our internal conflicts into interpersonal ones.

We inevitably encounter new feelings as we grow closer to our partner. Patterns of interaction and self-protection are constantly shifting. Now we may be merger hungry, but later we may turn merger wary, and back again. What we experience today, our partner may experience tomorrow, and vice versa. Once we understand that change is the norm, that no destination is final, then any particular experience along the way may be a little less disturbing.

The difficult but essential part is bearing our troubling feelings, and those of our partner. Fortunately, if we are willing, our tolerance for such feelings can develop—like a muscle that grows stronger with exercise. And this evolving ability to tolerate feelings can gradually make it easier to find our emotional bearings, even in the midst of the conflict and turmoil love has a habit of generating.

Necessary Conversations

Now suppose we find ourselves at an impasse with our partner—colliding emotionally or simply drifting apart. How do we collaborate actively to resolve such an impasse? The key, of course, is communication.

Partners need to communicate about the barriers, usually the defenses, that are keeping them apart. In the face of an impasse, it is vital that a couple think aloud about the probability that merging is scaring them and that they are trying to protect themselves in their characteristic ways. They may find it useful to approach such a conversation in the fashion we've previously described: by attempting to recognize, describe, and identify the motives for the defenses they are using individually and as a couple to fend off the perceived dangers of closeness. It may also be important to understand the price they pay for this protection as well as the hidden payoffs.

But this kind of communication between partners is usually intensely difficult. Revealing our fears, and the defenses we use to protect ourselves, can be uncomfortable and embarrassing. Discussing the hidden payoffs that help keep our defenses in place can feel even riskier. We may worry about being branded as sadistic or spoiled if we expose our secret desires for revenge-by-proxy against disappointing parents, or our covert efforts to collect the unpaid IOUs of childhood.

As therapists, our stock-in-trade is making it possible for people to communicate, even about their most difficult experiences and needs. We have learned that such communication is facilitated if people are given the opportunity first to have their experience clarified and second to have their experience empathized with.

In the context of two partners attempting to understand an impasse between them, clarification means that each partner makes room for the other to put his or her experience into words: not just the headlines ("I'm angry at you") but the story in detail ("I'm angry because you make so many emotional demands on me... and then I withdraw... but I feel guilty about withdrawing because you seem hurt..." etc., etc.). When partners disclose their experience to each other as fully as they can, the experience is clarified ("So *that's* what's been going on with you. I get it."). But in order for partners to feel a modicum of comfort with what they have disclosed, empathy must follow clarification.

To empathize is to put ourselves in our partner's shoes, emotionally speaking, by trying for the moment to feel what our partner might feel. The challenge is to temporarily *identify* with our partner's experience and to see how—from his or her point of view—it might make sense. Then, for our partner to feel our empathy, it must be communicated ("I can see why you'd feel angry and why you'd withdraw. I've been showing you my neediest side. . . and if you can't respond, I can see why you'd have a hard time expressing your anger directly. . . As you said, you don't want to hurt me.").

When the experience of two partners has been clarified and empathized with in the ways we have described, there are a number of very positive consequences. The tension in the couple is likely to have been released. The emotional gulf that existed will be easier to bridge. Two partners may again find themselves in touch with the love that is the bedrock of their relationship. Clarification and empathy can change the emotional atmosphere in which the couple live, and this, along with their heightened understanding, can make it possible for two partners to resolve their impasses.

Clarification and empathy are possible to the extent that we can trust in our own boundaries that keep us separate from others and thus keep our feelings about ourselves safe from the feelings others have about us. This protective separateness lets us put aside our own emotional responses in order to listen—which is a precondition for empathy. Without boundaries to define our experience as separate from our partner's experience, it is all too easy to feel threatened.

On the other hand, our boundaries also open to let our partner in on our private experience, and our boundaries expand so that we can put ourselves empathically into the experience of our partner.

Earlier we alluded to the "rich get richer, poor get poorer" quality to the dynamics of merging in love. Nowhere is this more evident than in the efforts of two partners to collaborate. The flexibility of their boundaries—which close to protect separateness and open to create moments of oneness—is invaluable when it comes to resolving the conflicts that keep partners estranged.

None of us is without boundaries, however. If we've had the opportunity to learn to use them early in life, we come to love with a distinct advantage. If not, one of the advantages of love is that it offers us as adults opportunities for learning that we may have missed when we were young.

THE JOURNEY OF MERGING:
WHAT CAN WE EXPECT ALONG THE WAY?

At each stage of this journey, we can anticipate both new rewards and new risks.

Falling in Love

When we are falling in love, merging rewards us with feelings of warmth, belonging, and comfort. Our new relationship feels infinitely promising—in part because the merging here is of the best of ourselves with the best of the person with whom we are falling in love. It is a healthy collusion to avoid what is problematic in the interest of capitalizing on what might be possible. Along with sexual attraction, the tender thrill of merging can enable us to overcome the fears that might otherwise keep love at bay. When we fall in love, we open our boundaries and enjoy a feeling of oneness with our new partner. It is the first half of the "merging without merging" equation that colors our experience with hope.

But there is also risk. The collusion that denies troubling differences can make us oblivious to problems that may in the end be insurmountable. Past loneliness may have left us so desirous of love that we are blind to reality. But there are self-deceptions that arise from fear as well as from desire. Paradoxically, merging with someone with whom we are falling in love can feel so good that we feel threatened. If our earliest experiences of merging were painful or inadequate, then the very *goodness* of this new merging may provoke feelings of guilt, disloyalty, anxiety, or mourning in relation to our parents. In the effort to protect ourselves from these painful feelings, we may deceive ourselves by deciding that what is good is bad, that what might be safe is actually dangerous. The risk is that we may sabotage love or flee from it.

Becoming a Couple

At this stage our merging involves more than feelings, more than the subjective experience of oneness or familiarity. Merging here means, in addition, the real-life, practical interweaving of two separate lives—for becoming a couple typically entails geographic changes (if we're now living together), financial changes (if we're sharing our economic resources), legal changes (if we're marrying), or some combination of all three. This practical level of merging often gives us a heightened sense of security and stability that lets us feel closer and more bonded to the one we love. We may feel more than ever that, once again, we are part of a family. And all this means, in turn, that we have a safer context within which to confront our fears and, hopefully, to grow as individuals and as a couple.

But the deeper merging that heightens security during the second stage of love may also inspire fear. Our characteristic merger-hungry or merger-wary defenses may be triggered—with the usual self-protective but ultimately self-defeating consequences.

Merger-hungry defenses will be activated when closeness provokes fears of exposure or rejection. To maintain oneness and dependency, we will sacrifice separateness and aggression: for us, the second half of the "merging without merging" equation will have fallen by the wayside, and our sense of personal security may well be undermined.

Merger-wary defenses, on the other hand, will be activated when closeness stimulates fears of dependency or loss of control. The "solution" here is for us to withdraw from our partner and to feel as little desire as possible. This reaction reinforces separateness and strengthens our boundaries, but it undermines merging. It also leaves us feeling lonely.

Deepening Love over Time

Self-transcendence makes possible a higher level of merging that enables us to remain in love over time, and we devote a chapter to this last capacity later in the book.

Briefly, the deepening of involvement that occurs with the commitment to raising children (and to other long-term, high-stakes joint undertakings) challenges our existing sense of ourselves at the most profound levels. We may feel reborn through such a far-reaching involvement (or at least we may feel our identity radically redefined). Or, in the most dispiriting case, we may feel that our life has virtually been ended by the sacrifices we must make in the larger interest of the couple or family.

Merging at this deepest of levels can reward us by kindling what Erik Erikson called the potential for "generativity." This means feeling a connection to the ongoing life and history of the planet and its people—rather than succumbing to the feelings of despair and meaninglessness that can arise out of the knowledge of our inevitable death.

Each of us confronts different challenges at different stages of love's journey. We bring strengths and vulnerabilities to our relationship that become obvious only as the relationship evolves. But at any stage along the way, we are likelier to be able to overcome the difficulties we face in love if we know how we contribute to them.

SELF-APPRAISAL: THREE PROFILES

How capable of merging are we? To answer this question we must start by recalling what lies at the heart of this capacity: being able to open or extend our boundaries to include the beloved. Just as important, we must be able to maintain our boundaries to preserve our own identity and autonomy. Second, our comfort with the twin desires for oneness and separateness—with our wish to be cared for and our impulse to exert our own will—determines how easily we can let ourselves be close to someone we love. Finally, when we have difficulties with boundaries, dependency, or self-assertion, then we use defenses that give us the appearance of being merger hungry or merger wary.

Sometimes it is easier to recognize ourselves in others than it is to see ourselves as others might see us. In the three sketches that follow, we may see reflections of our own capacity for merging.

Alex: Merging as a Resource

A veterinarian in his mid-forties, Alex had divorced after a marriage of eight years and remarried three years later. He possessed a relaxed quality, a casual friendliness with others that seemed a little too good-natured to be true. The impression, however, that Alex might be capable of only a narrow range of emotion was misleading, as those who had seen him sad and angry well knew. His older brother said of him, "You can see his heart." When Alex spoke his wedding vows, which he had written himself, those present were moved by the transparent depth of feeling with which he expressed his love.

Alex felt that his first marriage had replicated what was most problematic in his parents' marriage. Like his father, Alex had cast his lot with a woman who was volatile, needy, and demanding: merger hungry, exactly as his mother had been. And in relation to this first wife, Alex played the role his father had played with his mother: acting solicitously with her, reasonably, putting his own needs and feelings aside, in order to maintain her emotional equilibrium. Alex, in a limited and not very helpful way, was acting as his wife's therapist. But he was also playing out a merger-wary style of self-protection, colluding with his aggressively dependent wife to shield himself from the threat of his own aggression and dependency.

Eventually their collusion broke beneath the weight of his unrecognized needs and his wife's unacknowledged strengths. From this failed marriage, Alex learned some painful lessons about the price of hiding his needs and anger behind the traditional male role of protector. When he married again, he chose a partner who was less like his mother, and he behaved toward her less like his father. Coupled with his hard-earned commitment to reveal rather than conceal himself, his wife's slightly merger-wary style allowed more of his hunger for merging to be expressed.

Alex found himself turning to her for comfort in a way he had done in no other relationship. When his wife was responsive to his neediness, he was sometimes moved to tears. He felt that he was now crying for all the tears he'd kept inside as a child—and all the years he'd spent as an adult, hiding his pain behind a facade of self-sufficiency and a habit of tending to the pain of others. He also gave in to the unwelcome reality that in relation to his wife, he was a much more demanding, less well behaved, and at times angrier person than he had hoped. But he was also full of gratitude and tenderness toward her for loving the person he was, rather than the person he had pretended to be.

Both Alex and his wife found themselves a little surprised at how their candor with each other, their ready abrasiveness as well as their affection, seemed gradually to have made their relationship the easiest they had ever known. But there was a logic to it: The more they allowed themselves to be known by the other, the less pretense was necessary—or possible. And pretense, Alex had come to realize, drained the life from a relationship. Taking the risk of being real, on the other hand, deepened the feelings of love that were the relationship's greatest reward.

Tony: Merging That Is Compromised

Now a teacher in his early forties, Tony married for the first time five years ago. He had grown up with parents who seemed always to be fighting. His father was strong and charismatic but also angry. His mother seemed overburdened, as though dealing with her husband's machismo and the needs of three sons were more than she could handle. Tony, the middle son, took on the ambiguously rewarding role of confidant to his mother: this got him special attention, but the price was to hear his father maligned. Encouraged to make his mother's resentments his own, he was also taught to keep them to himself. The family rule was never to expose family realities. Sustaining a public pretense of private harmony was the most important thing.

Tony felt that the lesson of his childhood was to keep painful truths under wraps. He seemed wary and his emotions were tightly controlled. His wife complained that he was close-mouthed and remote. She pressured him to enter therapy with her.

To begin with, he felt the best he could hope for from therapy was "to get through unscathed." As time went on, he began to realize that his wariness of his wife was the inevitable outcome of his habit of hiding. He hid his resentments from her, his needs from himself, and his fears from both of them. Terrified of being the brute his mother told him his father was, he concealed his anger. Worried about being the helpless dependent that his mother was, he couldn't acknowledge his wishes to be cared for. Nor could he allow himself to recognize his fears, because these threatened to leave him feeling powerless and overwhelmed—just as he had felt when he faced a father who scared him and a mother who couldn't respond to his needs.

Tony had felt that, by his parents' standards, he was close to his wife—after all, they weren't at each other's throats. But with the therapist's help he became aware of how rigidly he maintained his boundaries and his secrets, and how this kept him lonely. Gradually, Tony found himself capable of somewhat greater candor and expressiveness. Both his self-assertion and his dependency began to find tentative expression in his relationship with his wife. Usually, however, in the wake of exposing his needs, he would withdraw or find himself angry at his wife's neediness. In due course, he was both disturbed and relieved to find that this angry perception of his wife's dependency was actually a defense against his own troubling wishes to be taken care of.

Tony's new awareness helped him to feel closer to his wife. He still had fears of losing control of his feelings, but he was capable of opening his boundaries and allowing more of himself to be seen than he ever had before. Because he was merging more, he felt more vulnerable to his wife, more exposed but also more alive. In his own words, he felt "more fully human."

Suzanne: Merging as a Struggle

Suzanne, now a successful trial attorney at forty-three, married at eighteen, had a child, and divorced before she was twenty. She has never remarried, though she's had a series of relationships, the recollection of which makes her angry and justifies her antagonism toward men. Whenever she finds herself tempted to love, she finds evidence in her past to bolster what she calls her "cherished hatreds." While this painful history can bring her almost to tears, it also keeps her desire for closeness safely in check. And yet she is lonely.

Assertiveness is far easier for Suzanne than dependency, but she is tired of battling. Abandoned by her mother, she was cared for by her aunt who, with nine children of her own, could give her only so much. In Suzanne's childhood fantasies, she was Judy Garland's daughter, and mom was away making movies. In reality Suzanne was fighting it out with her cousins to get a little of her aunt's attention, while her uncle was absorbed in running a small garage to support his extensive brood. To cope with feeling neglected, Suzanne decided that she was special: in addition to being beautiful and intellectually gifted (which she was), this meant that none of the rules that applied to others should apply to her. Her aunt disagreed, so she was always being punished. Adding it up, Suzanne decided that it made no sense to want very much from anyone. Yet now she is torn, her mistrust at war with her exhaustion at having always to do everything for herself, or for others.

Her relationships with men have been stormy. She has picked two kinds of lovers. There have been powerful men who helped her feel special, but she's ended up battling them, which is a frustrating kind of closeness. There have also been men she's taken care of, but she's wound up seeing them as unreliable and draining. She is wary of men who betray an interest in taking care of her. Suzanne is terrified that being dependent means being abandoned—and until recently she's always been more than willing to muster the evidence to prove it.

The anger and mistrust that serve her well in the courtroom have pushed away those who might love her—and now her lonely isolation is beginning to frighten her. After several decades of making the case for her suspiciousness of men, she is questioning whether this is a case she really wants to win.

CHAPTER THREE

***

The Capacity for Idealization: The Role of the Romantic Ideal in Love

Love does not spring up out of nowhere,
but has its source in the qualities of
the beloved...Love loves because it sees
that the object is lovable.
—José Ortega y Gasset

The beloved is the right screen for the
projection of something internal.
—Ethel S. Person, M.D.

We look for love. We find love. We're lovestruck. We're swept away.

In popular imagery love exists outside us, and falling in love has everything to do with locating or discovering the beloved. Given this view, we can either seek love the way a prospector seeks gold or wait for it the way a gambler waits to hit the jackpot. But starting with Cupid and his arrow, the familiar images convey only half the truth—for while falling in love depends on discovery, it involves creative imagination every bit as much.

When we fall in love all of us become artists—or at least we share the artist's task. The artist enlists an external reality (say, a flower-filled vase in a sunlit studio) to embody an internal vision—it could be the artist's intuition that all is right with the world.

In much the same way, when we fall in love we have usually found someone who seems to embody an internal vision of our own—in this case the internal vision of our romantic ideal. This ideal is the image (both conscious and unconscious) of the infinitely desirable partner crucial to our happiness. Our heart beats faster when we meet someone in the waking world who seems the real-life double of this dream partner.

It is idealization—the third of the six capacities—that allows us to experience love in just this way, as a rendezvous with our romantic ideal. Each of us has our own romantic ideal, its character and details unique, but for all of us this composite image of the partner we seek seems to spring from the same three desires— desires that originate in the need to strengthen the sense of self. We want someone we can love and admire. We want someone who loves and admires *us*. And we want someone with whom we share significant common ground. The hope that our partner will fulfill these desires may be the biggest part of what makes falling in love such an intoxicating experience.

However, if the wish for a partner we can admire is greatly exaggerated, it may generate a romantic ideal so spectacular that every real partner falls short—and consequently we wind up searching endlessly for perfection. If the natural desire for a partner who loves and admires us is opposed by a feeling that we are somehow guilty or undeserving, then a conflicted romantic ideal may lead us to pursue partners who are critical, rejecting, or unavailable. Finally, a romantic ideal shaped by an extravagant desire for commonality may make us intolerant of difference—in which case the dawning awareness that our partner is other than a twin may lead us to fall out of love.

Despite all our wishes to the contrary, no beloved we meet can ever be more than an approximation of our romantic ideal—for this ideal, blending details drawn from experience, fantasy, and hope, is always too individualized and too perfect to exist outside the world of our imagination. If we are to fall in love, therefore, what is required for a time is the ability to imaginatively exaggerate, to creatively embellish what is realistically desirable in the actual person we have found. And we need to exercise this ability without being aware we are doing so.

In the happiest case, when idealization's spell remains unbroken for a serviceable period, our acts of creative imagination in the service of love are recognizable only in retrospect. At the time, we are convinced that the seductive perfections of the beloved are more than enough to justify the intensity of our passion. In fact, as the following vignette suggests, our passion is always in part a response to our romantic ideal—the reflection of which we partly discover and partly imagine within the one we love.

Barry, a forty-year-old screenwriter, is on the verge of marrying a Danish woman with whom he has been involved for more than four years. He is keenly aware that his initial love for Kirsten was sparked by her resemblance to his preexisting ideal:

> Maybe I should be embarrassed to admit this, but it's as though Kirsten was typecast. Doesn't everybody have a "type" though? I just know when I first saw her it was like seeing someone I'd been looking for for years: one of these tall, athletic, almost masculine-looking Nordic women. Preferably with long, straight dirty-blond hair. I mean, let's get all the details right!
>
> The way we met, it was on the beach at Santa Monica...she was lying on a huge beach towel with all this equipment around her, very organized: her bike, a little backpack, swimfins, sunglasses, a book, food, drink. She seemed totally self-sufficient. It took two hours for me to get up the nerve to try and meet her. During which time I practically wrote a novel about her—actually about us. I'm exaggerating but the point is I had all these ideas about her, all these hopes, before we even spoke...
>
> And then when I met her, she was close enough to the mark so I could decide she was just about perfect. I remember a couple of things that really stood out for me. There was this

little girl on the beach, maybe three, who was lost and Kirsten was incredibly concerned, took care of her, got her reconnected with her parents. That really moved me—it was like, aha!: a mother. Also she had this book of poetry she was reading by a poet I really liked. That made me sure we were intellectual soul mates. I thought, She's it! And the ways she was different from what I hoped were easy for me to ignore. At least for the first few months. By which time we were already living together.

When Barry first encountered Kirsten, he "discovered" a real woman who genuinely possessed qualities he appreciated and admired. But as Barry admits, he "had all these ideas about her, all these hopes, before [they] even spoke." The fact that upon meeting her, Kirsten seemed "close enough to the mark so I could decide she was just about perfect," the fact that he could almost immediately peg her as mother and soul mate, the fact that he could so easily ignore his disappointments in her—all these reflect the role of Barry's ability to imagine, that is, to enhance his image of Kirsten with a wealth of flattering detail that enabled him to see her as his romantic ideal.

Our ability (like Barry's) to partly discover and partly imagine our romantic ideal in the one we love is at the heart of the capacity for idealization.

Mapping the Terrain of the Ideal

But if idealization is partly imagination, doesn't it map a terrain that doesn't "really exist"—and therefore doesn't it misguide us?

Not necessarily. Recall that our own internal map always contains a range of images of ourselves and others: actual, ideal, and feared images. The romantic ideal is a distillation of our most ideal images of the partner we desire. Like the first maps of early explorers (which were also partly products of imagination), the romantic ideal depicts an inviting terrain as yet uncharted but rich in promise. And like those early maps, the romantic ideal as an image of desire beckons us to risk voyaging into a new world.

In *A Lover's Discourse*, the French philosopher Roland Barthes wrote: "I encounter millions of bodies in my life; of these millions I desire some hundreds; but of these hundreds I love only one." Our internal map of the romantic ideal inspires some of us to search for our "only one." And the capacity for idealization (imagination in partnership with discovery) enables us to feel we have found this beloved. Then we are transported to that bewitching terrain where desire and reality seem to overlap. Though elusive and impermanent, it's a terrain we remember if we have ever fallen in love. But without a healthy capacity for idealization, it's one we may never visit.

To Idealize and Feel "Idealizable"

Along with erotic involvement and merging, idealization makes possible the intense bliss we feel when we fall in love. Of course, if there is to be an actual love relationship rather than only the frustrated hope for one, our feelings when we fall in love must be reciprocated by the beloved.

Because the romantic ideal includes the image of someone who loves and admires us (as well as the image of someone admirable to us and, to some extent, similar), the capacity for healthy idealization implies that we are capable of not only idealizing someone we love but also feeling "idealizable"—that is, comfortable and deserving when we are idealized.

To love and feel lovable, to idealize and feel idealizable, is a rare and heady combination. But it's also a necessary one if a love relationship is to get off the ground. Idealization enables us to break through the barrier of our fears. It allows us for a time to admire the one we love without qualification, to feel lovable enough to merit such admiration in return—and to share with the beloved a deep sense of commonality.

Love or Infatuation?

It might be objected here that we are confusing love with infatuation when we emphasize the indispensability of idealization. For isn't it only the young and immature whose relationships are based on such a romantic overvaluation of the partner?

No. Our experience has shown that love relationships that deepen and endure are usually initiated by a phase of profound shared uncritical appreciation. The mutual idealization of lovers makes for a too-good-to-be-true feeling whose intensity, to be sure, will wane. But if this feeling is missing from the start, the relationship may be companionable without being passionate, it may be labored, and it may not last. We don't assume that the intense idealization that makes falling in love an enchanted experience will remain perpetually at its early peak. But if idealization is present at the inception, even briefly, it can often be revived. And given the difficulties that invariably complicate intimacy, the capacity to reconnect (if only temporarily) with our initial idealization of and by our partner is a resource whose value cannot be overestimated.

THE UTILITY OF ROMANCE

The romantic ideal—which idealization enables us to feel we have found in the one we love—serves a number of useful purposes. Most important, our experience of love as a rendezvous with our romantic ideal exerts a magnetism that is hard to resist. It draws us to our partner in spite of our fears and keeps us in a relationship in the face of current difficulty and past disappointment.

But there is more to be mined in this very romantic vein, as the following story demonstrates. Alice is a twenty-nine-year-old accountant, recently remarried after abandoning the security of her first marriage for a relationship that promised more:

I was nineteen when I married Don. I don't think I knew it at the time but I was looking for a ticket out of my family—and then, my God, it seemed like a few minutes later we had a family of our own. Don was the boy next door who I'd known for years. Marrying him was like leaving home without leaving home. I loved him, I still love him, but I never fell in love with him. I don't think I knew what those words meant until I met Andy, my husband. Now, in retrospect, it seems clear that this was what was missing in that first marriage, why it felt incomplete.

With Andy it's the opposite. It's like, Oh yeah, this is what the songs and movies are about. I was incredibly drawn to Andy from very early on...maybe the second time we met. Almost from the start I missed him when we were separated, I really wanted to be with him. I remember picking him up at the airport and it really was like a movie somehow: the excitement, the feeling that we were somehow two special people meeting...it felt almost glamorous. I'd fantasize about us, about how people saw us, and it would just make me feel good. I felt great that this great guy loved me and that we were on the same wavelength. It's not that everybody would find him so amazing. It's just that he seems so right for *me* in terms of my ideas about the sort of man I always wanted to be with.

The only problem, and this is what I need to work out, is that I feel like I want Andy for myself. I feel reluctant to share him with my kids and they seem to like him as much as I do. It's sort of the reverse of the usual situation. But it's like there's something there with him that I never got in my family and never got from Don...I don't know, it's like this feeling that he's going to make everything right, that I'm going to really flourish in this relationship. But I want that all for myself.

Alice's words illustrate the power of idealization. Andy is her romantic ideal in the flesh—or rather, this is how he feels to her, how she's able to experience him. Whatever the blend of discovery and imagination that goes into it, her experience of Andy is compelling and profound. And all three of the motives that regularly energize love—pleasure, self-esteem, mastery—play a role in fueling her idealization.

When we discussed these same motives in the context of erotic involvement and merging, each one could be seen to play a distinct part, but with idealization it's hard to separate the three. The experience of a rendezvous with our romantic ideal makes for a potent combination of pleasure and self-esteem. As Alice says, "I felt great that this great guy loved me and that we were on the same wavelength." When our relationship is bathed in the rosy light of idealization, part of the high comes with the feeling that we are both similar to and seen as special by someone who we see as special. The emotional logic here is straightforward: If I'm similar to someone ideal who loves me, then I must be ideal too. So long as the spell of mutual idealization remains unbroken, we can ignore not only our misgivings about our partner but also our doubts about ourselves as well.

Never mind—for the moment anyway—that the whole experience may have an unreal quality about it ("like a movie somehow," says Alice). Idealization, as we now know, always depends in part on imagination. When it's in high gear, we experience a heightened responsiveness to what is positive about ourselves and the one we love—and a selective inattention to what is negative. Bad news, in other words, is censored. Idealization wards off whatever might disappoint or disturb us if it were recognized in ourselves or in our partner. But despite knowing that early idealization has an unreal, too-good-to-be-true quality about it, few of us would want to give it up—and for good reason: it serves us too well. Its pleasure and promise shield us from the recognition of love's risks. We forget for the moment how frightened of involvement or rejection we may actually be—how wounded we may previously have felt or how guilty, how our parents' love was not enough or how it smothered us. Idealization provides a specific antidote to these painful feelings: it fuels the belief that love heals.

Idealization stirs the hope that our partner might bring us as adults what we missed as children, might make up to us in the present for the pain we suffered in the past. It's as though we expect the new relationship to guarantee a happy ending to what might otherwise have been a sad story. Our idealized partner is cast as a better parent, a rescuer, or a healer with the power to make us happy, often in ways we've never been happy before. With this partner we begin to envision a future together in which most wishes are satisfied. We expect to be, as it were, bigger, stronger, less lonely, more taken care of, and more content than we've ever been in the past. Ironically, this utterly unrealistic expectation seduces us into a real relationship in which a great deal of healing may actually occur.

To feel we are loved by someone we love and admire is deeply soothing. But such an experience, if we allow ourselves to take it in, can do more than comfort us. Through experiencing as adults some of what we missed as children, we can modify our internal image of ourselves (so we feel more confidently lovable) and our internal image of others (so we feel more trusting).

In sum then, these are the uses of romance. When we fall in love, idealizing our partner heightens our pleasure and intensifies our passion. Idealization also makes our relationship a setting in which our self-esteem may be strengthened. And our idealized images generate a vision of love as a healing force—a vision that emboldens us to take the risks that may enable us to grow. Coupled with the capacities for erotic pleasure and merging, idealization allows us to *begin* a love relationship. It also equips us with the potential, when relationship difficulties arise in the future, to revive the precious feelings we first experienced when we were falling in love.

It sounds like a bonanza. And, unquestionably, when we can idealize our partner and feel idealizable, we possess a very significant resource. But we've been talking so far mainly about *healthy* idealization. In contrast, if our ability to idealize or feel idealizable is limited or problematic, then the capacity for idealization can be just as significant a liability.

WHEN IDEALIZATION MAKES LOVE VULNERABLE

To get a preliminary feel for idealization's potential to make trouble in love, listen to Sheila, a woman who came to a therapist for help in understanding her painful and inexplicable loneliness:

It baffles me. It frustrates the hell out of me. I'm just mystified about why at this stage in my life I'm still alone. I'm thirty-three and I have a lot that others would probably envy. Maybe it's not the most important thing in the world, but I've heard for years how attractive I am, how bright I am, how sensitive I am, etcetera, etcetera, etcetera. I've got plenty of friends and I'm lucky enough to have work I love that also happens to be very well paid. But all that sort of pales when I think about being single.... *Single*—I can hardly say that word without shuddering.

If I think about the relationships I've had with men, they all seem to have been basically disappointing. Eventually one of two things always occurs. Either the man turns out to be unavailable, or somehow I wind up feeling, I don't know, disillusioned? disappointed? It's like, at the beginning, for the first few weeks or whatever, I'm thrilled. I think, At last! The guy seems great—you know, everything: smart, appealing, honest, stable economically—I have sort of a list. But then, over and over again, I end up feeling dissatisfied. Like this latest guy, he just turned out to be *boring*. No sense of humor, no emotional expressiveness. But I don't know anymore: my best friend told me I was crazy. And other friends of mine really liked this guy. I think they've developed this idea that I'm too "picky." But that's really not how it feels.

The way it feels, I just have a very clear idea of the sort of man I want to be with. Maybe it's a little much...But I'm really not sure there's anything wrong with looking for a prince. Except I don't feel I have any control over events— you know, whether someone terrific turns up or becomes unavailable or turns out to be a disappointment. And I keep winding up alone...so I have to wonder.

Whatever else might stand in the way of her loving, whatever the events over which Sheila feels she has no control, there's much here to suggest that her own difficulty with idealization is a major part of the problem. She tells us that her search for a "prince" has always been doomed by the discovery of his flaws. A pattern like this usually has more than one meaning, but it's hard not to guess that her romantic ideal is "over-ideal" and that her ability to sustain admiration is limited by her need to find fault.

A romantic ideal involving a collection of traits too extraordinary to be found in the real world and a difficulty sustaining admiration are just two of the problems that commonly interfere with our capacity to idealize those we love. It's worth emphasizing that these are problems inside us that can be actively dealt with. They are not events over which we have no control—though this is how we may experience them, just as Sheila did.

The other two factors in the idealizing equation can also be vulnerable. First, we may find it hard to feel idealizable. As a consequence, we may become uneasy or even suspicious when cast in the role of our partner's romantic ideal. Or a variation on the theme: our need to be idealized (to protect us from our fear that we don't *deserve* to be) can be so desperate that any sign of diminished interest or of criticism from our partner sends us into a tailspin or a rage. Second, our desire for a partner with whom we experience a strong sense of kinship may be overamplified. If so, our wish for kinship can escalate to a demand for "twinship" and an intolerance of the differences between partners that inevitably become more apparent as intimacy deepens.

Whether we have problems idealizing those we love, being idealized by them, or maintaining idealization in the face of difference, our ability to fall and remain in love can be seriously compromised—but fortunately in predictable (and therefore recognizable) ways. Thus we can often identify the romantic ideal's influence on our own relationships.

We might become aware, for example, that we repeatedly choose partners whom we see as our romantic ideal but who can't or won't idealize us. We might infer, then, that it's our trouble feeling idealizable that leads us to "prefer" relationships in which we won't be loved or admired enough. It's as though we don't feel entitled to be loved by someone we love. Armed with such awareness, we're better equipped to understand and begin to take charge of events in our love life rather than feel (like Sheila) powerless to affect them.

Like each of the six capacities in love, our capacity for idealization originates in the particulars of our own personal history. But while the psychological landscape is different for each of us, the generic "terrain of the ideal" has been extensively explored and mapped by psychoanalysts. Work in this area has proven especially fruitful during the last two and a half decades, revealing that idealization occurs to strengthen the sense of self—and that our difficulties idealizing those we love have to do with our feelings about ourselves.

LOVE, SELF-LOVE—AND NARCISSISM

We can't love another until we learn to love ourselves: it's a cliché with some truth to it. But "loving ourselves" sounds subtly different from "self-love," which sounds too much like narcissism. And narcissism brings to mind other words, few of which have positive connotations. At best, someone who is "narcissistic" is self-absorbed and arrogant, at worst selfish. But this pejorative understanding of the term is incomplete.

In recent years, psychological research has expanded our definition of *narcissism* to accommodate the insight that as we mature emotionally, idealized or "narcissistic" images of our own perfection (and that of others) actually play a healthy role in strengthening our evolving sense of self. Once regarded only as an objectionable trait, narcissism has come to be understood as a feature of normal human development—and one that has particular significance in shaping the capacity for idealization and the experience of falling in love.

This new understanding grows out of the pioneering work of Heinz Kohut, the father of a school of psychoanalytic thought known as Self Psychology. Just as Freud made the exploration of sexuality respectable, Kohut brought narcissism out of the closet, where it had long been isolated from scrutiny as an unsightly and disavowed feature of human experience.

Kohut enabled us to realize that *both* self-esteem and trust in others—each equally necessary if love is to thrive—have their origins in part in our early narcissism, in our images of perfection. He explained that narcissism itself evolves in each of us as we grow up, undergoing a transformation that softens our original egocentricity but also leaves certain vestiges of this childhood quality intact. The evolution of our own narcissism—healthy or not so healthy—determines whether or not our capacity for idealization will be a resource in love.

How Healthy Narcissism Contributes to Love

Kohut theorized that in childhood there are three kinds of "narcissistic" relationships we must experience with our parents in order to develop a solid sense of self—and that this solid core self makes possible, in turn, a romantic ideal that enhances our ability to love. The three relationships Kohut describes register as images of ourselves and others that shape our own individual map of the "terrain of the ideal." Each relationship involves a central image. Kohut calls these images, in sequence, the Grandiose Self, the Idealized Object, and the Alterego. If we could interview a remarkably articulate and deeply self-aware little child regarding the personal meaning of these images, she might say of the Grandiose Self, "It means I'm perfect"; of the Idealized Object, "Whoever I love is perfect"; and of the Alterego, "Whoever I love is just like me."

The fundamental idea here is that each of us starts out as a little narcissist—as "His or Her Majesty, the Baby"—and that this wishful overestimate of our importance and power is actually our earliest version of self-esteem. When a little later we endow our parents with a comparably imagined perfection, this is an early version of trust and admiration.

When the reality of our relationship with our parents—our first love relationship—is "good enough," our narcissistic fantasies of the ideal become less and less necessary and can gradually be toned down. Just as we don't dream night and day of lavish feasts when we're well fed, we don't require the comfort of fantasy to sustain us when reality is nurturing enough. If, on the other hand, our relationship with our parents is not good enough, then we will cling self-protectively to our narcissistic images of perfection—not just to fill an emptiness but to offset the impact of the *feared* images that register in memory as the record of painful experiences.

The evolution of Kohut's three narcissistic images profoundly affects our sense of self and shapes our romantic ideal in the most direct way.

The Grandiose Self

In the first few years of our lives we display many of the traits associated with narcissism, narrowly conceived: we may see ourselves as the center of the universe, demand the attention of others, and act as if our needs come first.

Crystallizing in the Grandiose Self, our early childhood feelings of perfect specialness spring from two sources. First, there are fantasies of being all-powerful that arise to protect us from our actual experiences of helplessness and dependency. But during our earliest years we also feel more "realistically" special as we acquire an exciting array of new abilities. These feelings probably peak during the exhilarating progress from crawling to toddling to walking. We're no longer on our hands and knees and suddenly the whole world looks different.

Our original grandiosity (which has been called "normal narcissism") can be the nucleus around which a strong sense of self develops. But the evolution from egocentricity to esteem occurs only if as children—elated at achievements that fuel our fantasies of perfection—we are "mirrored" by our parents. *Mirroring* is the term Kohut, Mahler, and others have used to describe the empathic responses we receive from our parents that communicate that they, too, take pride in us. When our first steps or our first words elicit a cry of joy or a gleam in mother's eye, some very important things occur. We feel less helpless—because our parents' enthusiasm signals that through our actions we can have a positive impact on others. We also get the message that it's a good thing to feel good about ourselves. As a consequence of seeing a positive reflection of ourselves in our parents' reactions, we begin to develop realistic self-esteem, to feel idealizable—and to rely less on the fantasies of perfection embodied in our Grandiose Self. In the course of healthy development, these fantasies of perfection evolve into the ambitions that energize our hopeful efforts to achieve, to grow, and to find satisfying love.

The Idealized Object

The image of our parents as perfect arises partly in response to all the ways in which they actually meet our needs. But it is also an attempt to cope with the challenges reality has presented to our own fantasy of omnipotence and perfection. If we can't be all-powerful, then probably the best available alternative is to have caretakers who are. When we idealize our parents in this way we turn them into heroes. It's a comforting transformation, and one that not only calms us but also provides exemplary role models to whom we feel close and with whom we can identify. While reinforcing our ability to trust and admire others, seeing our parents as special also strengthens our sense of self.

If our parents are "good enough"—if they don't hurt, neglect, painfully disappoint, or abruptly disillusion us—then our image of them as Idealized Objects can be toned down over time to accommodate the reality that they may be wonderful even if they aren't perfect. Modulating our images of the ideal in this way makes it easier for us to love others even when they disappoint us.

The Alterego

Kohut had the least to say about this last "narcissistic" experience of childhood. But he observed that in order to feel capable and confident of our abilities, all of us must feel that we see and understand—and are seen and understood by—someone just like us: a kind of twin. Feeling connected through our similarity to a person we deeply admire is like seeing a flattering reflection of ourselves in the mirror. When we have this experience with our parents, peers, or imaginary playmates, it strengthens our optimism that we can successfully express our own individuality and exercise our own talents. Without this "alterego" relationship, we may feel not only that others are different but also that this difference means they are better than we are—immune from the foibles that make us all human. And if we equate our differences from others with our own inferiority, it can be hard to be close to someone who isn't a twin.

Idealized Images and the Romantic Ideal

There is a direct connection between our Grandiose Self, Idealized Object, and Alterego images on the one hand and our romantic ideal on the other: the three aspects of the romantic ideal parallel the three images that Kohut sees as central to the development of a healthy sense of self.

Recall that a healthy romantic ideal includes the image of someone who admires us (as, hopefully, we were admired by our parents), someone we deeply admire (as, hopefully, we admired our parents), and someone with whom we feel a sense of kinship (which, hopefully, we felt with our parents or others when we were young). The needs we look to our partner to satisfy in love are a later, more moderate, adult version of the needs that our parents had to satisfy for our childhood narcissism to evolve.

When we are fortunate, our narcissistic images of perfection have been allowed to mature through a good-enough relationship with our parents. Then our sense of self will rest on a solid foundation and our romantic ideal will, as a consequence, be realistically enticing. For it will include the image of someone who admires us (but not unceasingly), someone we admire (but not someone who must inspire awe or worship), and someone we experience as a kindred spirit (but not necessarily a twin). The rendezvous with such a romantic ideal can be especially intoxicating because it revives old narcissistic experiences. It enables us to feel again that we are endlessly deserving of love, boundlessly loving—and connected by love to a soul mate.

How Narcissism Complicates Love: The Movie Star's Daughter and the Homeless Crone

When the development of our childhood narcissism has gone awry, our internal map may mislead us because its imagery of self and other will be distorted. We will value ourselves too highly or not highly enough. Our romantic ideal will lead us to expect too much or too little of those we love. And as for idealization, we'll have difficulty either idealizing others or feeling idealizable. Let's begin by looking at how problems in early development distort our images of ourselves: the real, the ideal, and the feared.

If our narcissistic imagery has not had a chance to mature, we may comfortably confuse our *real* selves with our ideal self-images—and feel as though we're very special. Or we may unhappily equate our real selves with our feared self-images—and feel as though we're especially awful. In the first instance, we consciously identify with our ideal images and fool ourselves into believing we're exactly who we wish to be. In the second, we identify with our feared images and wind up believing we are exactly who we fear we might be.

Suzanne (see Chapter Two), an attorney and divorced mother in her early forties, confused the real with the ideal, as the following story shows. Frightened by her loneliness, Suzanne is trying to understand and overcome the obstacles that have kept her from having a satisfying relationship with a man:

> The only time I ever fell in love was with Daniel—and that was a catastrophe. It's only this last year that I finally feel I'm over him. I showed you his picture, you saw what a hunk he was...*and* he was brilliant...*and* he was sensitive. The only problem was that he was an alcoholic who didn't know he was one. Before that I never met a man I couldn't find something wrong with. But maybe it's an impossible quest I'm involved in. I mean, I think I'm looking for somebody who's a cross between Gandhi, Joe Montana, and what's his name, Harry Connick, Jr. Except that sometimes I wonder if maybe I just dislike men. Or maybe I don't want to be with anybody, like nobody's good enough.
>
> But am I so special? The reality is I come from Hell's Kitchen and I dragged myself up by my bootstraps after my mother dropped me with her sister right after I was born.

Nobody wanted me. I had to fight for whatever attention I got with the nine other kids in my aunt's family. And the way I dealt with it, I really believed I was Judy Garland's daughter and my mother was off making movies. So I didn't have to live by anybody else's rules and I never did. I got into a terrible fight though when I was six with a boy who called me a liar 'cause he wouldn't believe my mom was Judy Garland.

Children can be very resourceful when they confront threats to their emotional survival. While it's always difficult to get the historical past in sharp focus as we look back across the decades, Suzanne's story contains vivid details that speak for themselves.

As a little girl, she had to compete with nine other children for her aunt's attention. In that setting, she probably had very limited opportunity to receive the enthusiastic parental mirroring and empathy that enables an *ideal* self-image to mature into a *real* self-image. At the same time, she probably had a very great need to maintain her internal image of an ideal parent, rather than a real parent—especially given the alternative: to see her mother as the sort of woman who could abandon her own child. Far preferable to the pain of seeing herself as the abandoned child of that abandoning mother was to believe she was the daughter of a movie star—and when that story couldn't be sustained, to feel that she was special enough to be exempted from other people's rules. The tragedy of this sort of recourse to fantasy in childhood is that it equips us so poorly to deal with adult reality, especially the reality of intimate relationships.

When we've had to cling, usually unconsciously, to our idealized images of ourselves and others, the result is a wound to the sense of self. The "impossible quest" for a perfect romantic ideal (Suzanne's composite of "Gandhi, Joe Montana, and...Harry Connick, Jr.") reflects a misplaced and ultimately self-defeating effort to heal that wound. It may comfort us, as it comforted Suzanne, to feel special, to believe we are entitled to ignore the rules others must play by, and to hope that one day perfect love will come. But it's a lonely comfort.

Karen, like Suzanne, also a single working mother, confused the real with the feared, rather than with the ideal. She dreamed repeatedly of a homeless crone hiding in her basement. This dream image of a frighteningly helpless woman embodied every trait Karen most feared in herself—yet, as we'll see, it was an image of herself she could not escape any more than she could escape her own shadow.

A thirty-two-year-old administrator for a nonprofit foundation, Karen divorced shortly after her second daughter was born. Whereas Suzanne could not idealize the men she might love, Karen could not feel idealizable. Karen originally sought therapy in a crisis when her boyfriend's ambivalence threatened both their relationship and her own self-esteem:

> I'm totally scared and confused. Allen moved out about a month ago, telling me he still loved me but giving me a list of my shortcomings that left me feeling very hurt and very angry. Now he's talking about moving to New York where there's a great job possibility and he's telling me he wants me to come. I asked him how I was supposed to deal with the custody stuff with my ex—'cause I know Barry would go to court in a millisecond if he thought I wanted to take Beth and Hilary three thousand miles away from him. At which point Allen said he didn't want to be asked to choose between love and work. But I'm just about sure he'd pick up and leave me if he got this job.

Karen utters these last words with a laugh and a smile. It strikes her therapist as incongruous and he says so. Why might the possibility of painful rejection provoke smiling laughter?

> It's like, "See? This is how the story *always* ends." That's how it was with my husband, that's how it'll be with Allen. I mean, it's not like it brings me great pleasure to be left, but it's almost predictable and I get some weird satisfaction when it turns out like it's supposed to.

Again, this seemed striking to her therapist. " 'Like it's supposed to'? How did you decide this is how it's supposed to turn out?"

I just feel I have this veil up all the time. Like I can be there in the relationship and act like I really believe Allen loves me—and why shouldn't he? I'm a great woman, I really feel like that sometimes, I do—but behind the veil it's like, No way is he gonna love me. It's just like with my parents. I'm only realizing it now, years after the fact, but I had this two-sided attitude the whole time I was growing up. On the one hand, I felt like I had this perfect childhood and my parents were just great. And I think I believed that. But now I think about my mother—she's just sort of given up, she won't leave the house...But that was always part of the picture: I got attention, but mainly for taking care of her, this depressed woman. And then the reality is I was always being criticized: I'd be playing the piano after a lesson or working on stuff from school or reading and it would always be, "How come you're not helping your mother?" So I feel like, Okay, I'll take care of somebody and maybe then they'll love me. Great solution. I find a great guy like Allen and then he leaves 'cause I'm not taking care of him well enough or he's found something better. I think that's what the smile is about—this feeling like, Yeah, that's just how it is and that's how it's gonna be: at least I know the score.

Karen talks about her "two-sided attitude": She can feel she had a "perfect childhood" and "great" parents—and yet her mother was deeply depressed and Karen was "always being criticized." She can feel at times like "a great woman"—and yet she sees herself in dreams as a homeless crone and believes that she'll always be left. This double attitude, these contradictory ideas, reflect the painful distance between her ideal and her feared images, between her wishes for herself and her terror.

Most of us experience some distance between our vision of ourselves at our best and the reality of our limitations; we also confront the difference between, on the one hand, the perfection we might wish for in our parents and partners and, on the other, their reality as people who both gratify and disappoint us. The contrast between the real and the ideal is part of what shapes our aspirations and drives our ambition—including our ambition to love and be loved. But as Karen's experience shows, the gulf between the real and ideal can be extremely exaggerated, while the distance between the real and feared images can nearly disappear: in dreams, one's house often represents one's personality, and Karen could not get the homeless crone out of her basement.

When it comes to assessing the current influence of those images that originated in the narcissism of our childhood, these are the key questions: First, how extreme or exaggerated are our ideal and feared images, and how great is the gulf between them? And second, which are the images we tend to identify with more—the ideal or the feared?

In Karen's case all the images are rather extreme. Both her difficulty believing that she is really loved and her conviction that she'll be abandoned suggest that Karen equates her real self much more readily with her feared images: she doesn't feel idealizable. This may explain why she is inclined to become involved—and to remain involved—with men who (we might speculate) have a limited capacity to love and idealize her. In terms of the desires reflected in the romantic ideal, it appears that Karen is capable of wanting someone she can deeply admire. But the desire for someone to admire *her* is apparently fraught with conflict.

When it comes to reconstructing the past, we can speculate that Karen's childhood sense of her own specialness (her Grandiose Self) was not adequately mirrored—nor could she adequately experience the comfort of the Idealized Object when this "object" was a depressed mother who seemed to need her daughter to comfort *her*. Consequently, rather than develop a healthy level of self-esteem, Karen continued to see herself in terms of very contradictory images: ideal self-images that were too good to be true and feared images that were probably even more exaggerated. And rather than develop a solid ability to trust other people, she continued to see them as well in terms of a very divided set of images.

How did Karen—and how do all of us—come to feel identified more with one set of self-images than another? How do we "decide" that we more closely resemble either who we wish to be or who we fear we might be?

Largely, of course, the way we see ourselves is a consequence of our experience with our parents. In this regard, we might ask, Did our parents adequately and empathically mirror our childhood achievements—and our early sense of specialness? And further, Could we idealize our parents for a time, rather than experience them as neglectful, hurtful, or abruptly disillusioning? In addition, two other kinds of influence molded our view of ourselves: the role models our parents provided us with, and our parents' needs in relation to us.

Karen, for example, conveys an impression of her mother as a depressed, now nearly immobilized, woman who probably thought poorly of herself. It's very likely that now, when Karen drifts unhappily toward a view of herself as the helpless crone, she is identifying with her own childhood view of her mother. For to a significant extent, we become who we are in the process of responding to our parents' example. Thus the dream image of the crone, which Karen takes to be a self-image, may also be an image of her mother (who, as she says, "won't leave the house"). All of us (like Karen) create ourselves in our parents' image to one degree or another—or risk feeling disloyal.

Compounding this, it may have served her mother's needs for Karen to feel that self-esteem and attention could be attained not on the basis of her own gifts (for playing the piano, studying, or whatever), but rather from taking care of others, especially her mother. Now, as an adult, the imagery of herself that she learned as a child in relation to her parents exerts a problematic influence on her self-image, her romantic ideal, and all her life in love. As Karen puts it, "I'll take care of somebody and maybe then they'll love me. Great solution." She's being ironic, of course, but in the past the solution worked.

Karen's solution is ultimately no more of an answer than Suzanne's was. Both women were struggling with the pain of what psychotherapists call "narcissistic injury"—injury to the sense of self or to self-esteem. But they dealt with their pain very differently. To cope with similar problems, they used very dissimilar defenses.

DEFENSES AGAINST IDEALIZATION AND IDEALIZATION AS A DEFENSE

Suzanne protected herself by *defending against idealization* (as she says, "I never met a man I couldn't find something wrong with"); Karen protected herself by using *idealization as a defense* (she looks for and finds a "great guy" to take care of—and hopes his grateful love will heal her wounded self-esteem). These solutions can be seen as defining opposite ends of a continuum that represents the range of possible responses to narcissistic injury. When we feel that our self-esteem is vulnerable, most of us make use of responses that lie somewhere between the two exaggerated alternatives described below.

When Our Romantic Ideal Is "Over-Ideal"

Shouldn't we be a little suspicious of our conduct in love when we find that perfection just isn't good enough? This is an ironic way of describing the defensive style of those of us whose romantic ideal so exaggerates the desirable qualities we seek in a mate that he or she can be found only in our fantasies or dreams. On the surface such an "impossible quest" for the perfect partner would seem to guarantee nothing more than a life of perfect loneliness. But in pursuing a romantic ideal that can never be found, we always have the safety and comfort of fantasy to anesthetize the pain of wounded self-esteem. The reassuring mirage of our own perfection is protected through the conviction that if only we could find the right mate all our discontents would vanish, and through avoiding the kind of actual intimate involvement that might challenge our wishful fictions about who we are.

When our fragile esteem rests on fantasy, it is frightening to be really seen—especially by someone who matters deeply to us. And yet, because our self-aggrandizing fantasy is hard to sustain if we are always alone, we also *need* to be seen or, more accurately, seen at our best. We need, in other words, to be idealized.

This dilemma of need and fear can be solved only by finding romantic involvements and then withdrawing from them. We can afford to idealize those we might love, but only until they begin to matter enough to deeply affect or hurt us. At this point our idealization becomes a danger and we have to defend against it. To protect ourselves from the fear of exposure and the threat to self-esteem, those we have loved and idealized must now be depreciated or devalued. But for this "solution" to work, we need to remain ignorant of the real meaning of our pattern of involvement and withdrawal, idealization and depreciation—this pattern that keeps us alone.

It is not uncommon for therapists to hear patients struggling to understand whether their loneliness is the outcome of their psychology or their circumstances. Sometimes these patients talk about their fear of making a mistake, of choosing the wrong partner, of foreclosing their chances for something better. But there is often a significant element of self-deception here, which is evident in their apparent absence of worry about winding up alone.

The psychoanalyst Owen Renik put it this way: What would we think about a man who said he desperately needed a car but spent years without transportation while trying to decide which car to buy? This one's the wrong color, he might tell us, and the hubcaps on that one are a little odd, and something with more power would be preferable. Possibly. But meanwhile this earnest searcher for the perfect vehicle is still without a car. Clearly, beyond what's being said, something else is going on.

And something else is surely going on when we complain that we're loveless and lonely but spend years or decades searching for that partner who fits just like a glove.

Here is the problem in a nutshell: When our romantic ideal is "over-ideal," it may mean that we are hoping to undo our hidden feelings of imperfection by meeting a partner whose own perfection is contagious. But these hopes inevitably backfire. If we happen to connect with such a partner, we wind up feeling inferior in comparison, and painfully envious. To avoid this kind of emotional danger, we then find fault and withdraw. But of course, defending against idealization in this way also undermines love.

When Our Romantic Ideal Won't Idealize Us

Few of us deliberately look for partners who are rejecting or critical. And yet we may repeatedly find ourselves in relationships in which we are uncertain of our partner's affection, frustrated by the ambivalent responses we receive, or angry at how little love and appreciation for us our partner expresses. We may feel that this is a familiar but inexplicable state of affairs. Or we may decide, drawing on cultural stereotypes, that all men are simply ungiving and self-absorbed. Or that all women are demanding and needy. However, if we find ourselves playing the same frustrating role over and over again vis-à-vis our partner (or a succession of partners), then we may begin to suspect that the explanation for our discontent in love is largely an internal one.

Looking at the image of the partner we seek can clarify why we find and remain involved with partners whose love and admiration for us is so limited.

If (like Karen) our solution to the problem of narcissistic injury is to take care of others as a way to be loved, then we put their needs first. This works best when we feel our partner is better or more important than we are—and consequently deserves more than we do. Paradoxically, then, to feel better about ourselves in this way, we must continue to feel undeserving. But it's hard to feel undeserving if we're loved and admired without reservation. So we habitually choose partners whose feelings for us are at best reserved.

This absence of consistent caring usually seems, however, to be the only significant flaw of the partners we select. Otherwise we can idealize them wholeheartedly—which is not merely reassuring but nearly mandatory because idealization is the foundation of our defensive solution. We have unconsciously concluded that our best (if not our only) hope for securing a feeling of self-esteem is to be loved by someone we idealize. But since we don't expect to be loved for who we are, we must find our way to self-esteem through love by a route that is quite indirect.

Typically we find our way as adults by retracing the paths we knew as children. Two childhood roles—to be needed and/or to exaggerate our neediness—reaped rewards for us in relation to our parents, and now we play them out for a second time with our partner. The rewards for being needed are easy to identify: when we make ourselves useful to our partner in whatever ways we can imagine, when we help him or her to feel better, we can reasonably hope for grateful love in return. The benefits of being seen as needy are less obvious, but they really amount to the same thing in disguise—for by being needy, too, we enable our partner to feel better: when we display our weakness, we help our partner feel strong. In relation to our dependence (or anxiety), our partner can more easily feel independent (or calm).

But there are problems associated with this solution. Being needed and/or being needy are essentially *roles* we have adopted as alternatives to being loved for who we are. Because they involve a kind of play-acting, these roles distance us from ourselves and make it difficult for our real needs to be satisfied. If we have even an inkling of our hidden motives, we may feel inauthentic or manipulative when we take care of those we love or are taken care of by them. Our pleasure in these acts may then seem hollow. We may also feel resentful that we have to turn such emotional somersaults in order simply to be loved.

Most problematic of all, taking care of a partner we idealize in the hope that we'll be loved and then feel lovable is a strategy that can never actually work. Even when it succeeds, it fails. Suppose that this partner, whose love has been so elusive, now experiences a change of heart and we find that we are loved. Then it's hard not to feel that we have won our partner's affection through pretense—and that even now we are not *really* loved, but perhaps only needed. In addition, our anger at having to go to such lengths to be loved can generate reactions that undermine the love we appear to have won. Having come to feel needed, we may then turn resentfully withholding, reluctant to give, or, having come to feel genuinely needy, we may angrily refuse to allow our partner to satisfy our needs.

IDEALIZATION AND THE COUPLE

So far we've been looking at individual defenses that bear on the capacity for idealization. Now let's move on to explore how our individual defenses interact with those of our partner.

It's no accident that those of us with a more self-aggrandizing style in love frequently gravitate toward those whose style is more self-depreciating. In a sense two such lovers—one who defends against idealization and the other who uses idealization as a defense—are a perfect match, though not exactly a match made in heaven.

But even when our defensive style and that of our partner are the same, there is frequently a tilt toward polarization—a tendency for partners to parcel out the two roles between them. We may both have been defensively self-aggrandizing in the past (or we may both have been self-depreciating), but now one of us drifts toward idealization while the other seems to resist it. This is the occasion for that familiar sinking sensation when love that had seemed perfectly balanced is unexpectedly revealed to be at least a little one-sided. Now one of us seems to love or give or admire more than the other does—and abruptly the difference between our defensive styles seems to erase what we'd assumed was the similarity.

Naturally this kind of situation is disturbing, but it should not necessarily be regarded as fixed or static, nor as evidence that our relationship is basically flawed. As love evolves, our needs for self-protection inevitably shift—and as they do, the imbalances of idealization between two partners will likely shift as well. The admirer will become the admired and vice versa—and sometimes through these reversals a more idyllic balance will be restored.

But whether we're talking about erotic involvement, merging, or idealization, our individual ability to use our capacities in love is always affected by our defensive needs and is always changing. And when we're out of synch with our partner, it may reflect something about an existing collusion, it may be the occasion for a collision—or it may be part of what makes collaboration possible.

The Couple in Collusion

When it comes to idealization, three sorts of collusion are possible. The most common is the match between two partners, one of whom uses self-aggrandizing defenses while the other uses self-depreciating defenses. But two self-aggrandizing partners may also collude to maintain their self-protection. The same is true for two partners with self-depreciating defenses.

One Idealizes and One Doesn't: *Partners Whose Defenses Mesh*

In this common collusion, the more self-depreciating partner is openly thrilled to have found his romantic ideal. But secretly he's hurt and disappointed at not being idealized in return. He is reassured, however, by his hopeful fantasy that through meeting his partner's needs he will eventually be loved by her.[1]

The more self-aggrandizing partner initially felt exhilarated at the prospect of admiring her partner without reservation. But now that she's discovered his flaws, her early excitement at his resemblance to her romantic ideal has become hard to maintain. Still, she has hopes that he may improve, and for the moment her shaky conviction that she is special is unconsciously reinforced by her feeling that he is not.

This kind of collusion has several key elements, some or all of which may be part of what defines a particular couple's real relationship. First, the self-depreciating partner essentially accepts the

---

1. The two roles in this interaction and those that follow are not gender specific: each role could be played by a partner of either gender.

other partner's faultfinding. To do so makes it easier for him to put his partner's needs ahead of his own—which is key to his hope of being loved. In addition, accepting the criticism keeps his identification with his feared self-images in place—and this maintains old family loyalties. Next, the self-depreciating partner may collude with the self-aggrandizement of his mate, not only through expressing admiration but also in doing nothing to challenge her in areas where she is vulnerable. Lastly, the self-depreciating partner may actually accentuate those features of his personality (say, his difficulty coping with crises) that make it hard for his mate to idealize him.

As for the self-aggrandizing partner, she may continually find fault with her mate, especially in those areas in which she is painfully insecure herself, to bolster her self-esteem through feeling superior. She may avoid idealizing her partner—to avoid a dangerous degree of intimacy. In addition to finding fault, the self-aggrandizing partner may unconsciously elicit insecurity in her mate by withdrawing emotionally, provoking jealousy, or withholding expressions of affection. Or, the self-aggrandizing partner may look to other sources of security to dilute her dependence on her mate—which in turn makes him feel less needed, less loved, and less secure.

Although this might not sound like a very happy scenario, two partners may both derive great satisfaction from such a relationship. One enjoys the satisfaction of having her feelings of specialness confirmed through her mate's admiration. The other has the satisfaction of being the partner of such an admirable mate. And, of course, because our focus here is on the capacity for idealization, we're leaving out a variety of other pleasures such a couple may very well enjoy. The problem is that this collusion is based on self-protective illusions, on defenses, which keep a couple from realizing the full potential of their partnership. And like many collusions, this one has instability built in. When either partner becomes discontent within the confines of his or her role, the collusion is likely to become a collision.

Two Partners with Self-Aggrandizing Defenses

This collusion begins on a harmonious note of mutual admiration but rather quickly turns discordant when the partners begin to find fault with each other. The more exaggerated the romantic ideal of each partner, the more he or she is disillusioned and angry when the flaws of the mate begin to be discovered. At its best this collusion can be stably unstable: a roller-coaster ride of falling in and out of love that enables both partners to learn something about tolerating the limitations of others. At its worst the self-aggrandizing style of these two partners is so rigid that mutual faultfinding dissolves the love that briefly brought them together: now their collusion simply collapses like a balloon emptied of air.

Two Partners with Self-Depreciating Defenses

This collusion in which each partner takes care of the other can be stably companionable, but it lacks passion. Neither partner really expects or feels entitled to a great deal from the other. Neither is terribly disappointed. But for several reasons, the abiding atmosphere around this couple's collusion may be one of muted, sometimes hidden, dissatisfaction.

The self-depreciating defense relies on the idealization of the partner and the hope that one's own meager esteem might somehow be enhanced by the partner's love. But it's hard to sustain idealization, passion, or hope in the face of a partner's naked self-depreciation. Both parties to this collusion may wind up feeling that they are living in a kind of emotional cul-de-sac that guarantees them safety and comfort but holds promise for little more. In terms of idealization, this is the neighborhood of diminished expectations. But it makes for the stablest of collusions—the sort that led one wife to say of her husband of many years that he fit her comfortably, like an old shoe.

The Couple in Collision

Collisions between partners who have previously colluded may be provoked either by an atmosphere of security about the couple's relationship that encourages them to take risks or by an atmosphere of insecurity that encourages heightened defensiveness and conflict.

Security and Collision

When our relationship feels solid and secure, we may feel safe enough to use our defenses somewhat flexibly. The self-aggrandizing partner may risk letting his limitations be seen rather than focus on the real or imagined failings of his mate. The self-depreciating partner may feel freer to assert her strengths: desires or dissatisfactions she formerly felt she needed to hide can now be put into words.

But when in this unaccustomed way we begin to acknowledge our limitations and needs—or start to assert our desires and dissatisfactions—we may find our stable collusion disintegrating under the pressure of conflict. If we were the more admiring partner, we may now be angrily discontent. If we were the more admired partner, we may feel very resentful at being challenged just when we're becoming vulnerable. Each of us may experience such a collision as dangerous—for it brings into sharp focus precisely those uncomfortable aspects of our personality that our defenses ordinarily protect us from. For the same reason, however, such a collision may also represent an opportunity to experience a fuller, truer sense of ourselves.

Insecurity and Collision

When a couple faces external pressures, their need for the defenses they customarily employ with one another may be amplified. To deal with his own insecurity, the self-aggrandizing partner may escalate his faultfinding and enlist other measures to evoke the insecurity of his partner. Meanwhile, to take care of herself emotionally, the partner who is self-depreciating may adhere more desperately to her familiar roles of caretaking or clinging. Now each partner may begin to seem a little more impossible or intolerable to the other. In this atmosphere of stressful insecurity for the couple, the lid may come off their incipient conflicts. Then, once again, what started as a comforting collusion may evolve into an extremely uncomfortable collision.

But as we've said before, collisions can reveal what collusions conceal—and this revelation, though painful, may turn out to be a very good thing. The question, of course, is whether or not a couple can successfully collaborate to transform the crisis of collision into an opportunity for mastery.

The Couple in Collaboration

Our capacity to idealize our partner is challenged when we're confronted with conflict or disappointment. It may be hard to continue to experience our partner as our romantic ideal when any or all of the three needs linked to that ideal are being frustrated. If our needs to feel admiration for our partner, to be admired, or to experience a strong sense of kinship are not being met, we may feel very disillusioned. Most of us will be inclined to blame our partner, though some of us may blame ourselves. But blame misses the point.

When we find ourselves wondering if we might not be better off should our once-perfect partner become again a perfect stranger, we have to ask what's responsible for the intensity of our disillusionment. It may be our partner's realistic shortcomings, or it may be our own failure of imagination. Or both—for even if getting to know our partner better means knowing more about his or her shortcomings, the question remains why these should be so intolerable.

We know now that it is mainly our feeling about ourselves that determines our capacity to idealize others. If our early experience has led us to feel good about ourselves, then our idealization of our partner can generally withstand the challenge of conflict or disappointment. Not that our idealization won't wane—of course it will, but it will be readily revivable. By contrast, when the past has left our self-esteem vulnerable, our romantic ideal will be skewed or exaggerated in ways that make our idealization of our partner much more unstable. If, for example, we have a need to admire our partner to compensate for an inability to admire ourselves, then our partner's imperfections will be hard to tolerate. If we have an overdeveloped need to be admired, then our partner's criticism (or even lack of enthusiasm) can be so disturbing that our idealization of that partner will suffer.

The point is that our difficulty maintaining idealization as a revivable resource in love usually has as much or more to do with our own romantic ideal—and our defenses—as it does with the realistic qualities of our partner. Understanding this about ourselves can facilitate our collaboration as partners in a couple.

As individuals the key is to begin by identifying the specific needs that must be satisfied if we are to experience our partner as our romantic ideal: Just how important is it for us to deeply admire, to be admired by, and to feel akin to our beloved? It's hard to recognize needs that are being met. Frustrated needs stand out much more clearly. Consider, then, those unwelcome situations that may try our capacity for idealization: When our partner's limitations seem to come into focus, how difficult is it for us to sustain our feelings of love? When our partner's loving admiration for us seems to wane, how hard is it for us to continue to feel loving? And how difficult is it for us to experience our partner as our romantic ideal when we become aware of the differences between us?

Looking at ourselves in this way, we may come to understand, for example, that we easily continue to idealize our partner in the face of apparent limitations and differences—but that we are unusually vulnerable to feeling disillusioned when our partner seems unable to idealize us. Or we may learn that admiring and being admired are secondary, while our predominant need, our most acute hunger, is to feel a sense of kinship (verging on twinship) with our partner: realizing how deeply difference threatens us, we might now want to ask ourselves why.

Once we've identified the particular needs that make our capacity for idealization vulnerable, we can more easily rein in the worst of our conscious impulses to blame our partner—or depressively blame ourselves. Yet most of us, in the face of disillusionment or frustration, still turn reflexively to our usual defenses—which may exacerbate our problems rather than solve them.

Suppose, for example, that we have an overly intense need to admire our partner—and that now we have become painfully aware of his or her supposed imperfections. Will we withdraw, will we find fault with our beloved or fantasize about other lovers who might be more ideal? We would do better to wonder about the meaning of our own exaggerated need to admire a perfect partner—a partner, perhaps, with none of the flaws that go along with being human. We would do well to ask if our characteristic defensive solutions really "work" when our need for such a partner seems to be frustrated. Do our defenses actually protect us? From what? At what price? With what hidden payoffs?

Often what we do to protect ourselves is anything but protective in relation to others—hence the vital importance of trying to appreciate the emotional impact our romantic ideal, our needs, and our defenses have on our partner. When much of this is finally known and some of it communicated, it reduces blaming and enhances empathy. This can take the edge off those confrontations that, in anticipation, are always hard to bear—but are necessary nonetheless.

For just because we understand that our own psychology makes a contribution to what goes wrong in our relationship doesn't mean that we have nothing to say to our partner about his or her contribution. In fact, it is often the very process of putting into words our thoughts and feelings about our partner's impact on us that is most healing. As the following example shows, this kind of communication may be especially healing when it touches on those jarring aspects of our partner's personality that challenge our idealization.

Four years after marrying Kathleen, Paul became ecstatic after receiving word he'd been commissioned to design the layout for a new national magazine. Kathleen seemed pleased, but her enthusiasm fell far short of her husband's, and Paul became angry, then depressed. He felt old suspicions stirring that Kathleen was unable to enjoy his success. But, worse, when he confronted his wife with her inability to share his excitement, she asked, Do you really want me to applaud you wholeheartedly for getting more work when you're already completely overwhelmed by the work you've got? He was stung. Her response was evidence, he claimed, that so long as they were together he would have to suffer her habit of finding a cloud around every silver lining.

Typical of the unwelcome interactions that occur between partners in love, this one threatened Paul's idealization of his wife—but it also temporarily eroded Kathleen's loving feeling for him. A week later, however, they had a long and difficult conversation that restored (in fact, amplified) their old shared feeling that each had found in the other a reasonable approximation of their romantic ideal. Their talk was healing, in large part, because it had been preceded on each side by some thoughtful self-scrutiny.

Paul had become aware that his confidence in his work, indeed his confidence in himself, depended inordinately on Kathleen's support. It was as though Paul was always performing before a hostile audience whose criticism had to be countered by his wife's enthusiastic acceptance. From the perspective of the romantic ideal, Paul's overwhelming need to be admired made his idealization of his wife vulnerable. When she was other than admiring he felt deeply hurt, and to protect himself he tended to withdraw angrily. In this connection Paul also realized that Kathleen's inclination to pessimism was a personal threat to him, because it undercut her ability to be unreservedly enthusiastic on his behalf.

Kathleen had thought about her ambivalent reaction to Paul's coup with the new magazine. She was able to recognize that her husband's persistent anxiety about his work threatened an image of him that was very important to her: her idealized picture of him as a nearly perfect partner—not just successful but calmly confident. The possibility that a high-stakes assignment might leave Paul feeling still more burdened and more anxious filled her with dread. From the perspective of the romantic ideal, her exaggerated need for a flawless partner to admire made her idealization of her husband vulnerable. So she imagined the worst to protect herself from disappointment.

Paul and Kathleen knew their talk might be a hard one. Fortunately they had the luxury of choosing their time and place well: a Sunday with hours to themselves in a nearby woods. They agreed it was important to tell each other what it was about their respective personalities that had so troubled them during their recent fight.

Paul told Kathleen how much her pessimism grated on him and how disturbed he was about her apparent difficulty expressing excitement about his success. He was relieved that after expressing so much of his dissatisfaction at such length, Kathleen largely agreed with him rather than becoming defensive. She admitted that her tendency to assume the worst was a problem for her—and one that emerged mainly when she felt threatened. She went on to explain that Paul's anxiety about his work made her extremely uncomfortable, but mainly because she wanted to feel—and more often than not *did* feel—that he was very special. And this was important to her, she said, because she sometimes felt far from special herself.

He was impressed by her honesty and moved by her capacity to appreciate him in spite of his being critical. He was able to admit that he *did* feel unreasonably anxious—and that, in fact, he probably demanded her support rather than feeling grateful when it was spontaneously forthcoming, which it often was. Kathleen told him she understood how self-critical he could be and how hard it was for him when her ability to be supportive was undercut by her worry. All of us have probably had such conversations—but not all of them have gone so well. A portrait of a couple in collaboration, Paul and Kathleen can be seen as coping successfully with challenges to their capacity to use idealization as a resource.

HOW IDEALIZATION EVOLVES AS LOVE EVOLVES

Like all of the six capacities, idealization is a resource in love that holds a different kind of promise at each of the three stages of a relationship. But like all of the capacities, idealization is also vulnerable to different risks during love's successive stages.

Falling in Love

When we fall in love, idealization plays an indispensable role. By allowing us to experience our partner as the embodiment of our romantic ideal, this capacity enables us to overcome our fears and begin a relationship. Idealization makes possible that priceless alchemy which permits us for a time to experience real love as ideal love. This is love as "a point of intersection between desire and reality" (in the words of the Mexican poet Octavio Paz).

The danger when we fall in love is too much idealization or too little. When the projection of the romantic ideal comes to commandeer the entire psychological space between two people and we see our partner entirely in terms of his or her fit (or lack of fit) with our romantic ideal, this can be deadly. It can suffocate a new relationship, leaving it no room to really become itself or to grow. We are so absorbed in our dream of the ideal that waking to the reality of an actual partner is inevitably disillusioning. This is the problem when the map of the terrain of the ideal is thought to describe the totality of our experience in love.

But there is also a problem when we try to deny the need to idealize our partner. Then we may wind up in relationships that lack the electricity of a circuit between inside and outside, between our internal world and the external reality. If our real-life partner has no connection to the image of the romantic ideal inside us, then the relationship will lack a crucial kind of energy. We may have companionship but probably not lasting passion. We may share mutual concern but probably not the deep tenderness that comes from a love that richly unites what is inside and outside us—and makes a bridge between desire and reality, past and present, lover and beloved.

Becoming a Couple

Idealization usually wanes as a relationship progresses. Now we confront disillusionment. The intensity of our disillusionment is largely related to the extent of the difference between the real beloved we've discovered and the idealized beloved we've imagined. When our partner has been overidealized, our disillusionment can be extreme and painful. But even when the distance between fact and fiction is minimal, it is predictable that eventually we'll find ourselves feeling some disappointment. For as time passes and intimacy deepens, our knowledge of our partner grows—and at least in part, this means knowing more about our partner's limitations. How we react to disillusionment and disappointment has a great deal to do with our capacity for integration, the subject of the next chapter. (Integration is the capacity that enables us to see the big picture rather than focus narrowly and confuse the part with the whole.)

Though it wanes more often than not, idealization also has the potential to be rekindled. As such, it can be an enduring resource that helps us tolerate the unavoidable periods of difficulty in love relationships. When idealization is revived, we can be nourished as a couple by reexperiencing the joy we knew with our partner when we were first falling in love. And of course, our capacity for idealization can also deepen as we learn more about ourselves and our partner and become more trusting. In addition, our idealization may intensify as we watch our partner come closer, with the support of a loving relationship, to reaching his or her potential.

The threat to idealization in the second phase of love has to do mainly with our self-defeating need *not* to idealize our partner. If, for whatever reason, heightened intimacy represents a danger to us, then we may experience the revival of early idealization as dangerous. Making matters still more problematic is an interaction between two partners in which one becomes the keeper of the flame. This partner is motivated to keep the relationship afloat virtually no matter what the cost. Such a polarization, in which one idealizes and one resists idealization, endangers love. The risks of confronting the "de-idealizing" partner may be frightening—but sometimes to save a relationship we must be willing to lose it.

Remaining in Love over Time

In this third stage of love, idealization can remain a resource that helps keep a couple's relationship passionate and vital. The challenges to idealization arise with the joint tasks and difficulties—child rearing and aging, in particular—that two partners may confront together. More on this in Chapter Six, on self-transcendence.

All of us have different strengths and vulnerabilities when it comes to idealization. To the extent that we understand our own individual capacity for idealization—how it is likely to be a resource in love, or a resistance—we are better equipped to deal with the challenges that will confront us in this area as our relationship evolves.

SELF-APPRAISAL: THREE PROFILES

Cynthia: Idealization as a Resource

Cynthia is a music teacher who sees herself at thirty-nine as enormously fortunate. She has been happily married since her mid-twenties to a man she considers her soul mate. She is aware of her husband Malcolm's flaws—he can lose himself in his work, he can be irritable—but she feels generally unperturbed by them. What stands out for her always are his strengths. His creativity and intelligence stimulate her and evoke her admiration. His generosity, responsibility, and caring enable her to feel confident in him as a partner and as a parent to their children. She says she could choose to be distracted by one or another minor shortcoming of his, but to what end? She's so much happier simply enjoying him.

Cynthia contrasts this relationship to that with Philip, the man she left to marry her husband. Philip was a charismatic songwriter to whom her attachment, as she puts it, was "hormonal." He was physically beautiful and talented but incredibly self-absorbed. She felt he never took her seriously, that she had to struggle to get his attention. This first love of her adult life duplicated her relationship with her forceful and magnetic father, a career diplomat who divorced her mother when Cynthia was five. To Cynthia, her father's attention was a glamorous but scarce commodity. It could be won only by diligently seducing him with a combination of her charm and her achievements. Being herself never seemed sufficient—not for her father, not for Philip.

In Malcolm, by contrast, she found a man to idealize who also idealized her. He was smitten with Cynthia's verbal quickness and sensitivity, her exotic looks and her musicality. He had hopes, as an aspiring composer, that the two of them might collaborate. Briefly, his unabashed affection left her feeling suspicious: was he just too desperate to notice her flaws? But she soon came to realize that if anything deserved to be regarded with suspicion it was her idealization of ambivalent men.

Once she recognized her anxiety about being idealized, Cynthia's own ambivalence subsided and she was able to plunge joyfully into the relationship with Malcolm. Her admiration for him has deepened over time. Now, in particular, when she watches him with their two daughters, she can be overcome with feelings of appreciation for his specialness. Yet these feelings have a bittersweet quality, too, for Malcolm's strengths as a father remind her of her disappointment in her own father.

Martin: Idealization That Is Compromised

A thirty-three-year-old sales manager for a chain of hotels, Martin is married to a woman he initially idealized—but seeing her as exceptional, he winds up too often feeling ordinary. Only half in jest, he summarizes their history: "I wanted her in the worst way and that's just how I got her." What he means is that he adores his wife for her strengths (her passionate intensity, ambition, and commitment to family) but that these same qualities lead her to ask of him more at times than he feels capable of giving.

Martin came from a splintered family: His parents separated before he was born, leaving his mother to care for him while two older brothers were sent to live for several years with her uncle. Eventually his mother remarried and his brothers returned, but before long she divorced again. Though Martin felt close to her, the chaos of his upbringing (fathers and brothers disappearing and reappearing) left him feeling unmoored and unaccountably ashamed.

His marriage to Elizabeth, a strong and very attractive woman from a stable family, promised to relieve him of these feelings. It was as though he felt she'd rescued him from drifting through life. Elizabeth's desire to re-create the warmth and stability of her own family became his ambition to create the family he'd never had.

But whereas his initial idealization of Elizabeth cast her in the role of the perfect mate, now her ease with herself and her high expectations of him leave Martin feeling inferior. Earlier his wife's admiration had seemed to effectively offset the impact of the feared self-images that he so easily identified with. But now in the face of Elizabeth's difference from him (which he interprets as her superiority), these dreaded images of himself seem impossible to escape. More and more it seems as though the price of being with his idealized wife is to feel contemptible in comparison. And this makes him resentful.

On the other hand, he can see Elizabeth's pride in him. When he lives up to her image of him, a much more positive image than his own, he feels grateful for her confidence in him. It allows him to stretch, to aim higher than he might have without her support.

Martin is torn by the conflict between his impulse to idealize his wife and his inclination to hold her responsible for his feelings of inferiority and resentment. He'd like to believe that if only she expected less of him then he could feel more comfortable with himself. But he suspects that the real basis for his discomfort is his own feeling of shameful inadequacy, which he knows is rooted in his past rather than his marriage. To some extent, this awareness takes the edge off his tendency to blame his wife, but the conflict between his grateful love for Elizabeth and his impulse to blame her remains painfully unresolved.

Sam: Idealization as a Struggle

In his late forties, Sam divorced after a frustrating second marriage that had lasted for a decade. Now, five years down the road, he is disturbed to find himself repeating in new relationships the doomed pattern of infatuation and disillusionment he played out with both his ex-wives. He has become suspicious of himself when he feels he's falling in love. He's reticent with friends, anticipating their bemused skepticism: he knows they've heard it all before, from the auspicious beginning to the inevitable ending.

Time and time again, he has watched himself deciding that the new woman in his life is just about perfect. His idealization of her is complete. Yet after a period of weeks or months, he discovers that this woman of his dreams is very needy and often sexually inhibited as well. He is still very much in love with her, at least for a time, but finds his idealization gradually eroded by his partner's presumed dependency, while his own sexuality seems hard to maintain in the face of her inhibition. He stays in the relationship longer than he's inclined to because he wonders if his disappointment might not have as much to do with his *own* frightening dependency and sexual guilt as with the qualities of his partner. But eventually, feeling trapped, depressed, and a little panicked, he pulls away. And before long he meets someone new with whom he can fall in love—and the cycle of idealization and disillusionment begins again.

Sam is right about himself: his fears about his own dependency and sexuality are dealt with by defensively finding these problems in his partner. But this knowledge alone has been inadequate to dislodge his self-defeating defenses. After a period of psychotherapy, however, he is beginning to understand two more things about himself that may help.

The first is that he arranges his relationships in such a way that he is bound to wind up feeling disillusioned and, to some extent, exploited. Often quite consciously, he chooses partners who have the potential to be very dependent (financially and otherwise) and then, albeit with some ambivalence, he encourages their dependency. He also chooses partners who are sexually inhibited and decides that, in addition, they are critical of his sexuality.

Second, he is beginning to see that his relationships assume the dead-end form they do because he is committed to re-creating the ambivalent relationship he knew with his mother. Reliving this old relationship means both that no new relationship can survive and that, therefore, what will be preserved is his loyalty to his alternately seductive and furious mother.

Like many people whose capacity to fall and remain in love is shaky, Sam with the passage of time is becoming intolerant of his old self-destructive habits of self-protection. He has become aware that his dreams of love are no substitute for a lasting relationship. He now knows that his search for a partner who won't disillusion him will be endless—unless he comes to terms with the fears from which his defenses enable him to hide.

CHAPTER FOUR

The Capacity for Integration: The Role of Acceptance in Love

*S*arah, a thirty-five-year-old restaurant owner, has just broken up with a man she had expected to marry:

At first I couldn't believe it, and then I was incredibly pissed off when I found out Ed was actually leaving on this business trip he'd threatened to take. He knew how important it was for me that he be around for this holiday. I spelled it out for him: I explained that I wasn't just being sentimental, it's that the restaurant is going to be a nightmare that weekend and I needed his support. He knew I'd flip if he were to leave me now...but apparently that's not important enough to him. I guess he felt he just had to let me know who's in charge. Well, if that's so vital to him, fine, that's it. But I feel totally betrayed... So we had this huge fight, and finally I told him to just get lost, to get out of my life...Lovely way to wind things up. God, I feel like such a fool.

Three months ago, even a month ago, I had a totally different picture of this guy. I thought he was solid as could be. And sensitive and emotional and available. We had practically decided to get married. I was feeling like we were made for each other. It seemed like he had everything I wanted and I had everything he wanted and it was going to be, I don't know, perfect. Or at least workable.

Maybe I just lose my mind when I see somebody who seems right, maybe I can't see straight. But I really thought I could trust him. And then to make matters worse, I was talking to Judy, this friend of mine, explaining the situation to her, and I couldn't believe it! She was totally unsympathetic...She said she thought I had blinders on when it came to my relationships...that my last relationship, with Matthew, had ended on exactly the same note...According to Judy, I wasn't seeing my role in this thing...My role! Do I have a role? Do I control whether he goes on a business trip or whether he can be trusted? It's not something I have the slightest control over...in any case, he obviously can't be trusted. Isn't that what he's just demonstrated?

Maybe in these crises you find out who your real friends are...I mean, Judy, of all people, should be able to understand...*She* just broke up with her boyfriend...Doesn't it ever occur to her that this might simply be the way men are?...She thinks Ed is different? That's ridiculous. He's turned out to be a ringer for my father: Mr. False Promises, number two.

I hate the fact that this whole thing seems so clichéd...but I guess clichés reflect reality, and the reality here is the man makes commitments, makes promises he doesn't live up to, and the woman gets screwed...I'd love to trust men, but guys like Ed make it totally impossible...You're supposed to trust people, if you don't you're paranoid...But I don't feel paranoid, I feel like a fool.

Like Sarah, all of us confront disappointments in our relationships. But Sarah's reaction is particularly intense. Her disillusionment, anger, and fear of abandonment all reflect vulnerability in her capacity for integration. It is possible to fall in love without integration, but remaining in love without it is nearly inconceivable.

Falling in love is a kind of honeymoon, but like every honeymoon this one ends. Idealization always wanes, and when it does we confront our partner's limitations, and often our own as well. Whatever our hopes may have been for perfect love, now we feel frustrated and disillusioned to one degree or another. How we deal with these feelings depends on the extent of our capacity for integration.

The challenge is to reconcile our positive and negative experiences in love. Integration is crucial here because it helps us see the big picture and thereby protects us from confusing the part with the whole. Without integration, love is either positive or negative: with integration, it can be both.

Integrating what is "good" and "bad" in our experiences of ourselves and of our partner lets us sustain empathy and affection even as we confront imperfection and disappointment. The capacity for integration means that we can be angry with someone we love and love someone with whom we are angry. In short, integration enables us to feel ambivalent and still proceed in the relationship.

On the other hand, by allowing us to be aware simultaneously of the positive and the negative, integration also enables us to thoughtfully evaluate a relationship and to leave it when there is good reason to do so.

FROM AMBIVALENCE TO ACCEPTANCE

The advantages that integration brings to a relationship include, but go well beyond, the tolerance of ambivalence, that is, the ability to live with our mixed feelings. With integration, our view of what love is and what love can be is far deeper and more complex than if this capacity were lacking.

With integration, our appreciation of our partner becomes both more real and more dimensional, as if our map of present love now has topography: we can see in greater detail the peaks and valleys, the graduated slopes and curves of the romantic landscape. Without integration, our view of our partner and of ourselves will always remain limited, like a picture in black and white, with no shades of gray. When the world of love is black and white, yesterday's hero can become tomorrow's villain, depending on whether he or she continues to gratify us. Where relationships are concerned, this is a very unstable kind of world.

Integration stabilizes love, but it can also deepen it in a number of ways. In making use of this capacity, we mobilize a larger sense of self. We take our experience of merging with our partner a step farther. And we have the potential to explore dimensions of intimacy that might not ordinarily be available to us.

At its most rudimentary, integration may allow us to stay in a relationship while still sitting on the fence, withholding real commitment. When integration is more fully developed, however, we experience acceptance. In this reconciliation of our "good" and "bad" feelings, we stretch emotionally to embrace what is difficult about our partner. We don't deny or ignore what we don't like. Instead we seek a point of balance. By embracing the polar opposites of contradictory emotions, we even out the intensity of either extreme.

Integration also encourages a more mature and larger sense of ourselves. To accept aspects of our partner that feel alien to us, our personal identity must stretch. Suppose, for example, that we are intolerant of anger. Then it will be hard for us to acknowledge our angry feelings—and hard, at least initially, to accept our partner's anger. But to the extent that we can accept our partner when he or she is angry, it often becomes easier to accept ourselves when we're angry. In this way, our sense of self becomes larger.

Integration gives us the potential, as partners in love, to come to terms with our differences, accepting and sometimes even celebrating them. Gradually, more of what each of us finds difficult in the other can be accommodated. And with more freedom to be ourselves, shared closeness can be heightened. In this way, integration takes the capacity for merging a step further, for we can now bring to the relationship a greater range and depth of emotional experience.

Integration also affects our inner map. When our capacity for integration is poorly developed, our map paints relationships in black and white and describes a very limited spectrum of options, as if love could only follow one or two paths. Sarah, for example, could think only of betrayal when her lovers failed to live up to her expectations. When they frustrated her, these lovers became villains—rather than individuals with needs of their own that might sometimes conflict with hers. Like Sarah, we are confined to a very restricted terrain in love as long as our capacity for integration is limited. For then we see our partner in all-or-nothing terms: he or she is either all good ("Let's get married") or all bad ("What am I doing here?").

By contrast, once integration allows us to accept our partner as he or she really is (good *and* bad), we open up a range of possibilities in love that might otherwise have remained inaccessible. Even when these aren't always the possibilities we would have chosen, they have the potential to deepen our capacity to love.

Consider Joe, an unmarried man in his late forties who fell in love with Cheryl, a single mother involved in struggles over parenting with her ex-husband. Prior to meeting Cheryl, Joe's map of intimacy did not include stepparenting, much less battles with a difficult ex. Yet now he finds that his deepening acceptance of Cheryl, which also means acceptance of some responsibility for her child, is showing him parts of himself that he never expected to see.

Joe had to alter his ideal image of himself in love, and all his expectations of his future, so that his image might include a stepchild. He needed to open his heart to loving a child who was not, by blood, his own. He had to face, and learn to tolerate, the sacrifices that having a child imposes on the romance of the couple.

As our mapping of expectations and possibilities in love becomes melded with the map of our partner, the whole is greater than the sum of the parts. Joe's experience of the pain and conflict—as well as the joy—of making his new family "work" was like an unexpected, undesired trip to a foreign country. His growing capacity for acceptance, however, turned it into a life-transforming and deeply satisfying journey.

LOVE WITHOUT INTEGRATION

Intimacy without integration is a series of emotional roller-coaster rides. When integration fails, feelings become intense and out of control. Disappointment turns to hopelessness, anger becomes rage, and the fear of rejection escalates to a terror of abandonment.

How can you disappoint me so? How can you let me down? How can you expect me to care for you when I feel I've been misled? How can I still love you when it turns out you've got these problems and weaknesses? These are the kinds of questions that come up when our capacity for integration is problematic. Without integration, we may have plunged into the relationship when it felt good, but now we're tempted to run for cover as soon as the slightest difficulty arises. These are the consequences of an inner map with images of love that are overly simplified.

STRENGTHENING THE CAPACITY FOR INTEGRATION

As is true with all the capacities in love, we can place our capacity for integration on a continuum ranging from experiences of deficient or missing integration to experiences of successful integration. When we grapple with the ambivalent feelings that inevitably arise in love, then integration continues to develop. But if we always respond to ambivalence as a signal to abandon ship— if we automatically tilt toward an awareness of the negative and act on it—then this capacity may remain dormant. Of course, our response would be just as "unintegrated" if we persistently ignored the negative side of our ambivalence—and stayed in a relationship regardless of the cost.

Integration can evolve when we choose to persevere and confront problems in love rather than engage in wholesale retreat. Every such predicament can be an opportunity to exercise (and strengthen) this capacity: to see the whole rather than the part, to take into account the rewards of the relationship as well as the difficulties that currently seem to plague it.

But integration can be a struggle. When we feel hurt or let down, it may seem easier to push away from the person we believe to be the source of our pain. "I hate you," said in the midst of a fight, may be both an exclamation of frustration (not to be taken at face value) and a momentary statement of fact. But if we allow ourselves to be driven by this hatred, then the relationship will be finished. Integration can help us pause before acting on our immediate feelings. If we give ourselves this interval between emotion and action, we may find ways to grapple with the relationship's difficulties.

There were many times when Joe felt he couldn't tolerate the conflict between being a stepfather (who had to set limits with Cheryl's son) and a lover (who wanted to stay in Cheryl's good graces). In moments of frustration, when the tension between these roles seemed almost unbearable, he had been tempted to bail out. But each time, he managed to struggle through his difficulties by using integration; to him this capacity meant recognizing the importance of his choice to stay or go. Appreciating all the implications, positive and negative, he was able to get a grip on impulses that threatened to overwhelm his judgment. As a consequence, he felt more aware of his own strength. He also felt more loving toward Cheryl. And this translated into a change in his inner map: more and more he was able to see himself as someone with the ability to stay in a relationship, even when confronted with considerable difficulty.

The crux of the matter is to keep the whole picture in mind: the depth of our love as well as our feelings of hurt or anger. When we use the capacity for integration, we can avoid being pushed around by our momentary impulses and globally negative judgments. In so doing, we reach a higher level of understanding and acceptance not only of our partner but also of ourselves.

HOW NOT TO BECOME A COUPLE: SARAH'S BLIND SPOTS IN LOVE

The capacity for integration opens the door to the second stage of intimacy—becoming a couple. When the idealization we associate with falling in love begins to fade, integration helps us deal with our disappointment. We may face the loss of the high hopes and wishful fantasies that we've projected onto our partner. We may find ourselves waiting in vain for the changes we expected love to bring. At this crucial juncture, integration is an indispensable resource.

Integration can make possible a comfortable acceptance that differs from merely "settling." It can help us feel content with our chosen love and enthusiastic about deepening our involvement. If there is a single capacity that enables us to remain in love and become a couple, it is integration.

Sarah, whose story opens this chapter, entered therapy feeling desperately unhappy about the state of her relationships with men. Nothing seemed to last. Sarah saw herself as unusually attractive, intelligent, and successful. Given these advantages and her intense desire to settle down, it was a complete mystery to her why she was still alone. It was less of a mystery to her friends.

Originally Ed had impressed Sarah as having everything she was looking for in a man: sexy good looks, emotional sensitivity, intelligence, self-confidence. At forty, he was a successful clothing designer. After the two of them slept together for the second time, Sarah made up her mind to marry him. Falling in love had never been her problem.

Sarah easily idealized Ed. In her eyes he was the perfect man and together they made the perfect couple. Ed was almost as full of admiration for Sarah. His thrill at finding such a woman made it easy for him to push his own needs, and his differences from her, into the background. For Ed and Sarah, the future together looked very bright and very certain.

Three months into the relationship, however, Sarah became disenchanted. She couldn't forget her feeling that a special bond between the two of them had been forged the second night they slept together. Lying in his arms, Sarah had confided to Ed that a childhood of neglect and unpredictability had left her with a terrible fear of being abandoned and a strong need to feel in control. Impressed with her openness, and wanting to take care of her, Ed had responded reassuringly. He promised he would always try to make her feel secure and be sensitive to her needs for control.

But now two things had occurred. First, Ed was beginning to chafe at Sarah's need always to be in charge. Second, Ed took a business trip at a time when the pressures of Sarah's restaurant made her feel she could not bear for him to go.

When Ed was no longer content letting her plan their time together, Sarah felt that he was betraying his promise to respect her need for control. And his leaving when she wanted him to stay left her convinced she could never rely on him again. Suddenly the "emotional sensitivity" that had drawn her to him began to look like immaturity. If he could betray her and prove unable to appreciate her needs, then he was plainly incapable of mature intimacy. If he could leave her as he had, it must be because he was unable to be close—or worse, he no longer cared about her.

Sarah's tendency to think and feel in black-and-white terms, to mistake the part for the whole, made it nearly impossible for her to tolerate the frustrations and disappointments that are unavoidable in love. In short, her problem with integration undermined her feelings for a man she had initially seen as perfect.

To protect herself from the rejection she believed was coming, Sarah destroyed her love for Ed. All at once, she could barely remember anything she liked about him. She decided that, like so many before, he just couldn't pass the test. He had betrayed her, and was really a hurtful, immature, and "neurotic" man. As an act of revenge, she was tempted not only to stop seeing him but also to tell him that she was already seeing another man. What she believed were his lies would be met by a final lie of her own.

Of course, Sarah was defining *their* problems as *Ed's* problems; she was only an unfortunate victim. People with a poorly developed capacity for integration usually respond to a failed relationship not only with disappointment but also by feeling intentionally victimized.

Ed was shocked by Sarah's all-or-nothing view of their relationship. His own real difficulties with intimacy, and his trouble handling her sensitivities, were overridden by his need to protect himself from the barrage of her blaming and projection. He felt trapped, controlled, and unable to negotiate. He was at a loss to understand her sudden and total depreciation of him. When she accused him of being unresponsive and needing to control her, he was furious. The more frustrated and angry he became, the more Sarah believed her judgments of him were accurate. In fact, she had provoked the fulfillment of her own prophecy.

Sarah's example illustrates how problems with integration emerge as intimacy deepens. When we are falling in love, two factors—our idealization and our collusion with our partner to avoid conflict—combine to generate a feeling of relative safety. When we become a couple, however, we may no longer be on our best behavior, muting our differences and deferring to the needs of our partner. Now we must begin to trust (as Sarah could not) that someone we love can really "be there" for us, even if he or she sometimes acts on the basis of needs that differ from ours. We must begin to trust that someone who is not perfect can still be reliable, can still empathize, can still be a dependable source of love.

Yet this necessary trust develops in a difficult new context. We know more about our partner now, which usually means knowing more about his or her limitations. And we are also known better by our partner. In addition, our feelings are more mixed—and so are those of our partner. We are aware of our differences and must accommodate them within a more complex view of the couple.

What is required at this phase of love is an expansion of our inner map—for the journey now taken by two partners together almost never follows the routes described in the map of one partner alone. Now we are compelled to take into account not only our own images of love but also those of our partner. Without integration, this is nearly impossible to do. For integration is the only capacity that can turn a world of "either-or" into the world of "both."

As Sarah's experience shows, when we believe that there's only room for one, we will have a hard time remaining in love. Without room for two, for an integrated view of the couple, our part-ner's differences and separate needs can become a threat. Then love (if it lasts at all) is either submission, domination, or a never-ending battle.

SPLITTING AS A
DEFENSE AGAINST INTEGRATION

Once we see our partner as a threat, the logical course of action is to protect ourselves. When we lack a well-developed capacity for integration, this self-protection usually takes the form of a defense that psychoanalysts have called "splitting." This defense divides (that is, splits) a whole experience or image into two con-tradictory parts.

Splitting divides our world into heroes and villains—and usually others are the villains. When we use splitting as a defense, we make a resource out of a liability. The liability is our shaky grasp on integration; the resource is our determined, rigid separation of good and bad in the interest of self-protection.

If we are good and others are bad, our esteem suffers less when a relationship fails. If we are good and others are bad, we don't have to envy them for what they possess and we lack. If we are good and others are bad, then we don't miss them when they are gone. Splitting also simplifies the world of relationships: "if they're not with you, they're against you" and "if they've got lia-bilities, dump them" are some of the harsh conclusions that flow from splitting.

Above all, when we use this defense, we absolve ourselves of responsibility. We believe we are responding justifiably to the treachery or inadequacy of our partner. We may blame, exaggerate, or use all-or-nothing thinking (and feeling) to clinch the case against our former beloved. But while splitting protects us, the price we pay is that love never lasts.

The longer we make use of this defense, and the attitudes and behaviors that go with it, the more we distort the actual emo-tional reality of our intimate relationships. And the distortion is often dramatic and extreme. The target of splitting, the partner, may be seen as monstrous, while we usually see ourselves as hapless and innocent.

When splitting turns someone we've loved into an enemy, we may feel confused. If on the other hand, we're on the receiving end of this defense, the experience can be bewildering—and sometimes infuriating. To be seen as we are not by someone who matters to us is intensely disturbing, particularly when what is "seen" is so negative.

Sarah's previous love relationships had all been dominated by her use of splitting. With Ed she used the same defense—and she went one step further. Once she decided that Ed had betrayed her, she began to treat him in such a way that he became unclear about what he really felt. Under the onslaught of Sarah's accusations, Ed found it increasingly difficult to connect with his feelings of love and concern for her. As Sarah raged at him about being uncaring and hurtful, he found himself identifying more and more with the image that she was projecting onto him. He began to *feel* very much like the angry, uncaring lover she accused him of being.

In this interaction with Ed, Sarah was making use of an additional defense, one that often compounds the problems associated with splitting. Psychoanalysts call it "projective identification." In this form of self-protection, we induce others to identify with the images we project onto them. Through enlisting Ed to play the role in which she cast him (the lover who breaks his promises), Sarah brought the external reality into line with the images of her inner map. In this way, she reconfirmed her suspicion that men were not to be trusted. She also reinforced her attitude that if a relationship failed, she was not the responsible party.

Sarah's revenge, in telling Ed she was not only disappointed in him but also involved with someone else, was a way of ensuring the finality of their breakup. In acting out her vengeance, she left no room for him to consider or understand her feelings, for now he had to contend with feeling betrayed himself. Without the modulating influence of integration, Sarah's feelings had an all-

or-nothing quality; when feelings are felt this strongly, action often takes the place of words.

Like many of her other suitors, Ed believed at first that he'd found a woman who sincerely wanted her relationships to work. She was bright and successful. She gave the impression of being both curious and knowledgeable about her own psychology. Later he was amazed to discover how little she understood about her patterns in love. She explained away her undistinguished relationship history as a run of bad luck, a reflection of the times, or a consequence of men's inability to commit themselves. Her own rather obvious emotional extremism was never factored into the equation.

INTEGRATION, SPLITTING, AND EARLY PSYCHOLOGICAL DEVELOPMENT

The capacity for integration has its roots in the toddler's learning to contend with, and eventually finding a balance between, loving gratification and painful frustration in relation to his or her parents. There is no such thing as "perfect" parenting. Rather, what we hope for are "good enough" family environments that provide adequate emotional resources for children. These are families where good experiences predominate over bad ones, and where parental love is, for the most part, predictably available. Compare this to families in which the parenting is more likely to be unpredictable, overly aggressive, and excessively frustrating. In these families, the bad times may overshadow the good. Coming from such a family can leave a child with an abundance of anger, and considerable anxiety about love.

Margaret Mahler's work has suggested that between roughly fifteen and twenty-four months of age, the toddler begins to develop the capacity to bring together (that is, to integrate) the all-good and all-bad images of himself or herself, as well as the all-good and all-bad images of important others like mom and dad. Prior to this, the child can only react as though each parent were really two parents: the all-good parent who gratifies and the all-bad parent who frustrates. And the child's own emotional states (blissful or angry) seem to reflect a comparably divided self-image.

This difficult period, which Mahler called the "rapprochement phase," is critical for the child's development of the capacity for integration. The child's task is particularly challenging because he or she is struggling during this period not only with integration but also with the disturbing realization that the psychological umbilical cord has been cut. Now the child no longer feels magically connected to his or her parents. It is a very early kind of existential awakening.

Parents know this phase well, for it is marked by difficult, often contradictory behaviors: one moment the toddler is very clingy and dependent, the next he or she is rejecting the parent, as if asserting independence. The wish for reassurance seems to vie with the need to push away and say no. This period has been called the "terrible twos," partly because it's difficult for the child, but also because it's difficult for the parents.

If during our earlier development we were adequately nourished and cared for, both physically and emotionally, then the rapprochement phase presents challenges that can be largely resolved. We learn to accept that our parents are both good *and* bad, and that we cannot completely control their responsiveness to our needs. Parents empathize with our feelings, give in and let us have our way some of the time. But they also set limits as to how far we can push them around. This is valuable role modeling, for we are going through an intense phase of learning about how to cope with our contradictory feelings about ourselves and those we love.

During rapprochement, we learn to deal with ambivalence for the first time: we want to be close, but we also want to be separate. When mom and dad respond evenhandedly to our contradictory impulses, it helps us integrate our images of ourselves: we are both dependent *and* independent. This evenhandedness also helps us integrate our images of our parents. They seem like the *same* parents whether we cling or push away; their relative consistency works against our earlier tendency to see them as all good when they gratified us and all bad when they didn't. Ideally, these early experiences set the stage for us to tolerate the whole range of complex feelings that will later confront us in our intimate relationships.

While the critical period for developing the capacity for integration is the toddler years, integration can continue to evolve throughout our life. As adults we experience a variety of situations that challenge our ability to tolerate, empathize with, and understand mixed feelings. As the children of "good enough" parents, what we learned—but probably still have not finished learning—will be put to the test again and again.

When, however, our earlier experience with our parents was not "good enough," the developmental tasks of rapprochement are experienced as traumas rather than as manageable challenges. In difficult family settings, our wishes for comfortable merging with our parents are often frustrated. Our hunger for mirroring and admiration can go unsatisfied. Instead of trusting that we will be loved, we may be overwhelmed by fears of abandonment. With too much aggression in our relationship with our parents (or in their relation to each other), we can feel intensely insecure and, frequently, full of anger. If our parents' responses are erratic, we can be anxiously uncertain about which of our behaviors result in loving attention and which lead to punishment or neglect. With too much frustration and unpredictability, and too little love, our imagery of intimacy will reflect a preponderance of painful rather than pleasurable experiences. In this unhappy context, it is emotionally disastrous for us to put together—to integrate— our all-good and all-bad images of ourselves and others. Why should this be so?

Imagine that a child's positive and negative experiences are represented by white and red paint, respectively. When childhood intimacy was troubled, it's as though the child is left holding a little touch-up jar of white paint and a gallon can of red. If the two were mixed, the white paint would simply disappear. When our bad experiences outweigh our good ones, and bad images outnumber good images, the only possible outcome if we combine them is to lose touch with the good—and so we don't combine them. To preserve hope, to salvage a sense of goodness, integration is avoided and splitting becomes the defense of choice. The advantages here are considerable. With good and bad kept apart, whatever goodness there is now can be felt to belong to the self, while the badness can be banished to the realm of the hurtful, sadistic other. But the disadvantages are also considerable—for without integration, sustained intimacy becomes impossible.

REAL, IDEAL, AND FEARED IMAGES

Integration has a profound impact on our real, ideal, and feared images of ourselves and others. With a healthy capacity for integration, we can see ourselves and others reasonably clearly. Our real images (those that reflect our view of actual reality) are fairly stable and faithful to the facts. Our ideal (or wished-for) images, though they reflect our ambitions and desires, are earthbound rather than spectacularly grandiose. Our feared images, though they reflect our anxieties about ourselves and others, are neither overly exaggerated nor paranoid.

With such images it's possible for us to have healthy self-esteem, because our real and ideal self-images are not worlds apart. With such images it's also possible to trust others, because our feared images of them are not overwhelmingly frightening nor are our ideal images intimidatingly grandiose.

In part these balanced images are the legacy of early childhood experience that was "good enough." In part they are the result of the subsequent influence of integration, which tones down the extremes of experience by combining them.

Sarah's view of herself was at odds with how she was seen by friends who knew her well. Sarah's real self-image had gaping holes in it. She was aware of her strengths, her attractiveness, and her competence, but she was blind to the most damaging aspects of her personality. Friends could see how her suspicion and anger doomed her relationships; she could not. In her view she was greatly deserving, but unlucky in love.

Sarah's "real" images of others (particularly men) were no less distorted than her image of herself, though the distortion was in the opposite direction. Sarah believed that all men were immature, untrustworthy, and emotionally unavailable. If they appeared otherwise, it was only an illusion that time would dispel.

Sarah's greatest vulnerability—and that of most of us for whom integration is a problem—was that she so easily confused her exaggeratedly ideal or feared images with reality. At times she could see herself as very nearly extraordinary: smarter, more beautiful, more successful than almost anyone she knew. But at other times, she felt hopelessly fearful, doomed to abandonment and loneliness, poisoned by her mother's rage and her father's unfulfilled promises.

In just the same way (that is, unstably), she could see someone like Ed as virtually flawless, a dream lover. But before long the same man would become identified not with her ideal image but with her feared image: now he was only a boy disguised as a man, a breaker of promises, like every other man.

All of Sarah's relationships were initiated by her wish to bring her ideal images to life. To the extent that she could feel special, and be loved by someone special, she was protected from her fears. But her solution was untenable. Her exaggeratedly ideal images of herself and her partner always proved impossible to sustain in the crucible of an ongoing relationship. When the ideal images faded in the face of routine or, more often, exploded in the face of conflict, they were invariably and completely replaced by her feared images. And these feared images, unmodulated by integration, were overwhelmingly intense. Looking for ideal love, Sarah repeatedly found betrayal.

Why were these extreme images so difficult to give up? For Sarah, like many of us, unmodified ideal images represent a promise of salvation. The fantasy of a perfect self and a perfect partner can look like a kind of emotional oasis in what might otherwise appear to be a desert. If we can just get to the oasis, we'll feel the comfort of closeness, and relief from our fears about ourselves. Beckoning like a mirage, our ideal images indicate a direction in which to go. Even when experience teaches us that going in this direction leads nowhere, it's hard to give up hope of reaching the oasis. Moreover, the very pursuit of the ideal is itself a kind of boon: it distinguishes us from the ordinary masses who are willing to settle for less.

We can be just as attached to our feared images, no matter how unrealistically threatening they may be. Feared images function as a kind of early warning system that can protect us from pain. So long as these images of danger remain in place, they can steer us away from situations that might hurt us again as we feel we were hurt in the past. The problem with these images, to put it lightly, is that "once burned, twice shy" becomes "once burned, never enter a house with a kitchen."

Giving up (or modifying) our ideal and feared images requires awareness, mourning, and courage. Understanding that these images of ours are not realities is itself a giant step. Then we need to mourn, for mourning is the natural human process by which we come to accept painful reality and loss. When we lose the ideal images, in a way we lose a hope for heaven on Earth. But giving up the feared images also represents a loss, for these images always reflect interactions (though painful ones) with people who have mattered deeply to us.

Giving up our ideal and feared images takes courage: without them, we are in uncharted territory. Relinquishing a big part of our inner map can be wrenching. We all try to keep our map intact in an effort to maintain consistency between the past and the present, between our internal view and our external experience. Doing so, we stabilize our sense of identity. This can mean holding on, psychologically, to a distorted map simply because it is *our* map.

The courage to let go of our unmodified ideal and feared images need not come all at once. We can relinquish these images slowly, detail by detail. But relinquish them we must, if our relationships are to last. With unintegrated ideal and feared images, it's possible to fall in love but impossible, as Sarah's experience confirms, to remain in love.

REVENGE AND OTHER REWARDS

Splitting, like other defenses, has hidden payoffs that make it even harder to relinquish than we might expect. First, splitting helps justify revenge. Second, it simplifies our choices in an ambiguous, complicated world, which can be reassuring.

Once Ed was no longer the hero of Sarah's romantic dreams, he became the villain. As the embodiment of her feared, rather than her idealized, image of a partner, he was now a legitimate target. Sarah felt that he was only the most recent in a series of men who had betrayed her. The first was her father, whom she scornfully referred to as "Mr. False Promises." Now, however, she would take her revenge: turning the tables, she would make sure that Ed felt the pain of abandonment as much as she had.

Sarah's wish for pleasure had shifted from the erotic to the aggressive in relation to Ed. Having felt victimized, she found it satisfying to strike back—in fact she relished the opportunity. Her anger at men and her frustration with relationships that always seemed to disappoint her could now be expressed without a trace of guilt.

This guiltless impulse to take revenge frequently accompanies splitting. If our former partner has become all bad, there is an emotional logic that seems almost to compel revenge. This logic has been called the law of Talion: "an eye for an eye, a tooth for a tooth." Without integration, we can experience a persistent pressure to exact our pound of flesh for misdeeds committed against us in the past. Now whenever an opportunity arises that justifies the expression of our anger, we may seize it with pleasure.

A second subtle payoff in splitting is that it simplifies our choices. A computer engineer felt that his mother and sister had both been unpredictably cruel to him. Now he thinks it's wise always to assume the worst about the women he's involved with. Rather than give his girlfriend the benefit of the doubt, and feel anxiously uncertain about the outcome, he prefers to assume that she can't be trusted. At a certain point, this engineer realized that some of the initial appeal of computers for him had been their "on/off, yes/no" logic. This was part of his dawning awareness about how deeply he could be reassured by the either-or of splitting. Through simplifying the alternatives, this defense protected him from ambiguous situations that he considered potentially dangerous.

At the cultural as well as the personal level, we can see the broad appeal of this simplification through splitting. Ronald Reagan's vision of the Soviet Union as the "evil empire" (juxtaposed against an idealized view of the USA) struck a responsive chord among millions of people. Apparently the splitting that separates "us" from "them" is a comfort to many. In a similar vein, the success of such films as *Star Wars*, which enable us so readily to identify the good guys and the bad guys, may derive in part from the appeal of the split view of complex human reality.

But this kind of comfort comes at a high price, whether in relations between lovers or nations. Once we have a more integrated view, we can become aware of the distortions splitting imposes: we can see that the "other" is rarely as "bad" as we believed and that we are not often as "good" as we might wish.

Giving up the defense of splitting means losing some of the impulse, and a lot of the justification, for revenge. It also means sacrificing the comfort of a simplified view of relationships. Integration, by contrast, makes possible some very complicated experiences in love including empathy, acceptance, and forgiveness.

THE DANCE OF DEFENSES:
COLLISION, COLLUSION, OR COLLABORATION

The idyllic honeymoon that distinguishes the first stage of love is fertile territory for the kinds of collusions we would expect when there are problems with the capacity for integration.

When the thrill of falling in love is amplified by splitting, for example, we indeed "fall hard." Splitting renders irrelevant whatever might conceivably trouble us about our new beloved, while whatever is good feels all the better. Recall that for Sarah and Ed, falling in love felt like a fantastic, potentially perfect romantic journey. Unfortunately, in colluding to deny the possibility of present or future difficulty, both partners set themselves up for disappointment. But their collusion took another important form as well.

Sarah's lack of integration inclined her to an either-or view of relationships. Either her needs would be met or his would, either her will would be expressed or his would, either she would have control or he would. Sarah stressed this point with Ed early in their relationship when she made explicit her need for control: If there was room for only one, that one had to be Sarah. Ed's collusion was in submitting. Because he had his own problems with integration, he shared her either-or view. In a sense it was a perfect fit, for Ed was accustomed to playing the role that complemented hers. He had learned to yield control to his partner as an indirect route to meeting his own needs.

But this collusion could not be maintained. When Ed's "betrayal" of Sarah exploded her dream of perfect love, her disappointment was almost too painful to bear. In large part this was because her new view of him contrasted so profoundly with the idealized image that splitting had helped her maintain for the previous three months. Now her intense anger toward Ed protected her from tremendous feelings of inner loss, for she was losing not only a lover but also her hopes for love as well. After all, Sarah had been convinced that she and Ed were "made for each other," and now, in spite of that, she was alone again.

Sometimes the feeling of being "made for each other" reflects a collusion like Ed and Sarah's. Perhaps, as a rule, it is more realistic to say "made for each other at this moment" or "made to work it out with each other." Collusions of splitting, in which difficulties are denied, are inherently unworkable and unstable.

There are, however, certain relationships that appear to be stabilized by defensive collusions. The most common example are those skewed partnerships that have come to be called "co-dependent." Here the tacit agreement between two partners is that one will support the other's dependency, in order that both are protected from discomfort and change. An alcoholic and a "co-alcoholic" partner, for example, will collude to avoid dealing with their individual pain. In these couples, integration is stalled because each partner provides the other with something that he or she is missing inside: two halves now form a very problematic whole. As long as neither partner complains too loudly nor demands real change, these relationships can last a lifetime. But the psychological development of both partners may be frozen. Integration, in particular, will remain a dormant resource until one partner or the other confronts the "co-dependent" pattern.

When what has been hidden by collusion is revealed, collisions can be expected to occur. Sarah and Ed collided in such a way that her defenses obliterated any trust she might have had in him. At first Ed's defenses led him to withdraw and disengage in response to Sarah's attack, but eventually he became angry. And the more he used his anger to shield himself from the impact of her furious criticisms, the more convinced Sarah became that he was the dangerous trickster of her catastrophic fantasies: a man like her father who would manipulate her with false promises.

When we have significant limitations in our capacity for integration, our collisions with our partner will always be complicated by splitting. Splitting provokes a heightened emotionality and patterns of "fight or flight" characterized by angry blaming or cold withdrawal. This defense is especially likely to dominate conflicts that involve issues of commitment, separation, or loss.

Recognizing splitting as a problem is critical to containing, and ultimately resolving, the conflicts couples face when their defenses collide. Once we are able to take responsibility for using splitting as a defense, we are on the road to diminishing its devastating impact. Then it may be possible to resolve through collaboration the conflicts that collision has revealed.

Psychotherapeutic work with couples has shown that enabling partners to empathize with each other becomes the crucial turning point in modifying or resolving their defensive collisions. One partner's initiative is all it takes to lead the dance of defense in a new direction.

Let's imagine how this might have occurred between Sarah and Ed. Upon being confronted by Sarah, instead of mounting a defense against feeling criticized, Ed could have tuned in to Sarah's feelings of hurt and betrayal. He could have tried to understand her experience. He might have asked how his words or behavior had led her to feel so hurt. He could have tried to grasp the emotional logic, from her side, that left her feeling abandoned by him. In receiving this quality of empathic attention, Sarah might have been able to feel less threatened and less vengeful. And then she might have become more receptive to Ed's version of their experience. Recall that empathy is a way of listening to our partner in which, emotionally speaking, we put ourselves in their place, with the aim of understanding their point of view. Empathy doesn't require that we agree with their point of view, only that we take it in: in particular, we're not required to agree with their point of view about who we are.

Now let's look at how Sarah might have encouraged empathy and collaboration by responding differently to Ed. Suppose she had noticed that her fears and concerns about Ed were taking on an all-or-nothing quality. This could have been a signal to her that, if she didn't change course, she'd soon be feeling overwhelmed and, potentially, explosive. She might then have tried to contain her tendency to overreact. If she were able to do so, she could then consider what was provoking such intense feelings and try to open a discussion with Ed. She was certainly entitled to let him know how much pain she was feeling, and how grave her concerns were about their future together.

Containing our most extreme reactions does not mean denying our feelings or concerns. In muting the intensity of these reactions, we are simply trying to increase the likelihood that we will be heard and understood. Ideally, even in communicating our anger, hurt, or disappointment, we can also convey our love for our partner and our desire to resolve shared problems.

Often the first five minutes or so of any conflict establishes a blueprint for the rest of the interaction—and the outcome will be either constructive engagement or a battle. When we express concern and take some responsibility for our own role, we enhance the odds in favor of resolving the conflict. In effect we're using our capacity for integration. Even when we're upset, integration can help make it possible for us to see that our relationship with our partner is worth protecting. Regardless of our feelings of hurt or anger, integration can sustain our desire to collaborate.

For most of us, this kind of collaboration represents an ideal, a standard to aim for but not always to reach. Partners can have the best intentions in the world and still find their desires to collaborate overwhelmed by intense emotion or the drift toward familiar patterns of collision and collusion. With time, however, couples can learn more about their defensive interactions and can recognize them before they get destructively out of hand. Hopefully, as love deepens, so does the capacity for integration. As our experience loses its all-or-nothing quality, we can become more capable of tolerating our own intense emotions, instead of feeling pushed around by them. In the same way, we can also become more capable of bearing the emotions our partner expresses toward us. With a greater capacity for integration, we can look beyond, rather than feel dominated by, the impact of any particular interaction in our relationship. Then, even in the heat of conflict, rather than feel overwhelmed, we will be able to sustain our desire to collaborate.

Couples who have gone through conflicts, and not only survived these struggles but also deepened their involvement, often feel they know the territory of love better than those who seem to have had it easy. These are couples who are likely to have worked hard on evolving and making use of the capacity for integration. And indeed, with such persistent effort there is a sense of wisdom gained, a knowledge of what it really means to fully accept one's partner.

Deepening our capacity for integration not only enables us to remain in love over the long run but also strengthens our confidence in our ability to meet love's challenges. The result is a larger, stronger, more expansive view of love and of ourselves.

PSYCHOTHERAPY AND INTEGRATION

A few weeks before she broke up with Ed, Sarah began to feel anxious. Their relationship was then the center of her life and it seemed to be going just fine. So what could possibly be bothering her so much? She felt almost panicky.

It was this feeling that led her into therapy. In trying to understand her anxiety, she wound up talking with her male therapist about her relationships with men. Though her relationship with Ed looked as if it had a future, she was insecure. She had learned that men couldn't be trusted—or was it just the men she picked? Perhaps Ed was different; she hoped so. But for her, bitter disappointment followed high hopes: this was the pattern she couldn't seem to escape. Before long, it became clear that Sarah's anxiety reflected her terror that the old pattern was about to be repeated.

Early in the relationship, Ed had reassured her with his empathy. He had seemed to understand her need to feel in control. But now there were disturbing hints that he wanted to exercise more authority. Very quickly the tension in Sarah's relationship escalated. And then the relationship was over.

In therapy, Sarah gradually began to understand how the either-or quality of her emotional extremism could generate an incomplete and inaccurate picture of her relationships: at the start by erasing whatever was problematic; at the finish by attributing all the problems to her partner. And then, not surprisingly perhaps, the pattern was repeated in relation to her therapist.

Initially Sarah's feelings about her therapist had seemed entirely positive. But then an emergency made it impossible for him to meet with her at their regular hour. An appointment was scheduled for later that week. When they met, Sarah was hurt, mistrustful, and angry. Her therapist couldn't really be concerned about her needs. Perhaps she'd been foolish in letting herself rely on him. Maybe therapy itself was an empty promise: it got your hopes up but then your therapist let you down.

The therapist empathized with Sarah's feelings, reflecting how hard it must have been for her to feel that he couldn't always be relied on to meet her needs. As the two of them discussed the meaning of her distress, Sarah saw how vulnerable she was to feeling abandoned—and how easily her angry suspicions could be aroused when she felt threatened or hurt. She found it disturbing, but also illuminating, to see herself playing out the old scenario with a man like her therapist, whom she had no obvious reason to mistrust. Just beneath the surface apparently, requiring only the slightest disappointment to bring it to light, was her attitude that men were guilty until proven innocent.

As her problem with integration began to be clarified, Sarah started to monitor responses in her relationships that until now had been automatic. Her therapist supported her growing disinclination to take her feelings unquestioningly at face value. Over time, it became clear that when Sarah was disappointed by a man, she experienced one of two alternatives: either she angrily blamed him, sometimes jeopardizing the relationship, or she blamed herself and felt worthless. Choosing the lesser of two evils, she had always sacrificed love to salvage self-esteem and hope.

The way out of this unhappy dilemma was to open up the emotional gray area between the extremes of black and white. This meant being aware of her love for a man even when she was disappointed in him. She also had to recognize that she could be at fault, that she could be flawed—and still be lovable.

Slowly Sarah began to make a major shift in her self-image. Taking responsibility for her part in what had gone awry in her past relationships was both very painful and very healing. It let her see that she could have an impact on her life in love, rather than believe that if she loved, she could only wind up the victim. She had regrets about the past but also began to believe that her future was largely hers to create.

This transformation in Sarah's attitude about future relationships reflected a shift in her understanding of the past. For years Sarah had been angry about her mother's unpredictable rages and her father's empty promises. Now she was able to mourn the past and to understand its impact on the present.

Mourning and Integration

As Sarah's feelings and images lost their all-or-nothing quality, she was able for the first time to grieve over the shortcomings of her relationship to her parents. When that relationship was no longer experienced as all bad, what *was* bad about it could be tolerably grieved—and what had been good could be missed.

Once we mourn we usually discover that what we feared would overwhelm us is tolerable. Sarah learned that she could tolerate her feeling of disappointment in relation to her parents. This meant, in turn, that love's disappointments could be tolerated: they no longer needed to be quarantined or split off; they could instead be integrated.

SELF-APPRAISAL: THREE PROFILES

Helen: Integration as a Resource

At fifty, Helen has been married for nearly three decades to an intense, charismatic, somewhat volatile attorney. Leonard, her husband, has long been regarded as a charming, but difficult, man. Both of Helen's parents were stable and supportive but restrained emotionally. When Helen looks back at the twenty-one-year-old she was when she married, she sees a young woman superficially serene and full of love but also very unsure. She had looked to Leonard's brash self-assurance to compensate for her own insecurity; she had hoped the example of his confident expressiveness would help her overcome her inhibitions. From Helen's point of view today, the growing strength of their relationship over the decades can largely be understood as the reflection of her evolving capacity for acceptance.

During the first years of their marriage, Helen felt as if she were riding the waves of Leonard's moodiness. When his cases were going well, he was extraordinarily loving. When they were going badly, he acted as though Helen were responsible. Her self-esteem rose and fell with his moods and the quality of his attention to her. With the birth of their first child, however, all this changed.

Helen saw that Leonard's behavior toward their daughter could be just as inconsistent as his behavior toward her. While this disappointed and infuriated her, it also freed her: Leonard was apparently a capricious man, there was no way around it, but she certainly didn't have to be overly preoccupied with *her* role in provoking his moods.

Over the course of several years, as her own self-esteem stabilized, Helen's estimate of her husband sank. Once she no longer held herself responsible for Leonard's emotional comings and goings, she became angry and exasperated. Working out his moods was like trying to pick up mercury with a fork. She began to regard his unpredictability as adolescent.

But she never stopped appreciating him. No one else excited her as Leonard did, either physically or intellectually. When he was present, she felt a depth and passion to his love that never failed to move and comfort her. He encouraged her ambitions and was supportive when these led to a career managing political campaigns.

Because Helen never felt any need to throw the proverbial baby out with the bathwater, she began not only to be less tolerant of Leonard's moodiness but also to set limits with him. This seemed to take the edge off the worst of his withdrawal and irritability. Over time, Helen's ability to be both angry *and* loving— that is, her capacity for integration—wound up enhancing his. He grew to meet her.

What she called her capacity for acceptance enabled her, much later, to weather Leonard's near-fatal heart attack without despairing. And when there was a painfully prolonged conflict between Leonard and their teenage son, she could empathize with both of them while taking sides with neither. The evolution of Helen's capacity for integration generated an upward spiral in her relationship with her husband. For this couple, integration made possible an atmosphere of acceptance in which both conflict and intimacy could be aspects of love.

Andy: Integration That Is Compromised

A lively computer engineer in his early forties, Andy is on the verge of marrying a woman with whom he has been living for almost five years. Their relationship has been stormy, punctuated by several separations, but now the two of them seem to have settled in.

At times Andy has seen Lorraine, his pretty wife-to-be, as a fine match for him. At these times Lorraine has impressed him as a woman of substance. The editor of a small magazine, she is bright, creative, and caring; she is, he asserts, at least his equal.

But at other times, Andy has become very angry at her, and suspicious. He has easily been convinced that her interest in him had to do only with her need for a man to father a child. Her desire, at least in his mind, has been a function mainly of what he could or couldn't give her. At these times he no longer saw her as powerful or competent. She became instead someone who'd use her considerable allure to exploit him, because she couldn't take care of herself.

But as time has gone on, Andy has bounced back more quickly from these episodes of angry worry and devaluation. In the past his dramatic shifts of feeling in relation to Lorraine had led to fights between the two of them—and several separations. Now Andy understands that his shifting reactions have much more to do with his own fears than with Lorraine's character. He trusts her more, and usually believes that they can weather their con-flicts together. He feels less need to cling to his wariness, to his secret suspicion that women are a threat. Yet when there is too much stress in their life together, his angry suspicion still briefly emerges. But he feels it with far less conviction than in the past.

His old way had been to assume the worst. If Lorraine were sometimes an angel, sometimes a vamp, then the safest course was to decide that even when she appeared to be angelic, she was only a vamp in disguise. Eventually he understood this need to protect himself as the legacy of his growing up with an absent father, and a tyrannical mother and older sister who treated him, he felt, like a male version of Cinderella: underappreciated and overexploited.

Andy's strengthened capacity to integrate his loving and his angry feelings toward Lorraine came about in large part through their separations. Initially, in keeping with an all-or-nothing style of thinking, Andy had felt that when the two of them separated, one or the other was always to blame. If Lorraine wasn't at fault, then he must be—and so, to protect himself, he felt compelled to blame her. But with each successive separation, he was more aware of missing her, and more aware of her caring for him. Through these experiences, he learned as an adult what he hadn't learned as a child: that emotions need not be either-or. He could be angry at Lorraine and also love her; she could be angry at him and still miss him.

Raphael: Integration as a Struggle

Raphael, a strikingly handsome park ranger in his mid-thirties, has been involved with many women but has never lived with one. He has a disturbing awareness that when he makes love to a woman, she always feels more than he does. The relationship means more to her. He'd like to be able to feel for a woman what he thinks certain women have felt for him. But there's a kind of emotional barrier when he's with women that separates him from them, and separates him from his feeling. At times, he thinks that the barrier is fear, that he's afraid of being hurt or rejected. At other times, he thinks that if only he met a woman with the right combination of qualities, then he could break through.

Raphael suspects that his problems with women are a carryover from his past. His father, alcoholic and usually remote, beat him angrily on many occasions, and beat his two younger brothers as well. His mother seemed relatively uninterested in children: Raphael recalls that her attention was expressed mainly in her desire to keep the children clean and to maintain their appearance. His parents fought frequently, and once their three sons had left home, they divorced.

Raphael's most recent romantic involvement, his longest, lasted for nine months. Karin appealed to him in many ways, but he was eventually frustrated with her because she wouldn't join him on a trip around the world that had been a dream of his for years. This was the straw that broke the camel's back. He had been in love with her only briefly at the start of their relationship, and if she couldn't share his dream then the relationship might as well be over.

This last involvement ended in much the same way as those that had preceded it. Typically Raphael would be quite taken with a woman, but only briefly. Then he would find fault with her, or she would frustrate him in ways he found intolerable: she'd be critical because he wanted to smoke, or she'd demand that he stay overnight. He didn't like to feel controlled. He'd rather be alone.

Sometimes in the course of these unhappy endings (unhappy primarily for the women involved), Raphael would become angry, feeling that he was being "guilt-tripped." His notion was that everyone was free to make his or her own choices. No one was beholden to anyone else. He could understand a woman being disappointed, but it was outrageous that he should be held responsible for her feelings, as though he had committed some kind of crime.

When Raphael was alone, he could become very depressed. He started to wonder if there was something very wrong with him, something that would always keep him feeling incomplete and unfulfilled. But then, once he was with a woman, it was like being in the sun again after a cold gray winter. His concerns about himself would quickly fade. And he could usually find women with whom to become involved.

He wasn't lonely, exactly. Given his parents' example, he had no burning desire to be married. Yet Raphael couldn't stop asking himself why he had such difficulty making a relationship last.

CHAPTER FIVE

The Capacity for Refinding: The Role of the Past in Love

We shall not cease from exploration
And the end of all our exploring
Will be to arrive where we started
And know the place for the first time.
—T. S. Eliot

The finding of an object is in fact
a refinding of it.
—Sigmund Freud

Andrea's father's hobby was woodcarving. Once he spent a year carving a chess set: all the pieces, black and white, and a board inlaid with squares of different woods. By Christmas Eve, Andrea remembers, the chess set was completed. The first game he played was with Andrea's mother. They sat before the fireplace, the chessboard between them, as Andrea watched. Her mother won the game. Whereupon, in a rage, Andrea's father threw the chess set into the fire. When Andrea met her husband-to-be, she played chess with him and won—twice. He fell into a dark mood. Thereafter, for much of her marriage, she inhibited her very considerable strengths; she "played dumb," and not just at chess.

Refinding, however, is more than the ability to reexperience aspects of the past in the present, for we do this as involuntarily as we breathe. As a resource that enhances love, healthy refinding is the capacity to appreciate what is positive in this partial revival of the past while mastering, or at least tolerating, what is negative.

If integration has enabled love to last, refinding will deepen it. The ability to rediscover in our partner qualities that were pivotal in our initial love relationships adds a dimension of depth to our capacity to love. Refinding allows us to feel passionate intensity, familiarity, and effortless rapport with our partner. Yet it can also represent the ultimate turn-off, the pain and heartache of love's disappointments, the re-creation of past conflicts ("Oh God, not again") in the present. While refinding enables us to experience depth in relationships, it is often the dynamic that people most consciously seek to avoid: the rediscovery of aspects of mother and father in our lovers is not generally felt to be desirable or to generate sexual chemistry.

Refinding is at work when our relationship begins to feel like a rendezvous with the past. As an undercurrent that imbues present love with what was desirable in the intimacy of the past, pleasurable refinding draws us to our partner. Refinding that is laden with conflict, on the other hand, casts a shadow over our relationship. Overwhelming the defenses that shield us from the impact of painful, unresolved experiences with those we have loved in the past, it can provoke a potential revival of these experiences in the present.

This superimposition of past on present can be very problematic, especially when it occurs outside our conscious awareness. But when conflicts with mother and father that may previously have been too painful to resolve now reemerge with our partner, we have a second chance to work through troublingly familiar scenarios, and perhaps master them.

WHAT IS REFOUND IN REFINDING?

What we experience in the present is almost never a picture-perfect replay of the past. Andrea's husband, for example, was not a perfect reproduction of her father: what Andrea refound in her husband was her internal *image* of her father.

Consider the experience of Justine, a recently divorced woman of thirty, whose own parents divorced when she was nine:

> I've always been very suspicious of men, including my ex-husband. For years I thought that they were all exactly like my father, who I saw as an unscrupulous manipulator, a guy who just exploited women. I'd see what I thought was my father's lack of conscience in my husband Lowell and I'd feel like, hey, the guy's capable of anything. Which in retrospect I think was a terrible distortion. The thing is it's only in the last two years or so that I've finally gotten to know my father for myself. Before that, after my parents' divorce, I hadn't spent that much time with him. I'd just absorbed this picture of him from my mother...which was like a guy on a wanted poster, one of the ten most dangerous or whatever...I just saw him through her eyes.
>
> Now I feel really angry at my mother, because she made it impossible for me to have a relationship with my father... she just spoiled him for me, I guess because she was so enraged at him for leaving....

Justine implies that in her husband she refound her father—but her father as seen through her mother's eyes. Justine's experience may not be typical, but it emphasizes that what we refind in our partners are our internal images. Interestingly, when her image of her father changed, what she refound in the men she loved also subtly changed.

Sometimes, as in Justine's case, the images that describe the landscape of intimate relationships are conscious: "I'd see what I thought was my father's lack of conscience in my husband Lowell." Much more commonly, we are aware of the results of refinding (as Justine was aware of her suspiciousness), but without being conscious of the process that has provoked them. Instead of recognizing the influence of refinding, we simply feel that our partner bears an unfortunate and uncanny psychological resemblance to our father (or mother, or whomever).

While the process of refinding often distorts our perceptions of our partner in the present, refinding is impartial in terms of what it carries forward from the past. Consequently, refinding is both desired and dreaded: we want to relive what we have consciously found to be the strengths of our past loves, but we dread the repetition of the painful difficulties that marred these same intimacies. It is the emotional complexity of this conflict that makes refinding, for many of us, the single most powerful and problematic force in love.

A Case of Refinding

Mark was a forty-one-year-old corporate manager who came to therapy for help with his difficulty in making a decision to marry. He had spent his twenties and thirties in a series of "committed" relationships, each of which had eventually unraveled. The women he'd been involved with had appealed to him in different ways, but they all shared a common trait: they were, in his words, "unusually sweet and nurturing." This quality was a significant aspect of their initial allure for him, but later Mark reacted to it as though it were a shortcoming:

> I feel like all my past girlfriends were too mushy, too yielding. I never felt I was coming up against someone I could fight with, someone who could take me on. I'd usually get my way and then feel disappointed or guilty, and also alone, somehow. It's as if something was missing, something about me or something about them, I'm not sure which. There was a lot that was good about these relationships...I learned a lot about accepting the ups and downs of living with someone...But this feeling of missing something was so strong I always wound up leaving, or else the woman got fed up and she'd leave me.

Now Mark was worried that, once again, he was about to leave or be left. He had lived for the past six months with Lauren, a thirty-four-year-old organizational consultant who had been hired by his company to resolve some interdepartmental tensions. Almost immediately, Mark had been intensely attacted to Lauren, but also somewhat intimidated by her. She was strong, assertive, and very adept at reading people. Once Mark became involved with Lauren, he quickly fell in love:

> From the start, I thought she had what was important to me. She was powerful, she cared about me, there's a whole lot we share. And unlike the other women I'd lived with, she was more than willing to argue with me. . . She didn't feel like she had to yield to my every whim. At the beginning, everything seemed unbelievably great. We loved to talk to each other, we both liked to cuddle for hours, sex was intense. . . Every time we were about to get together, I'd feel my heart start to pound, anticipating what it was going be like. . . I'd feel this weird combination of longing for her and being afraid. . . Being with someone like Lauren was exactly what I'd decided I wanted, but for some reason it was scary.

Lauren seemed to embody many aspects of Mark's romantic ideal. It was easy to admire her, and the two of them had enough in common that he could see himself in her, which made him feel comfortable. He could both argue with her and enjoy feeling "merged" with her.

Mark said that when he was with Lauren, he felt that he was "home." This had a double meaning for him. He thought he had finally found the person with whom he could make the home he wanted. And there was a feeling that she was familiar, which reminded him of his first home.

Lauren was both different from and similar to his mother. She was much more independent than his mother had been, and she was less demanding. But like his mother, Lauren was genuinely interested in him, and enjoyed the same playful aggression his mother had. He and Lauren could banter for hours. There was usually an ironic edge to their humor. It was an oblique way of being close. Mark's mother had constantly tried to connect with him in the same way, through irony and playful argument. At the time, he had engaged with her, but without getting much pleasure from their verbal jousting. Secretly, he hated the feeling that his mother couldn't do without this kind of involvement with him, as if it were the only form of intimacy with which she was comfortable:

> My mother was always in my face. I loved her a lot, and I'm sure her admiration, her desire to be involved with me, all that stuff gave me a lot of confidence...But I got sick of the endless arguments she'd instigate about politics or how you should lead your life or some stupid TV show or the food at a restaurant...Sometimes she'd preface these beloved debates of hers with something about playing the devil's advocate. The devil needs an advocate? I never understood that concept. Anyway, I just felt like I had to get very far away from her and as soon as I could, I did.

Prior to Lauren, Mark had chosen women with personalities as different from his mother's as he could find. This freed him from his mother's kind of intrusiveness. But in these relationships, he never felt challenged or stimulated. By the time he was forty, he had determined that he wanted to find someone who was more of a peer, someone, in his words, "who could handle him." Mark's intensely ambivalent relationship with his mother had apparently left him with a significant problem: How could he be with a woman who was strong and challenging like his mother without feeling he was with someone who wouldn't let him be? In Lauren he felt that he had found the ideal solution. But a year and a half into his relationship with her, he was dismayed to find himself standing again at a familiar crossroads, simultaneously drawn to her and eager to get away.

The Refound Past: Positive and Negative

Mark's dilemma—how to reconcile the positive and negative aspects of refinding—is one that many of us face in love. Mark wanted to refind in his partner only those aspects of his mother that he believed were worth reexperiencing: her unfailing interest in him, her nurturing domesticity, her intellectual energy and feistiness. At the same time, he hoped to avoid aspects of his relationship with her that had left him feeling invaded and corralled. But no one has this kind of control over refinding. Because so much of the process is unconscious, refinding works its problematic (or magical) effects regardless of our conscious wishes or intentions.

The impact of refinding on our love lives will differ depending on the nature of the images that make up our inner map and on whether our internal images, positive and negative, are integrated or not. The more integrated our images of past love, the more these images facilitate love in the present. Why should this be so?

Recall that integrated images have a both-and rather than an either-or quality: they let us see other people as possessing a mixture of positive and negative attributes. Integrated images of past love that are neither overwhelmingly positive nor frighteningly negative draw us to new love, and enhance it, for at least two reasons. First, we're motivated to refind in the present what was *pleasurable* in the past. Because we aren't comparing current love with an impossibly idealized version of childhood love, we aren't acutely vulnerable to disappointment. Second, we're motivated to refind in the present what was *problematic* in the past, for the purpose of mastering it. We aren't so dominated by images of old disasters in love that we compulsively re-create them—or, to protect ourselves, avoid love altogether.

As for Mark, his images of his mother were integrated, but only barely. He "loved her a lot" and he "had to get very far away from her." He didn't have an image of her as either all bad or all good. Yet his positive and negative images of his mother were both very highly charged. He was capable of ambivalence, but not acceptance. "Can't live with them, can't live without them" summed up Mark's feeling about refinding in relation to women like his mother. This unresolved tension between his desire to refind and his dread of refinding dominated his romantic involvements.

Mark's conflict of wish and fear is a version of what most of us experience. Perhaps, given this conflict, the most auspicious romantic match is one with a partner who is similar enough to the "original" to encourage pleasurable refinding, but dissimilar enough that problematic refinding does not overwhelm us. This "moderate" choice may heighten the potential for mastery as well as pleasure; similarity to the original love helps bring the past into the present, while dissimilarity may help us differentiate the past from the present. When one lover says to another, "I feel as if I've known you all my life," he or she is probably responding to the factor of similarity. But if the past is refound without enough dissimilarity, it may only be repeated (or fled) rather than mastered.

WHAT MOTIVATES REFINDING?

Refinding is driven by the same three motives that energize all six of the capacities in love: the desire for pleasure, the need for self-esteem, and the urge for mastery. Our understanding of these motives in refinding derives in part from what may seem an odd source: the exploration of transference in psychotherapy.

Transference and Refinding

In treating his patients, Freud found that most people were inclined to transfer onto their physician (or analyst or therapist) feelings, thoughts, and behavior that they had originally experienced in relation to significant figures during childhood. The child saw the parents as all-powerful and responded with intense and contradictory feelings. Now, with very much the same mixture of feelings, the patient empowers the doctor.

Early in this century, Freud wrote about an especially hazardous form of transference in which the patient falls in love with the analyst. The "erotic transference," in Freud's initial assessment, was an obstacle that had the potential to derail treatment altogether. Over time, however, Freud and others came to recognize that if transference (including erotic transference) were explored rather than acted out, it could provide, alongside dreams, a second "royal road to the unconscious."

Freud's observations of the erotic transference crucially informed his understanding of refinding. He saw that romantic and transference love alike were new editions of original childhood love. In the decades since Freud first wrote, explorations of transference have continued to deepen our understanding of the role of refinding in love.

The study of transference reveals that people bring the past into the present in various ways in order to satisfy various needs. The first evidence of a patient's transference may be glimpsed in his or her choice of a therapist. Similarly, refinding exerts its initial influence on love as it shapes our choice of a romantic partner. In general, patients choose therapists, and lovers choose their partners, to satisfy needs for pleasure, self-esteem, and mastery that stem from their most significant early relationships.[1] When we fall in love, we are usually aware (albeit dimly) of the kinds of refinding, positive and negative, that our partner will provoke—and the needs that this refinding will satisfy.

The Pleasure of Refinding

The refinding of experiences that were positive is usually pleasurable. Paradoxically, perhaps, there can also be pleasure in the refinding of experiences that were negative.

Positive refinding fuels passion, as we reexperience the excitement, mystery, and allure of what was longed for but unobtainable in our earliest love relations. It's as though we revisit the past

---

1. Nearly every student of psychotherapy has an opportunity to research this matter informally when he or she watches a film that has become a staple in training programs across the country. In this film, the same patient is shown in successive therapy hours with three different therapists: Fritz Perls, Carl Rogers, and Albert Ellis. After the film, it is common for students to speculate about which of the three they would select as their own therapist: Perls, who is often seen as a challenging, aggressive, erotically exciting father? Rogers, whose presence is suggestive of a calm, accepting, almost "maternal" father? Or Ellis, whose demeanor is rational and disinterested, calling to mind the image of a consultant, rather than a parent? Students with different pasts choose with different needs in mind.

by bringing it alive in the present: now there is the exhilarating potential to satisfy desires that, when we were very young, we could satisfy only in fantasy. We feel we are again with someone very familiar, but with whom, in the past, sexual closeness in particular was taboo. Unless anxiety or guilt is dominant, this mixture of the familiar and the forbidden can create a very powerful chemistry. Unconsciously, we may have chosen our partner precisely because he or she embodied certain qualities or physical attributes of the intimate other who was forbidden to us or lost: mother, father, a sibling, or someone else.

Positive experiences of many kinds can be relived through refinding. The closeness and support, security and stimulation, that we enjoyed in the past can be revived in the present where they add a dimension of depth to current intimacy. To the extent that pleasurable refinding dominates the picture, our partner becomes all the more appealing, and this in turn intensifies our desires for intimacy and commitment.

The refinding of pleasurable experience also enables us to make a bridge between our present love and our broad family legacy. When Mark fell in love with Lauren, he was responding not just to his recognition in her of his mother's strengths; he also saw his grandmother's wit, his uncle's shrewdness, his sister's sophistication. He refound with Lauren the best that his family had to offer, and through doing so, he made a statement about what he valued in his family heritage. In a sense, through refinding we honor our past: we carry forward what we loved in our original family into the new family we are now creating. This aspect of refinding may enable two partners to feel more comfortable with one another when they share a common cultural heritage and the values, beliefs, and rituals that go with it.

The legacy of our families, however, is always mixed. We refind in our partner the worst of our past as well as the best. How could this painful refinding possibly be a source of pleasure?

To answer the question, we must consider not only the conscious but also the unconscious aspects of refinding. Before he met Lauren, Mark had already become aware that his relationships

with women were marred by control struggles, for which he ac-
knowledged partial responsibility. He knew that his mother had
been very dominating and, therefore, that he was always much
too ready to see (or imagine) the same quality in the women with
whom he became involved. Mark hoped, a little too optimistically,
that with Lauren his self-knowledge would inoculate him against
the old fear of feeling controlled.

None of us consciously invites painful refinding. We hope to
avoid it or diminish its influence. Like Mark, we may hope that
understanding our patterns in love will protect us. But when it
comes to our own habits of refinding, our knowledge is always
incomplete. The refinding we confront in every particular relationship is unique; it brings to the surface new, sometimes unexpected aspects of the original experience. Mark had every reason
to worry that he might refind in Lauren some of his mother's
unwanted control—and in fact this is exactly what occurred. What
he failed to anticipate was how confused and angry he would find
himself feeling—and how compelled he would be to play out the
painful drama.

In the course of his struggles with Lauren (over everything from
whose tastes in decorating would prevail to who would be in charge
sexually), Mark became guiltily aware of the pleasure he took from
confrontations that were ostensibly painful. Whenever his will
and Lauren's were about to collide, Mark detected a strange sense
of satisfaction in himself. In trying to understand this feeling, he
realized that while he had hated the confrontations with his
mother, they had been charged with an emotional intensity that
felt very intimate. Battling with his mother had been a way to
feel separate while also feeling close. Now with Lauren, fighting
seemed to provide the same reward. In addition, there was the
undeniable pleasure of releasing pent-up anger. Lauren was the
immediate target, but Mark knew she was also a convenient stand-
in for his rather intimidating mother, in relation to whom his
anger had had to be suppressed.

Painful refinding often brings with it these kinds of unconscious,
or hidden, pleasures. But they are pleasures that often exact a

high price. In part, the failure of Mark's involvements can be understood in these terms: he traded love for the pleasures of painful refinding. When Mark said he now wanted a partner "who could handle him," he meant a woman strong enough both to tolerate this painful refinding and to help him transcend it.

Refinding and Self-Esteem

The relationship of pleasurable refinding to self-esteem is straightforward: self-esteem is enhanced when positive experiences are refound, whereas refinding negative experiences usually diminishes self-esteem. Under certain circumstances, however, painful refinding can protect, if not enhance, our self-esteem by enabling us to attribute the negativity in a relationship to our partner rather than ourselves. Once Mark decided that his first serious girlfriend was impossibly controlling, exactly as his mother had been, he had an explanation for his difficulty in the relationship that kept his self-esteem entirely intact. To the extent that painful refinding facilitates blaming, it preserves self-esteem. This is one more reason why, in current love, we may refind even those experiences we wish we had never had in the first place.

Refinding and Mastery: Repetition vs. Repair

With the hope of transcending our limitations in love, we often challenge ourselves by unconsciously choosing partners with whom the problematic past can be replayed. The opportunity in this refinding is to repair the emotional damage inflicted, inadvertently or otherwise, in the course of our earliest relationships. The risk is that the troubling past will only be repeated.

For purposes of mastery, it is usually our negative experiences in love that we refind in the present. But past experiences that are ostensibly positive, such as closeness and success, can also be conflicted. To master them, the unresolved aspects of such positive experiences often make their way into our relationships.

At thirty-three, Celine's relationships with men had been disappointing for as long as she could remember. Her assumption, which she traced to her relationship with her father, was that men didn't care. Her father had died when she was twelve; while he was alive, she believed, he hadn't really cared about her. An experience of refinding, however, was reparative: it helped her to see her father differently—and this in turn allowed her to trust a man's love for the first time in many years:

I was with my boyfriend Terry the night before he was leaving town for a three-week vacation. I'm not sure why, but it made me think about my father...I guess because Terry was leaving, and my father's death was a kind of leaving...I started talking about all these feelings I was having about him, about my father, that made me really sad...not so much about how he didn't care, but more about how I really missed him...how terrible it was for a girl to lose her father like I did, when I was so young, when I really needed him...And as I was saying this, I looked at Terry and saw his eyes welling up with tears...he was almost crying...He was feeling right along with me. Then we hugged. I started crying, and I felt, my God! he's really here with me, he really does care...And I'd never, ever felt this about him before. I'd always taken it for granted he didn't really feel that much for me...you know, my usual attitude about men, none of them care.

So this was a revelation...And then suddenly it triggered this old feeling, of being held by my father. I just started sobbing. I realized that the same way Terry cared for me, my father had really cared, too. I just *knew* it. I felt it. I'd been wrong about him, the idea that he didn't care. I took out this photo album I have that I'd never looked at much. Terry and I looked at it...I saw pictures of my father holding me when I was little...and his look, the way he held me, this big smile he had. It just said what now I know was true, that he really loved me...

I think when I was twelve I just had to pretend that he didn't...otherwise, I think I was afraid I'd never stop crying, that I'd never have a normal life, his dying would have ended everything.

Celine's experience with her boyfriend allowed her to refind her father. In this refinding, she was able to master her childhood terror of loss and grief that had forced her to deny her father's love, and the love of other men as well.

Mourning and Mastery

For there to be repair rather than repetition, the past must come alive, but with a difference. In Celine's case her boyfriend's tears were the difference. As evidence of his caring, they jarred Celine's assumption that Terry was just like her uncaring father. Once her basic assumption about men ("none of them care") was shaken, the door opened to a past she had denied. She reexperienced with Terry the love she had known from her father when she was a child. And this left her sobbing, moved by feelings of gratitude and loss. It also left her more capable of loving.

Celine's example makes the point that becoming aware of the goodness of love in the present can, unexpectedly, trigger grief. Like Celine, we may grieve for what we have had and lost. Or we may grieve for what the past has never given us. But this grieving can lead to mastery. Mourning frees us from the inhibitions imposed by the past and lets us love more fully in the present.

THE STAGES OF LOVE AND REFINDING

In the first moments of meeting, we register microcues that either stimulate our desire for deeper involvement or turn us off. Partly, the silent question we ask ourselves has to do with idealization: Are we in the presence of someone who could conceivably personify our romantic ideal? Just as important, however, we're unconsciously assessing whether this is someone who could play the various roles called for in our dramas of refinding. When we experience an exciting sense of possibility, it's often because we've found someone who fits the part (or parts) we're trying to cast.

Falling in Love

During the first stage of intimacy, refinding colors the relationship in broad strokes. We're becoming aware in a rudimentary way of the kinds of refinding that our partner will provoke. We're also unconsciously deciding whether we're willing to take on the refinding that we provoke in our partner. Usually, if the relationship is to survive the first stage of love, the refinding that we (and our partner) dimly anticipate must be more positive than negative. Of course, the accuracy of our conscious assessment may well be marred by the idealization of early love. By diminishing our awareness of whatever we might find problematic in our partner, idealization often distracts us from the potential for refinding painful experience.

Becoming a Couple

Refinding begins to exert both a more profound and a more obvious influence once we enter the second stage of love. In relation to love's early promise, refinding ensures that "what you see isn't what you get." Remember Adam and Rachel, whose story was summarized in the Introduction? Adam's view of Rachel had shifted 180 degrees: the smart, strong, and supportive woman he had fallen in love with now seemed to be a coolly castrating adversary who saw him as weak and clinging. Adam *and* Rachel had refound in one another their most painful images of their mothers. This dispiriting refinding provoked nearly overwhelming feelings of disappointment and resentment. What began for Rachel and Adam as a "made for each other" romance nearly unraveled due to the influence of the reanimated past.

In the second phase of love, refinding's themes emerge in sharper relief because we are now establishing a "family life" together that is likely to evoke the past. We may begin to live together, to set up a household, or to make joint, long-term plans. Our view of our partner, at this point, is likely to be overlaid with impressions of past intimacies, including but not limited to our images of mother and father. Often we begin to notice how similar our partner is to one or more past loves. These similarities are partly observed (for we chose our partner purposefully) and partly imagined or projected. Now that our partner is relating to us in a more overtly familial role, we're inclined to see him or her filling that role in a way that's consistent with our models from the past. When Adam began to see his mother in Rachel, therefore, he defensively reenacted what he had learned as a child: namely, to sulk and/or demand attention. When Rachel noticed Adam's psychological resemblance to her mother, she became increasingly critical and withdrawn.

Unconsciously, we also treat our partner in such a way that he or she actually comes to identify with the internal images we project. We enlist our partner to play a role in the old drama and, in so doing, we enhance the likelihood that our current relationship will replicate a previous one.

For many of us, the results of refinding are not as obvious or dramatic as they were for Rachel and Adam. We may experience its influence only indirectly, or in small and subtle ways. We may be aware of a nagging uncertainty about our commitment to our partner as we come to feel more and more "coupled." We may find specific behaviors of our partner increasingly annoying, without understanding quite why. Usually, we are not only struggling with the capacity for integration, attempting to accept the bad with the good; we are also experiencing the as-yet-unidentified influence of the ghosts of our past loves, hovering over a relationship that previously seemed free of such influences.

The challenge of the second phase of intimacy is not to resolve the dilemmas of refinding, this would probably be too ambitious, but to be able to recognize the impact of refinding for what it is: an incursion of the past into the present. Hopefully, we can also come up with ways to grapple with problematic refinding, so that its destructive potential is minimized.

Ultimately, we hope we can enjoy what is positive in the revival of the past while accepting what is negative. In this connection, our prior experiences as adults in love can be a considerable help. Previous relationships may have allowed us to become aware of our vulnerabilities to particular kinds of refinding. In addition, they may have helped us recognize the near-inevitability of refinding, and thus made possible a more relaxed and accepting attitude toward it.

Mark and Lauren shared the advantage of these kinds of prior experiences in love. Both had suffered in their past relationships from a lack of understanding of the role of refinding. After one particularly disappointing relationship, Lauren had sought the help of a therapist. Now she wanted to make use of what she had learned to help ensure that her relationship with Mark would not be similarly disappointing. Mark was in very much the same position. The two of them talked about the troubling impact of the past on their previous relationships. They realized that they shared a vocabulary and a perspective that made them more confident of their ability to resolve their problems together. There was something both realistic and romantic about this conversation. Talking together about their future as a couple symbolized a deeper commitment and helped them feel closer to one another.

Deepening Love over Time

The third stage of intimacy further heightens the potential for refinding. In part, this is because greater commitment means greater safety. Feeling more secure and more relaxed, we're more willing to take the risk of being fully ourselves, which can elicit more transference, more refinding. In addition, with marriage (or a comparable commitment), our living arrangement usually comes to resemble more closely the one in which we grew up—and this too evokes refinding. Finally, if and when children enter the picture, refinding our experience with our parents becomes an absolute inevitability. In this connection, consider the couples (old-fashioned couples, perhaps) who address one another as "Mother" and "Father."

In the third phase of love, we're hoping for a lifelong involvement with our partner. Often, this raises our expectations, and rising expectations heighten both the risk of disappointment and the wish to be close. We may want our beloved not only to be a good companion but also to continue to meet our romantic ideals. In addition, and this may be the most ambitious desire of all, we want our partner to remedy the injustices of the past, to compensate us for what we missed when we were young. We want our lover to be a healer.

Love's potential to satisfy and to heal is considerable but not unlimited. Finding ourselves again in the bosom of a family can stimulate very powerful longings, only some of which will be fulfilled. Whether our own refinding is merely a painful repetition or turns out to be reparative depends on the details of our personal history and, just as important, our reactions to them. If we only *experience* problematic refinding, without recognizing and understanding it, we're in trouble. If, by contrast, we can recognize the experience for what it is and learn from it, then refinding can become a resource for personal transformation and for enhancing our relationship.

PSYCHOLOGICAL DEVELOPMENT AND REFINDING

Healthy refinding enables us to experience with our partner both the passion that makes love exciting and the tenderness that makes it comforting. Aspects of every previous relationship that has mattered to us from infancy through adulthood can be revived through refinding; refinding is never limited to a single phase of development. For the most part, however, it is our first and most influential experiences of intimacy that shape our habits of refinding. It's not surprising that we most commonly refind experiences from the family in which we grew up, for this was the setting in which we first knew love, and the problems associated with love.

When our first relationships (especially those with our parents) were "good enough," they can be refound with our partner without too much pain, guilt, or disappointment. In this happy instance, refinding will be a subtle backdrop that mainly enhances our current relationship, rather than a factor in the foreground that dominates it. Our childhood involvements will have encouraged an optimism about the involvements to come and, consequently, we will have been able to develop deep and lasting adult commitments. To the extent that the original relationships are refound, they will bring to new love a reassuring continuity with the old.

But when our early relationships were troubling, refinding them can cause problems that are difficult to avoid because troubling experiences press for repeated expression. Partly, this allows mastery; as we've seen, however, painful refinding can also serve other less progressive purposes, such as defensive loyalty or revenge.

Refinding—When Earlier Capacities Are Vulnerable

Problems in refinding originate primarily in two ways. First, like Mark, we can be vulnerable in one (or more) of the capacities in love that precede refinding in the course of our development. Mark's Achilles' heel was merging:

> My mother was very loving and she expressed a lot of this physically. I'm sure physical affection is healthy for a kid, but when I was still pretty young, I began to feel like it was getting to be too much. She'd come and tuck me in, and I'd just feel like I had to get away...but I'd pretend everything was fine...otherwise she'd be hurt or angry. I remember how strong the smell of her perfume was...she'd be bending over me in bed and I'd almost feel like I couldn't breathe...Now it's ridiculously easy for me to feel smothered by women. Obviously, this goes back to my mother.

Mark complained about being smothered, but secretly he also loved his mother's adoring attention, even when it felt overwhelming. It was a heady experience to feel so utterly confident that he was the apple of his mother's eye. For Mark, merging came to have two contradictory faces: on the one hand, being close to his mother was to feel adored; on the other hand, being close to her was also to feel suffocated.

This conflict about merging was intensified by Mark's belief that in order to be adored, he had to submit ("I'd just feel like I had to get away...but I'd pretend everything was fine.") His mother's adoration helped him feel good about himself, but submitting to her was humiliating. It became impossible for Mark to separate his positive imagery of being deeply cared for from his negative imagery of being intruded upon and feeling compelled to submit.

As an adult, whenever Mark began to feel close to a woman, he invariably refound these contradictory images. He loved to feel loved, of course; but to the extent that he refound his mother's affection, as he did with Lauren, he was also burdened by the old images of intrusiveness, submission, and weakness. In addition, Mark felt that his mother had "spoiled" him. Living in the aura of her overwhelming affection had been very compelling—and because this childhood experience was impossible to duplicate as an adult man with an adult woman, he frequently wound up feeling disappointed. Mark's conflicted imagery of merging made him a very ambivalent lover.

In his twenties and thirties, his solution had been to dilute refinding by consciously choosing partners who bore little resemblance to his mother. But these relationships had felt incomplete. Now, in his forties and living with Lauren, Mark chose to grapple with the challenging refinding that he had previously sought to avoid.

Mark's experience illustrates the way in which a vulnerability in merging can make refinding problematic. Conflicts or vulnerabilities in the capacities for erotic involvement, idealization, and integration can create comparably challenging problems with refinding. Integration, when it is not securely achieved, can be especially destructive, for it gives all the old images we refind in adult love an exaggerated, black-or-white quality that makes them very difficult to cope with.

Refinding the Oedipal Past

When as children we compete with one parent for the love of the other, we play a high-stakes game. During this period (roughly ages three to six), emotionally charged experiences involving passion, tenderness, and competition register as internal images. Shaping our map of love, these early images have lasting consequences and are the other primary source of problems in refinding. Listen to two fathers describing the Oedipal triangle from opposite vantage points:

> I was talking to my four-year-old son, Lenny, the other day about who sleeps with who in our house. Very nonchalantly, he announced that he was going to sleep with his mother from now on. Then he was going to marry her. I asked him, What about your brother Mike? What's he going to do? Lenny said he could sleep with Marie. Marie's the au pair. Then I said, But what about me? Who am I supposed to sleep with? Lenny told me I could sleep with Byron. Byron's the dog.

> You asked me if I ever felt jealous of Brent, my son. I didn't think so. But then I woke up one morning, this was about six months after Brent was born. . . and I was feeling so upset that I was almost shaking. My wife asked me what was wrong, and I said, I just had a terrible dream. It's completely freaked me out. I told her that, in the dream, I'd gone to work—but somehow I'd discovered that she was at home having an affair with another man. To which my wife replied, "Was he short and bald?" Very smart woman, my wife.

Generally, people either accept the influence of the Oedipal triangle as a psychological given or reject the whole notion as preposterous. How could a little boy take seriously the possibility of displacing his father as his mother's mate? How could a little girl think she could replace her mother in her father's affections? Indeed, these kinds of wishes (which children regularly reveal, both in words and play) *are* unrealistic, but only if we look at them from our perspective as adults. Through the eyes of a child, as yet incapable of clearly differentiating fantasy from reality, the same wishes can seem entirely realistic, and as such they can be both very motivating and very frightening.

As children, it's scary for us to compete with one parent for the love of the other. What will the consequences be? Will our competition be tolerated or punished? What if we are successful? What if we fail? Can we have the love of both parents, or must we choose between them? These are the kinds of questions that are answered through the real and fantasized events of the Oedipal period of development. The playing out of these dilemmas is central to our imagery of ourselves and others in love. The Oedipal romance of childhood is the first edition of the romance that is refound when we love as adults.

When Oedipal Dilemmas Are Resolved

One of the rewards of healthy Oedipal development is the ability as adults to experience both passionate excitement and tender comfort with the same lover. The pathway to this happy destination is somewhat circuitous, for this potential is alternately encouraged and discouraged by the circumstances of development. At age three or four, we first experience affection and sexuality in relation to the same person, usually mother or father (or both). Boys and girls become aware of their genitals as a source of pleasure much earlier, but it is only at three or four that the child's genital pleasure becomes associated (in fantasy) with interaction with other people. Partly, it is this first fusion of affection and erotic fantasy in relation to the parents that animates the Oedipal romance.

In the healthiest case, our parents were neither seductively encouraging nor angrily rejecting when we tried to play out the childhood drama of romance and rivalry. Competition, then, will not have been experienced as a terrifying danger. Nor will sexuality have been frighteningly complicated either by overstimulation or punitive intolerance. Typically, in such an atmosphere, we can give up our romantic pursuit of the parent gradually, without feeling burdened by guilt or shamed by defeat. Our sexual feelings now go underground, for the time being, while our feelings of love for both parents persist. Our compensation for what we might feel we've lost is not only our parents' continuing love but also our identification with their strengths, especially the strengths of the parent of the same sex. The little girl, for example, might not marry her father, but she begins to experience as her own the strengths that enabled her mother to marry him.

Then, in adolescence, puberty threatens to revive some of the old erotic longings. Given a healthy passage through the Oedipal straits, however, these feelings will be redirected toward nonincestuous partners. The amicable divorce from our parents, emotionally speaking, frees us to choose new lovers. In this context, passion and tenderness, sex and affection, can once again be experienced in the same relationship. To the extent that our parents are refound in adult love, their presence will only, subtly, enhance it.

When Oedipal Dilemmas Are Unresolved

PRE-OEDIPAL PROBLEMS. As if the Oedipal situation weren't complex enough, there are pre-Oedipal difficulties that can complicate it still further. Consider the relationship we have with our parents in the first two or three years of life. Suppose, for example, that a little girl's mother was too depressed or too ill to give her the nurturing attention she needed early in her life. Then she will arrive on the Oedipal scene like a child who is desperate for dinner, having been deprived of the first two meals of the day. Her desire for her father to love her, as he loves her mother, will be much more intense than it would otherwise be. But the same early frustration that intensifies her desire, and propels her into the Oedipal rivalry, can generate intense anger. And this anger can make the rivalry much more frightening, by coloring it with themes of revenge and retaliation.

If, as children, our fear of competing with the same-sex parent prevails, we may pull back from the Oedipal rivalry, regressing to a preoccupation with earlier issues in development, such as dependency or control. And this can turn our passion as adults into something more closely resembling the relationship of parent and child.

A middle-aged man, for example, found it difficult to be comfortable with his wife. While he wanted her to take care of him, he was terrified of losing his autonomy. One night he dreamed that he was in the kitchen, while on just the other side of the wall his wife was in their bedroom with another man. He couldn't deal with this adulterous triangle, however, because he was too preoccupied with repairing a device that stood against the kitchen wall: a curious combination of a stove and a toilet. Whatever else it meant to him, this dream reflected his fear of competing with other men and his difficulty responding sexually to his wife—not to mention his preoccupation with concerns that predate the Oedipal period.

On the other hand, the intensification of our childhood desire for the opposite-sex parent may be more potent than our fear of competing. The inability to relinquish the object of our Oedipal desires can be reflected in our choice, as adults, never to pursue partners who are available. This keeps the original Oedipal pursuit alive. A forty-year-old man, never married and recurrently involved with unavailable women, told the following story:

> When my mother remarried after my father's death, I was very, very upset. It wasn't that I expected her to stay single, but I never thought that she would act as though this new husband was more important to her than her children. My brother and I used to be so important to her. . . she obviously loved her boys. It's weird, but now I feel betrayed. It's almost like I thought maybe she'd really be there for me even more, once my father was gone. But it turned out to be almost the opposite and it still really pisses me off.

OEDIPAL SUCCESS, OEDIPAL FAILURE. Freud said that the man who is unquestionably his mother's favorite has an inestimable advantage in life. While this may be true for some men, there are others for whom success with mother is no success at all. While it may convey certain rewards, the son's Oedipal victory (or more commonly the fantasy of Oedipal victory) always comes at a high price. When a man believes he has triumphed over his father in the contest for his mother, he is doubly disadvantaged. First, he bears the guilt of defeating a man who loves him and whose love he desires. Second, as a role model for the son to identify with, the father who is defeated is no great source of strength. A daughter who feels she has triumphed over her mother is comparably disadvantaged.

Mark tended to see himself as a victim of his mother's intrusiveness, but he also felt that he was very special to her. Mark's father was a formidable man, a successful surgeon, but he was largely absent. He ceded home and family to his wife. Mark's mother seems to have compensated for her husband's invisibility at home by turning to her son. Her loving attention, her endless interest, and her eroticized banter all reflected her efforts to find with Mark what was lacking in her relationship with her husband. Mark was vaguely aware that he occupied a place in her life that should have been his father's. But rather than focus on his special status, Mark preferred to concentrate on the ways in which he experienced his mother as a burden. This choice was a reflection of his guilty "triumph" over his father.

The same choice complicated his refinding in adult love. Unconsciously, he was compelled by his guilt to focus on the ways in which Lauren, for example, was a burden to him rather than a pleasure. This was both a defense (against his guilt) and an irrational penance for having "wronged" his father. As we'll see, Mark's guilt also affected his sexual relationship with Lauren. One of the most common manifestations of guilty Oedipal triumph is the enforced separation of passion from tenderness.

What is called "Oedipal failure" can reflect either of two different scenarios. In the less-damaging, the child feels helpless to make a dent in the parental relationship. Mother and father seem so utterly absorbed in their love for one another that the child feels there's little room for him or her and that, consequently, any romantic pursuit of the parent would be doomed. In the more-damaging scenario, the child is actually mocked, teased, or punished for his or her pursuit of the parent. To different degrees, these scenarios undermine the child's confidence in his or her sexuality and power. In terms of adult refinding, there may be a tendency to seek out rejecting partners with whom the Oedipal drama can be replicated or to pursue inadequate partners whose neediness ensures that they won't be rejecting.

INADEQUATE IDENTIFICATIONS. Without the opportunity as children to identify with the same-sex parent, we may feel that the labyrinth of Oedipal rivalry has no exit. When, by contrast, we can identify with our parents, we have a way out. Rather than continue to compete with mother or father, we can take on the strengths of our rival. When the little girl, for example, begins to feel that she is *like* her mother, she reaps a number of rewards: She maintains her love for her mother and ensures her mother's love for her. She avoids the risks of competition with a formidable competitor. She learns about reality (you can't always get what you want), which is different from fantasy (in which the little girl's omnipotence has no limits). Finally, in identifying with an admired figure of her own gender, the little girl solidifies her confidence in herself as a female. And this preserves the hope that someday she'll be able to possess a man like the father she's now "surrendering" to her mother. The little boy's Oedipal identification with his father serves the same ends.

For various reasons, however, the path of identification can be more or less closed to us as children. A mother, for example, may treat her husband with such utter contempt that it becomes difficult for their son to identify with his father. Or the father himself, through debilitating illness or some other misfortune, may simply be difficult for the son to admire. Sometimes a son may feel so corralled by his mother's need in relation to him that identifying with his father becomes a dangerous betrayal of his mother. To understand more about the consequences of inadequate identification, let's turn to the experience of Mark's partner, Lauren.

Lauren has told Mark that she can't separate her images of herself in relation to men from her image of her mother. From the time she was five, she has never been able to think very highly of this quiet, adaptable woman whose identity seemed molded around her husband's needs. Lauren felt loved by her mother, but she could never admire nor feel close to her. She always wondered why her father, a somewhat dominating man with a keen intellect and cultured tastes, had married her rather drab mother. In fact Lauren and her father were allied in their (mainly covert) depreciation of her mother, who seemed incapable of keeping up intellectually with the two of them. Lauren sometimes felt that the specialness of her relationship with her father depended on joining with him in seeing her mother as inadequate. The last thing in the world Lauren wanted was to feel that she was anything at all like her mother.

Now, however, with the benefit of some therapy, she has become aware of the consequences of this flight from her "maternal identification." First, it has left her with the disturbing feeling that men are the only game in town, for they're the ones with whom she associates intelligence, power, and sexuality. As defined by her image of her mother, being female means being nurturing and patient, but also weak, overcompliant, and asexual. As a result of this imagery, Lauren's relationships with men (including Mark) are full of psychological conflict.

She wants to win Mark's love, as she won her father's, but doing so fills her with guilt. To have a successful relationship is to surpass her mother once again. Lauren's compromise is to enjoy certain aspects of the relationship with Mark but to spoil others. She tells him that she suspects she picks fights with him to make sure that their intimacy "doesn't get too good." Lauren has learned that she has more than one reason to fight: if she doesn't, she's also worried that she'll become too much like her overcompliant mother. While she may not be aware of it, Lauren probably has a third motive for spoiling her relationship with Mark.

Because she couldn't comfortably identify with her mother, she remained overly involved with her father. As a result there may well be a profound dependency upon her relationship with her father. This leads her to re-create elements of that original relationship in all subsequent relationships with men. Unconsciously, it may also lead her to subvert these relationships, so that she might be able to remain psychologically "married" to her father.

The Partner or the Parent?

To the extent that our original romance with our parents remains unresolved, it is always either refound (or avoided) in our relationship with our partner. Mark consistently refound his mother in Lauren, while she refound her father in him. Their images of the past interlocked in a way that was initially stimulating and later unsettling. Originally Mark and Lauren were both excited to recognize in the other the best of their parents: the intellectual energy, the power, and the love. This was the pleasurable side of refinding. It easily enabled them to fall in love. They saw their power struggles during this period as minor skirmishes that only gave their intimacy an added electricity.

After a year they chose to live together. Six months later, however, it was not the pleasurable but the problematic aspects of refinding that had started to dominate. Mark was beginning to feel "claustrophobic," just as he had with his mother. A new image of Lauren crystallized. In his eyes she was now obsessively preoccupied with planning every detail of their lives together:

> We couldn't seem to do anything spontaneously anymore. It seemed like we were spending all our time haggling about how to decorate the apartment, or who was going to take care of what, or what we were going to do three weekends from now. I felt like I needed a Day-Timer for all the lists and appointments that our living together seemed to involve...And meanwhile, sex was getting to be sort of an obligation, almost like another item on the list. It was that old feeling again of being trapped.

While Mark was becoming more concerned about Lauren's intrusiveness, she was beginning to see him as self-absorbed and controlling. He acted, in her view, as if everything had to go his way. And this recalled a side of her father that she had found very unappealing.

Mark and Lauren's ability to experience passion and tenderness together was a casualty of their problematic refinding. Neither of them could completely separate the image of the partner from the image of the parent. And with the ghosts of old love in bed with them, it was increasingly difficult to feel turned on.

Juggling the demands of work and home life, and especially parenting, can challenge the capacity of many of us to keep passion alive, and this challenge is compounded by refinding. The presence of six people in the bedroom—the couple and the shadow company of two sets of parents—can be very inhibiting indeed. For passion to survive, there must be an emotional divorce from our past loves and rivals. Sometimes, however, it's easier to separate from our partner.

While acknowledging her love for Mark, and her desire for the relationship to continue in some form, Lauren suggested that perhaps the two of them should resume their lives apart, that their decision to live together might have been premature. The ghosts of refinding (and the pressures of everyday life) had taken their toll. Feeling rejected, Mark angrily dismissed her suggestion, telling her that she had a problem with intimacy and should get back into therapy. He said that if she were to move out, the relationship might just as well be over. He proposed that the two of them declare a truce and take a week apart from one another.

When Lauren left for a weeklong trip with a girlfriend, Mark found himself missing her a great deal. He became aware once again of how deeply he loved her. But while she was gone, he called an old girlfriend, implying that he was available for an affair. Eventually he chose not to act on his sexual impulse, but the strength of this desire, coupled with his renewed passion for Lauren, confused and troubled him. It was at this point that he decided to see a therapist himself. Caught in a tide of emotion, he was worried about how out of control he felt. He had used an affair to exit a relationship once before, and he was wary of his impulse to do so again.

DEFENSES AGAINST REFINDING
AND REFINDING AS A DEFENSE

When refinding threatens to generate painful feelings, we defend against it, just as Mark and Lauren did. The greater the threat, the more drastic the defense. If the prospect of refinding the past is truly terrifying, we may protect ourselves by avoiding romantic relationships altogether.

Short of this wholesale avoidance, we have several other alternatives. We can choose partners with whom there is little hope for a deep or lasting involvement (including partners who are married, uninterested in or intimidated by commitment, and so on). By selecting someone who is likely to remain unavailable, we ensure that our relationship won't develop past love's opening phase. Then, so long as the spell of idealization remains unbroken, we are relatively immune from the threat of problematic refinding. We can also try to minimize the likelihood of refinding by choosing partners who are as unlike our original loves as possible. Lastly, once we are in a relationship, we may protect ourselves by avoiding intimacy. Whatever we ordinarily do to avoid being close also helps us to avoid refinding. Merger-wary defenses, for example, can function as defenses against refinding.

Prior to her involvement with Mark, Lauren apparently made use of a combination of these protective strategies to defend against refinding. Her first line of defense was to choose men whose availability, or interest in her, was uncertain at best. Several of these men were married. Because their primary commitment was to their wives, Lauren's participation in these romantic triangles meant that her involvement with men remained relatively superficial. Whenever she found herself becoming more deeply involved with a man, she dealt with her unconscious fears of refinding by creating distance. To dilute intimacy she withdrew emotionally or retreated from her partner more overtly, going so far at times as to refuse to speak with him. And the consequence? Lauren could enjoy falling in love, but as long as she defended against refinding in these ways, she could never remain in love.

Refinding as a Defense

It is exceedingly common to refind one aspect of our past as an unconscious defense against another. For most of us, the past is a mosaic of significant experiences, positive and negative, and through refinding most of these have the potential to make their way into our current relationship. To protect ourselves from the *most* disturbing aspects of the past, we often refind experiences that are less disturbing, even though they may still be unwelcome.

In therapy, Mark began to develop some insight into his use of this defense:

> The combination of Lauren and me almost breaking up and some problems I was having with my boss at work had me feeling pretty overwhelmed. . . . I think I really wanted some support from Lauren but didn't quite know it. Anyway, we'd gone out to dinner and the place had booths, so the next thing I know she's sitting next to me—not across from me, *next* to me. And she's got her arm around me and I was just feeling like, Back off! It was just too much of this suffocating stuff I remember with my mother. So I kind of pushed her away, she moved around to the other side of the table, and meanwhile the waiter saw all of this, and Lauren and I were both sort of embarrassed. Then the waiter left, and I felt kind of tearful and apologetic, and Lauren was very understanding. And then I realized, I actually wanted her to hug me, prob-ably I'd wanted that before, but I always get this bad-mother thing going, you know, she's going to swallow me, instead of just letting Lauren take care of me sometimes. I don't know why it's so scary to just let that happen, but apparently it is.

As Mark would later become aware, refinding the image of his suffocating mother protected him from his early boyhood image of her as romantically exciting. This Oedipal image frightened him for several reasons: Because it made his mother (and the women who followed her) *too* enticing, the image left him feeling vulnerable and potentially dependent. In addition, because it drew him to her, this image made Mark feel guilty and fearful in relation to his father, whom he felt he had usurped in his mother's affections.

Refinding as a Defense against Change

When we enlist our partner (or a series of partners) in a repetition of old scenarios, we can convince ourselves that nothing new in romance is possible. This may then serve to justify our unwillingness to take risks or to seize the initiative in mastering our difficulties with intimacy. A variation on this theme is to use our "understanding" of the past as a story we hide behind:

> It makes sense to behave as cautiously as I do in relationships: just look at how unsafe I was in my relationship with my father [or mother, or whomever].

> Of course I tend to get angry at my mate now. . . I've got a lot of anger to express after all those years of being treated as badly as I was by my mother [or father, or whomever].

> I *do* expect more from a relationship than other people might —and with good reason: after getting nothing from my parents, I think I'm entitled to something special at this point.

Using the past to understand and come to terms with our self-defeating habits in the present is one thing. Using the past as a justification for maintaining these habits is an altogether different matter. The first is a vital part of healing; the second is a defense that can make it very difficult for us to heal at all.

The Romantic Triangle as a Defense

There are essentially two types of romantic triangles, either of which can serve defensive purposes.

The Rivalrous Triangle

Here we compete with an adversary for the lover we desire. This can be seen as a re-creation of the original Oedipal threesome, in which we competed with one parent for the love of the other.

Participation in a rivalrous triangle can have multiple meanings. Often, however, the choice to compete for a partner who is already "taken" is determined by self-protective needs. By diluting intimacy, threesomes shield us from whatever we have come to regard as the hazards of being part of a couple. When we regularly wind up as the excluded third party, the defensive motive behind our preference for triangles may become obvious.

For Lauren, being part of a couple was dangerous because of the refinding it invited. By pursuing men who proved unattainable, she protected herself from refinding the difficulties she'd known with her overly controlling father. She also avoided the old guilt of Oedipal success; in fact, her "defeat" in the triangular rivalries may have been a kind of penance.

The Reverse Triangle

The second variation on the triangular theme turns this Oedipal rivalry on its head. In the "reverse" triangle, rather than compete, we become the object of competition: *our* love is the prize for which two rivals now contend. When Mark considered having an affair after Lauren suggested they separate, he was (probably unconsciously) generating a reverse triangle. That is, he was defensively setting up a rivalry between Lauren and his old girlfriend. What a relief it would have been for Mark to feel himself the object of a romantic rivalry between two desirable women— rather than a child with his mother or a man about to be rejected by his lover.

As a reversal of the Oedipal rivalry, the reverse triangle is a defense against all the anxieties of Oedipal refinding. Perhaps most particularly, it is a defense against the humbling scenario of Oedipal defeat. Instead of feeling like the loser, the reverse triangle enables us to feel twice the winner—for two rivals now compete for our love. But the reverse triangle is also a defense against the refinding of Oedipal victory: to the extent that we are torn by the choice between two lovers, we are fully involved with neither. In this way the reverse triangle dilutes intimacy, just as the rivalrous triangle does. The difference, usually, is that the reverse triangle is more likely to bolster our self-esteem.

An important variation of the reverse triangle is the "split-object" triangle. This is the defensive solution for someone who is too frightened to experience a "whole" relationship with one person. Consequently, the whole is split in two: usually, then, sexuality is experienced with one partner and nurturing affection with the other. Like most romantic triangles, the split-object triangle is a defense against problematic refinding.

Whether we defend against refinding or use refinding as a defense, this capacity can be so influenced by our self-protective needs that instead of deepening love, refinding restricts it. Then the music of our relationships can begin to sound repetitive, as if the same songs were playing over and over, with only minor changes in instrumentation. It is crucial to assess whether we are trading the possibility of a passionate, tender, and lasting love for the limited rewards of psychological safety.

REFINDING AND THE INTERACTION OF DEFENSES

The fate of our relationship hinges on how our refinding—and our defenses against refinding—interact with those of our partner. In collusion with our partner, we may keep the most problematic aspects of refinding at bay but limit the intimacy and personal growth that our relationship can make possible. If and when we find ourselves in collision with our partner, some of the most painful aspects of the past are likely to be refound. In the worst case, this difficult refinding can make the relationship unlivable; in the best case, collision sets the stage for collaboration. If collusions involving refinding allow us to avoid the problems of our past, collisions compel us to relive them. Both ensure that our energies in love are largely absorbed in keeping the past in place. Only collaboration can enable us to work through these problems, diminishing their destructive impact and permitting love to deepen.

Collusions That Defend against Refinding

These collusions are the norm during the first phase of a relationship. Two partners who are falling in love usually banish the ghosts of the painful past by focusing on the pleasures of sexuality, closeness, and idealization. Later, when they are becoming a couple, partners can continue to defend against refinding by colluding to minimize intimacy—like a workaholic pair who spend the vast proportion of their waking hours absorbed in careers that keep them apart. For some partners this way of life is chosen for its own rewards. For others it is a choice based on the defensive need to avoid the refinding that comes with deeper involvement.

Collusions Based on Refinding as a Defense

Often, especially early in a relationship, we collude with our partner to refind exclusively those aspects of our respective pasts that are pleasurable. Lauren was happy for Mark's admiration of her for qualities she possessed that were reminiscent of his mother. Meanwhile, Mark played to Lauren's appreciation of his strengths, which reminded her of her father. Simultaneously, Mark and Lauren both ignored in the other traits that might remind them of difficulties in their past relationships. To complete the collusion, they also managed to hide from each other aspects of themselves that could conceivably evoke the painful past.

As intimacy deepens, such collusions become more difficult to sustain. What we may previously have concealed (by tacit agreement with our partner) now emerges as a source of conflict and tension. One partner may refuse to play his or her part as it was written, so to speak, by the other.

Recall Adam and Rachel again. When Adam revealed the depth of his vulnerability to Rachel, her sexual interest in him vanished. Adam had breached an unspoken covenant that lay at the foundation of their first falling in love. To help her defend against the painful refinding of her needy mother, Adam had been assigned to play the role of the "strong, sensitive" type: an up-to-date version of Rachel's powerful father. When Adam ceased to collude, he became in Rachel's eyes not her ambivalently loved father but her mother, a woman with no cachet whatsoever.

Our collusions can break down when we realize that our partner lacks qualities that are central to our refinding of the pleasurable past. Then there is danger that the problematic past may come rushing into our relationship. Disappointed and probably fearful, we may then complain, like Rachel, or we may try to change our partner, who winds up feeling criticized, hurt, and/or angry. In this way our collusion to avoid the past can quickly become a collision.

Defensive Collisions and Refinding

Our collisions with our partner are always painful, but they can reveal two interlocking dramas. We assign roles to our partner, while our partner in turn assigns roles to us. In the heat of collision, one partner may find himself protesting, "But I'm not your father!" while the other partner cries despairingly, "And I'm not your mother!" Of course, this scenario is an oversimplification, but it suggests how two partners simultaneously attempt to impose their internal images upon one another, and how this can lead to conflict.

Unconsciously, for the most part, each of us is the director of our own drama of refinding, and each of us tries to shape the performance of our partner. In this light, the complaint that "You're not the man/woman you said you were" can be reinterpreted to mean, "You're not playing your role as I imagined and expected you would." Projective identification, which was discussed in Chapter Four, is the primary defense that enables us to enlist our partner in playing the roles called for in our drama of refinding.

Through projective identification we unconsciously encourage our partner to identify with the internal image that we are projecting. Mark, for example, treated Lauren in such a way that she gradually came to identify with his image of his mother. In Mark's version his mother was a woman with no respect for his boundaries: she was contrary, controlling, and intrusive. Through various means Mark succeeded in eliciting from Lauren an aspect of her personality that duplicated his mother's. By acting at times as though he couldn't tolerate Lauren's independence, Mark evoked an angry contrariness from her which he could associate with his mother. He also led Lauren to believe that their shared life together would be chaotic unless she helped him get things organized. When she responded to this invitation to take a hand in his affairs, however, Mark accused her of being intrusive—exactly as his mother had been.

Like Mark, most of us unconsciously influence our partner's "performance" so that it conforms to our imagery of past intimacy. But as we play out the drama of refinding, there is always a "directorial tension" between our desires to re-create the familiar past and to master it. When our present relationship repeats the past, it can be exasperating but also strangely satisfying. And when something new occurs that represents a departure from the past, it can be a refreshing relief, but a little disorienting at the same time.

Mark and Lauren were aware of this tension in their relationship. Both of them knew that they had the potential as a couple either to repeat the past or to experience something new. The defensive collision that was nearly their undoing came about when their respective refinding dramas seemed to interlock and escalate. From Mark's perspective, he was battling with Lauren to ensure that he wouldn't suffer her controlling him as his mother had. From Lauren's perspective, she was battling with Mark to ensure that she wouldn't be victimized again by a self-absorbed and dominating man like her father. Each partner blamed the other, while minimizing personal responsibility for the conflict between them. Each fought for vindication, as if in a court of law.

Of course, love is never a trial in which one is found innocent and the other guilty. But we often act as if it were. Collision with our partner can leave us feeling that we're in a fight for our emotional lives. Eventually, in exhaustion and despair, we may call a truce, only to find ourselves colliding again a short time later. If there's an advantage to this painful repetition, it's that we gradually become clearer about the pattern of collision in which we're involved. Once we do so, we have three alternatives: The first two involve new versions of defensive collusion; the third is collaboration.

Collusion Revisited: Refinding as a Defense against Change

We can choose to look at collisions as an inevitable consequence of intimacy, a limitation that is simply built into relationships. We may say, in effect, "This is the cost of being close. There will always be fights, struggles, and misunderstandings." Through a combination of realism and resignation, we may come to accept that many of our desires will be unsatisfied. We may tell ourselves that we have a "good enough" relationship, troubled in the same way as everyone else's. But our aspirations for a more fulfilling love will have been surrendered to painful refinding and the belief that the present cannot possibly be better than the past.

Collusion Revisited: Defending against Refinding

Exhausted by the fight and getting nowhere, we may tacitly opt for distance rather than intimacy. By diminishing the emotional intensity of our involvement, we can push refinding into the background. Essentially, we are trying to remake a collusion of avoidance, of the sort that first helped us fall in love. Unfortunately, the intensely positive feelings that made the original collusion possible are now less accessible. Nonetheless, we can often create a semblance of intimacy that both stabilizes our relationship and minimizes the most problematic aspects of refinding. In exchange for a fulfilling relationship, we will have chosen one that is secure. At its best such a relationship can be companionable and warm. At its worst this is a marriage of convenience, with none of the pleasure or depth of feeling that motivated our romance in the first place.

Collaboration and Refinding

Collusions hide the intrusion of the past into the present. Because collisions have the troubling potential to strip away the veil, they present us with an opportunity to grapple with refinding. Without collaboration, however, the unwelcome past we refind is only repeated; it is never mastered.

Recognizing Our Own Defenses

Paradoxically, we set the stage for collaboration by shifting our focus from the couple to the individual. Collaboration is largely effective to the extent that, as individuals, we become aware of how we protect ourselves. Understanding (and diminishing) the impact of refinding on our current relationship absolutely depends upon this, for so long as we remain in the dark about our own defenses, they will continue to shape our relationship, as we either re-create the past or avoid it.

Often, to become aware of the role of our defenses, we must declare a truce, giving each partner the chance to consider his or her part in the collision. During Lauren's absence, Mark saw how easily (and with what relief) he could assign blame to his partner. He became aware that his insistence that Lauren return to therapy was a defensively disguised reflection of his own need. This awareness both propelled him into therapy and enabled him to become more reflective, less impulsively reactive, in his relationship with Lauren.

Obviously, one such step does not complete a journey. Our habits of self-protection are deeply ingrained. In one interaction we may demonstrate impressive understanding and restraint in relation to a defense. In another we may use the defense so unconsciously that its origins (in our needs for self-protection) are invisible. Our capacity to first understand and then manage our defenses exists on a continuum, from active awareness that enables us to acknowledge them, to reactive obliviousness that permits us only to act them out.

The Continuum of Awareness

The greater our awareness of our defenses, the more likely we are to reflect on our own role in creating the problems we complain about in our relationship. We're more inclined to consider the possible disparity between our first impressions and what we might see at second glance. First impressions usually reflect a view of the relationship in keeping with the imagery of our inner map. Taking a second look often reveals the impact of the past and the influence of our needs for self-protection. In the short run this kind of awareness can evoke anxiety, for it heightens our uncertainty about our perceptions. In addition, to the extent that we acknowledge what we know to our partner, we let ourselves be seen as the psychologically complicated and fallible beings we really are, which can leave us feeling vulnerable. In exchange for these short-term liabilities, the long-term reward is a greater likelihood that our relationship will be lasting and fulfilling.

When we're caught at the unconscious end of the continuum, our defenses can dominate us. Acting on impulse, pushed around by our feelings, we are likely to repeat self-defeating patterns in love. Taking our first impressions at face value, we may assume that our relationship with our partner and the emotional reality represented by our inner map are one and the same. This assumption leaves us trapped in the past.

The Benefit of a Truce

When a couple can interrupt their collision with a truce, as Mark and Lauren did, they often have room to become aware of their individual contributions to the conflict. Ideally, both partners can then acknowledge to each other what they know about their own role in the collision. The first order of business should be to clarify the experience of both partners, in as much detail as possible. To the extent that each partner can actively empathize with the experience of the other, the likelihood is enhanced that the couple's collision will be understood. Usually this understanding reveals the impact of the partners' defenses. Assuming that clarification and empathy have largely replaced the automatic defensiveness that led to the collision, we also want to understand the refinding that triggered the conflict in the first place.

Candidly exploring the impact of our images of the past on the present requires still more trust in our partner. The risk in this exploration is that what we reveal may later be used against us: "Aha! I get it: you're neurotically confusing me with your father again. . . ." If partners can agree in advance to refrain from this kind of misuse of what they learn about each other, the exploration of refinding can occur much more freely. In the absence of such an agreement, candor can feel unsafe—and a couple (without the help of a therapist) may conceivably be better off refraining from this exploration of the past.

Awareness and Change

To free ourselves from the constraints of painful refinding requires both awareness and a willingness to change. We must ask some difficult questions: Who are the figures from the past whose images we superimpose on our partner? Who are the figures from the past whose images have become blended with our images of ourselves? What beliefs and behaviors derive from these old images? What relationships from the past are we re-creating in the present?

Changing can be even more difficult. For a variety of reasons, we are usually very attached to the images that connect us to the world of our past loves. Without some willingness to change the beliefs and behaviors that flow from these images, our current love relationship will remain problematic.

Refinding both reflects and generates deeply held beliefs about intimacy. Refinding his mother in Lauren, for example, led Mark to believe that Lauren would be out to control him. Mark's underlying belief, derived from his childhood experience, was that women wish to control men. When, like Mark, we cease to take these beliefs entirely at face value, we can subject them to a new scrutiny, assessing their accuracy in the context of our current love relationship. Sometimes we find a particular belief doesn't hold up; it's simply contradicted by the "facts" of the current relationship. Sometimes we discover that the price for maintaining a belief is far greater than the payoff. All this may be enough to persuade us to change the belief. Once we are willing to do so— or at least experiment with doing so—the effects on our relationship can be profound. Changing our beliefs is tantamount to redrawing the inner map that defines what is possible in love. When we allow new experience to modify our images of our partner and ourselves, we begin to liberate our love in the present from the confines of the past.

In her collaboration with Mark, Lauren revealed both the awareness and the willingness to change that make this process of liberation possible. She believed that her romantic relationships had all been dominated by her conviction that she could never prevail in the face of strong-willed, intelligent men. This belief, a consequence of her experience with her loved but domineering father, had generated a very ambivalent attitude. The wish to refind her father's love led her to seek out men very much like him. But once she was involved with such a man, her fear of refinding her father's dominance led her to keep her distance. By the time she became involved with Mark, however, Lauren was aware of the price she paid for her belief. So long as she assumed that her only possible fate with a man was to be distant or to be dominated, no relationship could last. She knew she had a stake in challenging her own belief, but she wasn't sure how she should go about it.

Like many couples who wish to grapple with the impact of refinding, Lauren and Mark had a hard time agreeing on what was being refound: Was she superimposing the image of her domineering father on Mark—or was Mark simply a domineering man? Was Mark superimposing the image of his smothering mother on Lauren—or was Lauren simply a woman who had to control every detail of her partner's life?

Unavoidably affected by our own defenses, each of us would usually prefer to believe that we are seeing our partner accurately, while our partner's view of us is distorted by the past. Even when both partners acknowledge the inevitability of refinding, it can be difficult to take the risk of revealing what we know about our *own* refinding.

When one partner knows more about himself or herself, it may be possible for this partner (along the lines of "one leads, one follows") to take the first steps. One partner's courage here can be enough to *begin* to break the hold of refinding on the couple's interaction. To enlist the other partner's collaboration, we can (ideally) confide a number of things, beginning with what we know about the beliefs that refinding has generated—beliefs about our partner, our relationship, and ourselves. What can be still more helpful (if we have this knowledge) is to communicate how we have been influencing our partner so that he or she behaves in ways that are consistent with these beliefs.

For Lauren, this meant confiding to Mark that her choice of men had always been dominated by her ambivalent feelings toward her father. She had been drawn to her father's power but put off by his egocentric control; and this ambivalent conflict repeated itself in her attitude toward the powerful, somewhat controlling men she chose to be close to. She also let Mark know that without always being aware of it at the time, she behaved with him in ways that elicited exactly the stubborn control she found so intolerable. Part of her difficulty, she admitted, was that her parents' marriage, in which her mother had always acquiesced to her father, gave her a model of interaction between men and women that left her ill equipped to really stand up to Mark. This explained her inclination to withdraw from him, up to and including her suggestion that perhaps the two of them should separate.

Lauren was aware that her choice to be with Mark was a choice to grapple with the unfinished issues in her relationship with her father. She was also aware that her relationship with Mark was doomed if she only repeated with him what she had experienced with her father. With this motivating her, Lauren was able to *use* refinding, rather than be dominated by it. In communicating what she knew to Mark, she expressed her willingness to question her beliefs and to change. As it happened, the very act of communicating with such candor and clarity challenged her old belief by enabling her to feel both powerful in relation to Mark and close to him. In addition, her candor was an invitation to Mark to respond in kind.

Collaborating with our partner to understand the painful effects of refinding can be daunting, and so it's not surprising that many individuals and couples seek out psychotherapy as a source of consultation and support. With a therapist's help, it is often easier for couples to listen empathically to their dissonant versions of refinding and to move toward a view they share. This may mean that a couple will "rewrite the narrative" of their individual and shared pasts. For example, if a man has decided that his mate is exactly like his mother, psychotherapy can help him separate the truth from the distortion in his assessment. In the process, he may develop not only a different view of his wife but also a different view of his mother—and of himself. With the help of a neutral party, exploring the relation between past and present can result in an alteration of the internal imagery that we refind in our intimate relationships.

We will never fully know the "real past," but we can develop an understanding of our history, a version of our past, that seems both more useful to us and true.

In the everyday life of most couples, collaboration to resolve refinding is an ideal, a level of communication to be sought but not always achieved. In dealing with the collisions refinding provokes, we sometimes collaborate—but often we're either drawn irresistibly into the old dramas or we deliberately keep our distance from them. Not uncommonly, we cycle through all three of these responses trying to work our way through a single conflict. Whenever we can summon the courage, initiative, and patience that collaboration requires, this ability will be strengthened. Then, with perseverance and goodwill, we can often diminish the damaging impact of parts of the past on our present capacity to love.

SELF-APPRAISAL: THREE PROFILES

Eliot: Refinding as a Resource

Married for six years and the owners of a small landscaping business, Eliot and his wife, Amy, have just adopted their second child. Eliot himself was the middle child of seven, and the oldest boy. Marrying when he was not quite thirty, Eliot was happily convinced that, like his parents, he too would have a large family. Three years later, when it began to seem likely that his wife would never bear a child, Eliot found himself in turmoil.

His mother had been a calm and loving but somewhat aloof woman. Whether it was her personality or the claims on her attention of seven children, Eliot felt that she had never been able to give him as much of herself as he needed. All the same, he knew that she cared for him unconditionally. Eliot's father, whom he deeply loved, was a pediatrician. Their best times together were spent fishing at a lake where the family rented a large cabin during the summer. Warm and generous, possibly to a fault, his father was often exhausted by his work. Eliot remembers him dozing off in his big living-room chair, and occasionally falling asleep at dinner. For years, Eliot couldn't help holding it against his father that he seemingly gave the best of himself to other people's children rather than his own.

When Eliot was twelve, and away at camp, his father died suddenly of a heart attack. Eliot returned home, where he remembers feeling alternately comforted by, and comforting to, his mother. In the months and years following his father's death, Eliot grew much closer to his mother, although sometimes, as the new "man" of the family, he felt burdened by the need to take care of her.

For most of his twenties, Eliot had been unwilling to settle down with a woman for any length of time. He had several girlfriends he cared deeply for, but he'd always been frustrated with the feeling that something important was missing. When he met Amy, Eliot felt that he was finally home. She was calm and loving, quietly confident about her opinions and impressively bright. Eliot found her compelling. Talking to her, he felt alive and engaged. Amy, too, had come from a large family. Their backgrounds were similar and he found the very familiarity of her somehow stirring. A year after they met, they married.

The longer they were together, the more Eliot recognized in Amy a quality he'd admired in his mother. Amy was self-contained: she seemed to have a world inside that sustained her. But like his mother, she also seemed a little removed. Sometimes her aloofness frustrated him; sometimes it gave him a bittersweet taste of his own past. As time went on, however, Amy became less reserved, and Eliot could more easily draw her out.

When it became clear that Amy could not bear children, Eliot was overwhelmed with contradictory emotions. He had always hoped that with his own children he might improve on the experience he'd had with his parents, drawing on their strengths but making up for their shortcomings. As he felt these hopes shrivel, he couldn't help blaming Amy: like his mother and father, she couldn't give as much as he needed. But he also felt a surge of sympathy and concern for her that brought tears to his eyes. She had wanted her own children just as much as he had, and she was grieving. Thinking of Amy, of himself, and especially of his father, Eliot realized with clarity and relief that adopting children would not be a terrible compromise of their dreams, but another way of living them out.

In Amy, Eliot refound what was positive and mastered what was problematic about his relationship with his mother. In grappling with his own frustrated wish to improve on the past, Eliot also refound an aspect of his father, whose impartial generosity let him give himself to other people's children. In choosing to adopt, Eliot both reconciled with his father and made his father's generosity his own.

Maureen: Refinding That Is Compromised

Maureen has been married for more than twenty years to a minister-turned-psychologist. When they met, she was a critical-care nurse and Tom was visiting a member of his congregation on the unit where Maureen worked. She immediately took to him: more than his his obvious kindness, his good looks and way with words gave him a quiet charisma. Although the passion quickly went out of their marriage, Maureen was so absorbed in raising their only child that, until recently, she very rarely felt discontent. Now that their son is in high school, requiring less of her attention, she has become increasingly aware of the frustration she experiences with her husband. But what she sees as Tom's vulnerability makes her so protective toward him that she hides her discontent.

Maureen's parents had the most traditional of marriages. Her mother was a gentle, nurturing woman whose energies were entirely absorbed in caring for her husband and family. Maureen, as the only daughter among four children, shared a special closeness with her mother—but her feeling was one of appreciation rather than admiration. In contrast to her father, an eminent and compelling professor of theology, her mother always seemed tentative and unsure of herself. Maureen had the feeling that her mother put the needs of others first because she felt less deserving than others.

Maureen's father was the sun around which everything seemed to orbit. She thought of him as a scholar/hero, disappearing into his study to write or holding court for students and peers who seemed in awe of him. She remembers as a teenager feeling both thrilled and uneasy to hear from her mother that the only photo her father carried in his wallet was one of Maureen. When he woke her early in the morning to walk with him while her mother was still asleep, Maureen felt vaguely worried that this important time alone with her father was somehow wrong. She thought he was uncomfortable with it as well: either he acted as though he was trying to keep it a secret or he broadcast it as if there was nothing to hide.

Maureen remembers her feelings for her husband changing shortly after they were married. Originally, she now recognizes, it was the qualities that Tom shared with her father that had drawn her to him: the fact that he was eloquent, authoritative, the leader of a congregation. Like her father, at times, Tom seemed capable of focusing all his energy on her, and this exclusive attention was exciting and seductive. Once they married, however, Maureen became aware of her husband's insecurity. She wondered if she had only imagined the aura of charisma around him. She began to believe that Tom devoted himself to others out of a feeling that he was somehow undeserving. She became resigned to the idea that rather than finding a man with the strengths of her father, she had instead joined her life with that of someone whose vulnerabilities reminded her of her mother. As Maureen's involvement with her son waned, her resignation about her husband's shortcomings turned into depression.

Outside her direct awareness, Maureen's marriage had been compromised by the guilt of refinding her father in her relationship with her husband. Her "solution" to this conflict was to exaggerate the significance of Tom's weaknesses by associating them with her mother's perceived shortcomings. Maureen's capacity to love was inhibited by her use of refinding as a defense.

Beverly: Refinding as a Struggle

At forty, Beverly is frustrated by her difficulty in making a relationship work. A strikingly attractive and markedly overweight woman, she has never lived with a man for longer than a year. She has several close women friends, all faculty members at the middle school where she teaches art. But she feels she has spent her life essentially alone. Never having expected to reach forty without a child and a husband, Beverly continues to look for a "decent" relationship with a man, while feeling increasingly pessimistic. She meets men through the personal ads, for the most part. Though she suspects it has something to do with her father, she can't understand why the handful of men she has become involved with have all turned out to be both dependent and unreliable.

Beverly's father was a frustrated, remote, and unsuccessful filmmaker who had been alcoholic from the time she was a child. Her mother eventually divorced him, but the three of them continued to live under one roof. The relationship between her parents was alternately distant and tempestuous. Her mother was essentially the family's sole provider. Beverly admired her mother's strength and resourcefulness but felt sorry for her. As a child, Beverly very much wanted to be close to her, but her mother seemed too preoccupied to give her the attention she longed for. She also craved her father's love, but she felt she had to keep her eyes closed; otherwise she couldn't help regarding him partly as an embarrassment. Her love for him confused her: the feelings of intense longing, pity, and angry contempt were impossible for her to disentangle.

Her confusion notwithstanding, Beverly knows that she has been on guard against men like her father all her life. This vigilance makes it difficult for her to understand how she winds up with the men she does. The one with whom she lasted the longest was an attorney, apparently solid and solvent. He was nothing like her father—or at least he shared none of her father's most disastrous shortcomings. Like her father, however, he had creative aspirations, and this appealed to her. His desire to write fiction about the criminal law he practiced led him to spend a great deal of time researching the milieu in which his clients lived: racetracks, casinos, poker parlors. Before long Beverly realized that he was as addicted to gambling as her father had been to alcohol. This addiction explained his mood swings and his recurrent unavailability, but her awareness of it devastated her. She had become deeply attached to him. She didn't want to believe that their relationship could duplicate her parents'. It took half a year more (and his bankruptcy) to convince her she had to leave.

Beverly suspects that her weight and her overeating are related to her unhappy experiences with men. She guesses that the weight keeps men away and that food is solace when she feels lonely. Lately she has become so mistrustful of her ability to choose a man that it almost seems safer to protect and succor herself. But she can't stand the thought of spending the rest of her life alone, so she keeps looking.

It appears that Beverly's profound ambivalence about refinding her father has led her to play out two equally problematic alternatives. Either she finds men who are too much like her father and relives her early experience without mastering it—or she avoids men altogether.

CHAPTER SIX

The Capacity for Self-Transcendence

A good marriage is that in which
each appoints the other guardian of
his solitude.
—Rainer Maria Rilke

I am not thine. I am a part of *thee*.
—Percy Bysshe Shelley

*W*hen our psychological foundations are solid, self-transcendence can expand our sense of self and liberate us from what Aldous Huxley calls "that tiny island universe, within which every individual finds himself confined." At the deepest levels, self-transcendence in love transforms our feelings about who we are, adding to "I" the experience of "we." This is a profound alteration in the inner map that changes both the boundary between self and other, and the image of the self, as it has for Helen (see Chapter Four):

After you've been married for a while you have a sort of double identity. There's me, of course, but there's also an "us" which feels very different from just "me and Leonard." There's this other identity that's the two of us, and in the basement of my soul, I know I'm more willing to do things for Leonard

I might not otherwise want to do, because of the "us"...Deeply accepting that there's somebody else who's part of you makes you grow—you have to, to keep on valuing someone who's different from you but whose reality you welcome and nurture as much as your own.

The feeling Helen describes, that "there's somebody else who's part of you," is a direct consequence—and a reward—of the healthy exercise of the capacity for self-transcendence. The same feeling can be associated with both self-enhancement (it "makes you grow") and self-sacrifice ("I'm more willing to do things for Leonard I might not otherwise want to do, because of the 'us' ").

Self-transcendence affects us, and potentially transforms us, through the twin processes of empathy and identification. When they are fully developed, empathy and identification enable us to put our partner's needs on a par with our own—and at times to feel one with our partner.

EMPATHY: FEELING *WITH* OUR PARTNER

Empathizing in an ongoing way with our partner's subjective experience gives us a vantage point that we lack when we're alone. While letting us see through our partner's eyes as well as our own, empathy also gives us access to our partner's private inner world. Thus we see and feel what would otherwise have been invisible and inaccessible to us. Empathy with our partner encourages compassion and helps us transcend the confining boundaries of our own subjectivity.

IDENTIFICATION: BECOMING *LIKE* OUR PARTNER

While empathy enlarges our moment-to-moment experience, the process of identification can permanently change us. Judith, a twice-married psychologist and mother in her late forties, describes this process of change in herself:

The other day I was comparing Jake with my first husband, Bobby, and how I was with the two of them. . .I realized that with Jake I've discovered this freedom to take chances and bet on myself, to take steps forward even if I don't quite know whether I'm capable of them. And this is very much a function of Jake. It's not the same as learning from him. I mean, you can pick and choose what you most love about someone and try to make that part of yourself, but what I'm talking about is much deeper. I saw this new part of myself, this freedom to be bolder, and it just dawned on me: *I* didn't use to do that, this is Jake!. . .It's amazing to me at this age how you can just keep on developing. It doesn't seem to stop.

Judith's language ("I saw this new part of myself. . .and it just dawned on me. . .this is Jake!") reflects precisely the means by which identification with our partner changes us. When we identify, we take in (internalize) an attitude, ability, or perspective that is our partner's—and we make it a part of ourselves. Thus, identification is an aspect of self-transcendence that transforms and enlarges us. It is often, though not always, an unconscious process, and generally it occurs over a lengthy period of time. Identification may be the key psychological mechanism through which, at the deepest levels, we continue to grow as adults.

Outside our awareness, the wish to be transformed through identifications with our partner is one of the most powerful sources of our original attraction. We often have an intuition about possibilities in ourselves that have been stifled, important abilities or qualities of character that we've never been able to develop. When we sense the presence of these nascent qualities of ours in a potential partner who has developed them more fully, it can be very alluring. For we have the instinctive awareness that, through identification, we could make these qualities our own.

Brenda, a professor of literature in her late thirties, describes the unfolding of this process in her relationship with her partner:

When Linda and I first got together I was very much aware of her ability to express her anger. It impressed me and scared me both. I hated it when she was angry at *me*, but I could see that there was a kind of power there that I lacked. I was too damn contained...I knew that about myself...I couldn't be any other way. Most of the time I didn't even *know* that I was angry, I just got sort of depressed....Linda was the opposite, sort of volcanic...she couldn't contain her anger even when she wanted to...She was too angry and I was too "unangry." Looking backward, it's obvious to me that part of my attraction to her was this anger she could express. But as time's gone on I've gotten better at being like her and now she's more like me. She's less angry and more contained and I'm less contained and more angry. Basically, we're more similar now.

Over time, as Brenda's account suggests, our identifications with our partner change us. The process, however, is two-sided: our partner, through identifying with us, is also changed. Mutual identifications transform us as individuals and transform the identity of the couple. As partners transcend their individual boundaries of the self, the area of their "overlap" and similarity tends to grow. Self-transcendence gradually diminishes the polarization between two partners, remaking their inner maps, so that more and more, they come to coincide.

SELF-TRANSCENDENCE AND "CO-CREATION"

Through empathy and identification, the capacity for self-transcendence transforms our internal experience and alters our identity. In addition to these psychological changes, however, self-transcendence changes what we do. To the extent that two partners in a couple strongly experience themselves as "we," they often have a desire to create something together in the world. Just as most of us desire to realize our creative potential as individuals, we may wish to realize our creative potential as partners. Often this desire for "co-creation" leads a couple to conceive and raise a child, but the shared project we choose can take many forms.

For Alex, a veterinarian, the project of co-creation with his second wife is a farm:

> There's something natural about doing a project together. Across species, males and females, creatures in general share tasks for a common purpose. It's part of the nature of union, why people get together. . . . if lives are tangential, if people just get together for dinner, to me that's aberrant. . .The project is the current "live" thing. . .For us, it's the farm.

Self-transcendence "gives birth" to collaborative efforts that often go beyond the individual capabilities of one partner or the other. This collaboration reflects our shared values and dreams as a couple. Sometimes it involves a commitment less to a project than to a practice, such as following a spiritual path or engaging passionately in joint political activism.

In many modern marriages, partners, living parallel lives, do relatively little in collaboration. The shared commitment, project or practice, can both anchor and invigorate an intimate relationship; it may even be vital for the health of that relationship. Listen again to Judith, the psychologist:

> Jake and I had to find a way to be *partners* together. Both of us have been married before and we knew that the "relationship" alone wouldn't do it. This isn't the only reason we wanted a child, but it's one of the big ones. If it hadn't been a child, it would have been something else. Part of my greatest joy is watching Jake as a father, but if it hadn't been as Ellie's father, it would have to be as the father of something else. It's a funny word to use, but there's this reflected glory in watching someone you love participating with you in something you both love.
>
> I'm sure this is part of what sustains us when our interactions start to get too complicated at the "who took out the garbage" level. . .You've got this larger thing to keep you on track, and remind you what you're doing, what's really important.

The jointly created project or practice has a two-way relationship to the capacity for self-transcendence. On the one hand, the couple's urge to generate something together in the world is an outgrowth of this capacity. Our desire for co-creation reflects the longing to express ourselves *as a couple*, to make good the promise that in a relationship the whole is greater than the sum of the parts. On the other hand, our collaborative efforts as a couple also provide a setting in which our capacity for self-transcendence can be strengthened. By generating a context in which we "overlap" as partners, the process of joint creation multiplies our opportunities for empathy and identification, and profoundly deepens the shared feeling of "we."

SELF-TRANSCENDENCE AND EROTIC INVOLVEMENT

Self-transcendence enables partners to cross the boundaries that keep them separate. For many of us, it is our sexual encounters with our partner that allow us most readily to transcend the limits of our psychological separateness. To make a bridge between two solitudes, we use our bodies.

Having sex per se has relatively little to do with self-transcendence. By contrast, making love with our partner, over and over again in the course of a sustained involvement, makes possible profound experiences of empathy, identification, and oneness. When sexuality becomes a way to express self-transcendence and our bodies bridge our separateness, then we can "feel along with" our partner. Our hearts open and the walls come down. We can be equally and simultaneously aware of our emotion and our partner's emotion, our touch and our partner's sensation in response to that touch. The heightening of mutual sensitivity in these transcendent erotic encounters is such that the two partners' separate experiences seem to become one.

In pleasing our partner, we please ourselves, which pleases our partner, and so on. "Sex feels better to me when it feels better to my wife. It also feels better to my wife when it feels better to me" is the way one man put it. To clarify this point through a contrast, consider the experience of another man, who said, "I don't like to come at the same time as my girlfriend, because then I can't pay as much attention to myself."

Sexuality can be a key context within which partners solidify their sense of shared identity. Erotic involvement deepens the feeling of "we" in several ways. Partly it is a matter of intention: Some of us think of the long-term emotional commitment we've made to our partner as, additionally, a pledge to a partnership of sexual pleasure. The feeling of safety that comes with commitment can also facilitate sexual flexibility and openness. With the freedom to experiment, partners can develop a sexual history and identity that is very much their own. Here's one woman's version of this development:

After the years of being together, the time-after-time of it, there's the strange awareness of being both in the moment and having a whole film library of resonant images and memories. It's kind of a giggle...Being pretty experimental, I think there's been a lot of stuff in bed that neither of us expected to do or feel...We've broken out of our childhood stereotypes together...which is part of the bond between us at this stage. It's not a question of good sex or bad sex, it's just part of our life...it's only bad if it goes out of our life...

As this account suggests, there can be a synergistic, upwardly spiraling relationship between commitment, sexual flexibility, and self-transcendence. Feeling secure in our commitment permits a more complete expression and exploration of our sexuality. And this fosters, in turn, a heightened empathy and identification with our partner. This kind of upward spiral means that contrary to the conventional wisdom—that erotic interest always wanes over time—sexual passion actually has the potential to become more fulfilling as a relationship matures.

WHAT MAKES SELF-TRANSCENDENCE POSSIBLE?

Whether we can make use of this capacity depends, not surprisingly, on both individual and interpersonal factors.

Separateness and Self-Transcendence

To transcend our individuality, we must possess a solid sense of self, as reflected in our ability both to tolerate separateness and to enjoy our closeness to another person. If being alone is bearable and being intimate is no serious threat to our autonomy or identity, then we are capable of temporarily dissolving the boundaries that separate us from our partner. With a secure feeling of "I," the new experience of "we" can expand and enhance our sense of self.

The paradox of self-transcendence is that without a separate sense of self, there can be no transcendence, but only surrender or submission. Without a separate identity, we may become a slave to our partner, or a burden, or a nonentity. Recall that we transcend the boundaries of the self through empathizing and identifying with our partner. If we are without a separate sense of self, there is no distinct, independent subjectivity with which our partner can empathize or identify. In surrendering or submitting, we deprive our partner of ourselves—and of the opportunity for self-transcendence.

Each of the capacities in love is influenced by the others, but self-transcendence uniquely rests on our relative mastery of all five prior capacities. More than any of the other capacities, self-transcendence expresses a synthesis of our abilities and reflects our overall capacity to love. Our strengths in the earlier capacities all support self-transcendence in different ways. The capacity for erotic involvement contributes to self-transcendence a pleasure in physical closeness and the ability to slide across boundaries in the context of sexuality. Merging adds the permeability of boundaries that is crucial to self-transcendence. Idealization contributes the basic desire to empathize and, particularly, to identify with our partner. Integration enables us to accept our own imperfections and those of our partner, thus preserving the desire to identify. Lastly, healthy refinding furthers self-transcendence because it promotes our desire to revive or create with our partner a new "family feeling."

Self-Transcendence, Commitment, and the Third Stage of Intimacy

Only when we've emerged from the second stage of intimacy are we in a secure position to mobilize the capacity for self-transcendence. Until this second stage is concluded, we are still grappling with our uncertainties about commitment. When our grasp on integration is solid, however, and when the most pressing conflicts of refinding have been recognized and understood (if not resolved), then we can say that we have finally "become a couple." With the issue of commitment settled, we experience a heightened feeling of security and involvement during the third stage of intimacy. Often, couples experience the beginning of this period as a "honeymoon." There is a revival of the intense feelings we first knew when we were falling in love. Once again, the relationship can have a "dream-come-true" quality. Sometimes this stage of a relationship is initiated by the decision to marry or by marriage itself, sometimes by pregnancy or the birth of a child. At other times, it is a crisis such as the death of a parent that crystallizes our awareness of the depth of our commitment.

Whatever the catalyst, several factors can now converge to activate our capacity for self-transcendence. Primary among these are a solid sense of self in each partner, a good-enough grasp on the five earlier capacities, and the security, longevity, and multidimensionality of a deeply committed relationship. In addition, each partner needs a willingness to be profoundly involved with and influenced by the other. The psychological "overlap" that self-transcendence entails virtually guarantees that each partner's inner world will be profoundly affected, if not transformed, by the other. Not uncommonly, one or both partners question whether this will be a change for the better or the worse.

SELF-TRANSCENDENCE:
SELF-ENHANCEMENT OR SELF-SACRIFICE?

Consider the experience of raising children. By no means the only setting in which the capacity for self-transcendence plays a vital role, it is certainly a vivid one. In large part, the strength or vulnerability of this capacity determines whether the experience of having children feels more like an enhancement of the self or a sacrifice. Listen to two points of view that represent opposite ends of a continuum. The first is expressed by a mother of two children, a social worker in her early thirties:

> When you have kids, you can't do everything you want to do, you put someone else's needs first...But I don't feel this as a loss. At worst, it's a postponement. There's so much more that you get in return. When Jenny was born I said to myself, I'm not going to wish for her to grow up faster, even though things get frustrating and hard...And it's been easy to stay with that because being with her, and watching her, and seeing Jack be a father is so amazingly satisfying...You change your priorities and expectations...If you're going to try and be the same person you were before becoming a parent you're gonna be resentful and sad...but if you know you're creating something bigger, it's remarkable and wonderful. It's way beyond anything that's gone on for me before...

A different viewpoint is that of a former dancer, also in her early thirties, a mother with one child:

> I love my child, but as soon as he was born, I felt like my own life was over. My pregnancy took my body and I've never gotten it back. Dance was the most important thing to me before I married Nathan. Now I have my marriage and my son, but the thing that gave my life its specialness, what I had that was unique that I could contribute as a person, I've lost that...it's gone. I know I had something to give, through my dancing...and now I'll never be able to do that. I can choreograph and I can teach—I'm doing those things now,

but it's not the same...that's other people dancing. I feel about my life that the climax has already come...and that's too soon.

A love relationship invariably involves compromise; because all of us are different, the compromises we make will be different. Nonetheless, the way we *experience* our compromises—as trade-offs that benefit us or losses that deplete us—depends largely on our capacity for self-transcendence. The social worker's experience of raising children ("It's way beyond anything that's gone on for me before") and the dancer's ("I felt like my own life was over") reflect opposite extremes. For most of us, however, the capacity for self-transcendence is not an either-or proposition that defines our compromises in love exclusively as enhancements or as sacrifices. Usually our feelings are more mixed.

In the optimal case, the empathy and identification at the heart of self-transcendence shift the balance toward self-enhancement and away from feelings of painful sacrifice and loss. When our own identity has expanded to include our partner, then our partner's experience becomes as important as our own. To the extent that we empathize and identify—that is, "feel along with" and "feel one with" our partner—then sacrifice may not be sacrifice.

When we care for a partner who is ill, for example, is this a sacrifice? And when we do our best to take care of ourselves when we're ill, is this a sacrifice? The point is that self-transcendence can promote a feeling of "we," a feeling of oneness, so compelling that it places the needs of the couple and of our partner on a par with our own. When we possess such a feeling, the choices we make in deference to our partner's needs are made freely and naturally, rather than out of a sense of duty, obligation, or guilt.

On the other hand, conflicts of interest always arise in a long-term love relationship. Self-transcendence can enable us to feel one with our partner, but not steadily: at times partners will invariably find themselves on opposite sides of the fence. In these instances, the awareness of the *possibility* of self-transcendence may take the edge off the struggle, as Helen, whose reflection began this chapter, tells us:

> There are times when I don't *want* to put myself in Leonard's place. I don't want to make room for him. But I also know we're better off together when we stretch to accommodate each other. As we've done that over the years, it's gotten easier. There's the feeling now that we've built something together . . . But I've also got to have the freedom to complain. There has to be lots of room to bitch and moan. . . . 'cause if you have resentment, you have resentment. There's no way around it.

Sometimes what looks from the outside like a sacrifice can also *feel* like a sacrifice. Striking a balance between our own needs and those of our partner, of the couple, or of the family is almost never easy. A well-developed capacity for self-transcendence, however, can make this balance a great deal easier to find.

INTIMACY WITHOUT SELF-TRANSCENDENCE

A forty-four-year-old architect with three children, Tom has been married for nearly twenty years. He thinks of himself as realistic and reasonably happy. The experience he describes in his relationship is not an uncommon one:

> In the very best of times, I'm able to get pleasure from Annie's triumphs, but most of the time I'm in my own head. . . In terms of seeing things from her point of view, I get rare glimpses, and then it's really fun. . . the more I can get into her frame of mind and see things from her point of view the more fun we have. But then there's the fear of being consumed or losing identity or giving it up. . .
>
> I think there's less empathy as time goes on. You think you already know someone, so you don't make as much effort to know them better. This is my experience anyway, and also my parents'. . . Sometimes I feel guilty about it and sad. . . But sometimes I feel like, Oh well, that's just the way things are. . .

Once you have kids, it's mostly figuring out the strategic issues and making sure we're taking care of the basics, so it's a lot of practical stuff, practical compromises.

For many of us, self-transcendence through empathy and identification is an ideal; for others it is a fiction of questionable value. Like Tom, we may have joined our partner in taking on the challenges and pleasures of a shared commitment. But while it may be deeply satisfying, the experience of raising children—or of any other joint project or practice—does not require, nor does it guarantee, that our capacity for self-transcendence will be engaged. Unfortunately, many relationships, perhaps even the majority, succeed or fail without the benefit of this capacity.

If we have difficulty transcending the boundaries of the self, or if our partner does, then the intimacy of love's third phase can have a superficial quality. We may find ourselves committed to a relationship that lacks passionate involvement. We may feel a frustrated longing for common ground that seems impossible to locate. More and more, our partner's interests and values may diverge from our own. We may begin to feel that we're going through the motions. Or we may find ourselves entrapped in endless competition or battles for control.

Partners with a limited capacity for self-transcendence are less likely to successfully weather the ordinary crises of adult development. Frustrations within the relationship may provoke affairs. Major shifts in work or lifestyle are more likely to result in separation or divorce. The couple struggling with infertility may be unable to generate a comparable involvement to take the place of the longed-for child. While the capacity for self-transcendence certainly offers no guarantees, it helps us to cope with the stressful changes, planned and unforeseen, that can place a relationship in jeopardy.

Intimacy without self-transcendence may keep the structure of a love relationship intact—but without the passionate involvement, the emotional overlap, that fosters the deepest growth and personal fulfillment.

THE BARRIERS TO SELF-TRANSCENDENCE

For most of us in intimate relationships, the capacity for self-transcendence waxes and wanes. Once the conditions for its emergence have been met, the capacity can be awakened. There will be times when we feel one with our partner; our destinies seem irrevocably joined and we can act on our partner's behalf as easily as we act on our own. But then, unexpectedly and often inexplicably, we may find ourselves again feeling divided from our partner, burdened with the awareness of our divergent natures and conflicting needs. Like a muse that comes and goes, the capacity for self-transcendence graces our love less steadily than we'd like.

These fluctuations in our ability to empathize and identify are no mystery, however. They can be understood in terms of three distinct influences. First, limitations in one or more of the prior five capacities can inhibit the capacity for self-transcendence. Second, our culture's idealized and devalued images of love can be a barrier to the self-transcendence that is part of real love. Third, the problematic fit between two partners can set up obstacles to self-transcendence.

Self-Transcendence When
Earlier Capacities Are Vulnerable

If we're not entirely confident in our ability to swim and we find ourselves in deep water, our stroke can become uneven and, in a panic, we may head for shore. This is roughly the situation we confront at a psychological level during the third stage of intimacy. Emotionally speaking, the water is deeper now and we can be overcome or panicked by feelings associated with the capacities we haven't fully mastered.

Suppose, for example, that we have problems with merging. As a rule, these will be manifest either in merger wariness or merger hunger. Tom, the married architect with three children, has revealed that his problems with self-transcendence in relation to his wife Annie are associated with merger wariness: "The more I can get into her frame of mind and see things from her point of view the more fun we have. But then there's the fear of being consumed or losing identity or giving it up. . . ." In contrast, the experience of Danielle, a singer in her late thirties, married without children, illustrates the impact of merger hunger on the capacity for self-transcendence:

> I'm a little too good at putting myself in the other guy's place. I think if I'd been less empathetic I'd only have stayed with my first husband for five years instead of ten. . . My own ambitions get kind of submerged in the other person because the relationship's so important to me. Only then I get resentful and eventually I'm out of there.

A limited capacity for integration can also undermine self-transcendence. The either-or thinking associated with poorly developed integration makes reciprocity and collaboration very difficult. One husband described his wife's problem with integration in this way:

> Junie makes a joke of it, you know: "It's my way or the highway" is what she says. . .but she acts like she means it. She can't get with the idea of "our way." The other thing is that when we have a fight, it seems to put the whole relationship in jeopardy, at least in her mind. My feeling is more, we're going through ups and downs and that's just how it is. . . her attitude makes it tough. . . I feel like I can see things from her side sometimes, but she can't seem to see things from my side.

If one capacity compromises self-transcendence more frequently than any other, it is our capacity for refinding. As we enter the third phase of intimacy, it is nearly impossible to avoid a reencounter with the past, particularly if the relationship with our partner involves marriage and children. The unfinished emotional business associated with our first family experience almost always reemerges when, once again, we find ourselves living in a family.

Ron and Joan had their first child in their late thirties. After his son's birth, the intensity of Ron's feelings took him by surprise:

Sex took on this momentous significance once we were trying to conceive. We were creating our future together and it felt thrilling and very close, but it was also scary...Then when Josh was born, I remember looking into his eyes and most of that fear dissolved...in the amazement of having a son, my own son...I was filled with a kind of love I'd never felt before...Holding him that first day, I felt so complete...But then a few days later I got very scared again...I had this feeling that was sort of ominous really, that who I was before Joshua was born, I would never be again...I only had an inkling of this when Joan was pregnant...And now the reality of it...shocked me. I felt overwhelmed.

Even though the birth of their son was a well-planned, long-awaited event, Ron was utterly unprepared for its emotional impact and its effect upon his marriage. That Josh was a colicky baby left both parents feeling frayed with lack of sleep. But whereas Joan seemed to be nourished by her bonding with Josh, Ron found his initial euphoria replaced with a troubling perception of his son as an intruder into his marriage.

Alongside his own deep love for Josh, Ron also felt that he had somehow lost his wife to the baby. He hated this feeling but couldn't escape it. He was tormented by his ambivalent emotions. He wanted very much to be a good father, but he was angry at feeling displaced by his son. He also felt inadequate as he compared his performance as a parent with his wife's. Her mothering seemed natural and unforced, and her bond with Josh seemed effortless. Ron was deeply ashamed of all these feelings and did his best to hide them. Before Josh was six months old, Ron was finding reasons to spend more and more time away from home. He sought refuge in work, exaggerating his role as the primary breadwinner to justify his withdrawal from his wife and son. When Joan wanted to make love, Ron could hardly maintain an erection. Shortly after Josh's first birthday, the distance between Ron and Joan became so unbearable, and the deterioration of their sex life so undeniable, that they sought therapy.

In therapy, Ron came to understand how the birth of his son had provoked the reemergence of buried childhood feelings about another, earlier birth. When Ron was five, his brother had been born. Feeling painfully displaced at that time, Ron had suffered a number of simultaneous losses including the loss of his status as the revered "only child," the loss of his grandparents' special attention, and most acutely, the loss of his mother's exclusive love for him. He remembered his rage at his brother and his effort to talk to his mother, which seemed only to provoke her impatience at his jealousy of the new baby. These childhood events had left Ron feeling devastated. Now, years later, with the birth of his son, Ron's grief, rage, and sense of betrayal were all refound with his wife. And this painful refinding made it temporarily impossible for him to exercise his capacity for self-transcendence.

When Joan became aware of the depth of her husband's old and new pain, she was able to empathize with him in a way that his mother had not. This enabled him not only to reexperience the past but also to reexperience it with a difference—and to grieve. The healing combination of his wife's empathy, his own insight, and his grieving permitted Ron to feel like a husband and father again. Grappling successfully with the crisis of unresolved refinding freed Ron to experience a strengthened feeling of oneness with Joan. Fortunately, the same crises that provoke our awareness of limitations in one capacity or another can also provide us with opportunities for mastery.

Self-Transcendence and Culture's Conventional Imagery of Love

All of us are affected by our culture's imagery of men and women in love. As we marry or "settle down," we tend to be increasingly influenced by the social norms and expectations that express the conventional values of the culture. While the force of conventionality can contribute, at times, to keeping relationships afloat, the culture's idealized and devalued images of love can also act as obstacles to self-transcendence.

Idealized images of love glamorize the rewards of relationship and downplay its difficulties. These images are seductive, but when we compare the reality of our own relationship to the ideal, the glamorous images usually wind up casting our own experience in a very unflattering light. If we are too much under the sway of these unrealizable ideal images, we may react in ways that work against the empathy and identification central to self-transcendence. When the cultural ideal becomes our own ideal, it encourages at once an overabsorption in ourselves and a lack of respect for ourselves as we are—both of which can compromise our capacity to be *with* our partner. Feeling that we fall short of the ideal, we may too easily blame ourselves and hide. Or we may blame our partner and withdraw. Or, denying the reality and importance of our actual experience, we may lose ourselves—or our relationship—in the vain struggle to live up to the ideal. Couples can be driven apart by their efforts to "keep up with the Joneses" or to maintain a harmony more fictitious than real.

Like the conventionally idealized images, our culture's devalued images of men and women in love also discourage empathy and identification. These images stereotype women as dependent, sexually passive, and so on; they stereotype men as indifferent, sexually obsessed, or exploitative, and so on. To the extent that we are unable to free ourselves from dependence on these sorts of images, our impulses to "feel along with" and to "feel one with" our partner will be inhibited.

Self-Transcendence When the Fit between Partners Is Problematic

The fit between two partners can be less than optimal in a number of ways: The particular characteristics of the partners' personalities can be poorly matched. The unfolding of their psychological development can be discontinuous. Or their timing can simply be off.

The Partners' Personalities

One of the rewards of self-transcendence is personal growth. We choose our partners for many different reasons, among which is our intuitive recognition that our partner possesses, in a more developed form, crucial qualities that are only nascent in ourselves. We are instinctively aware that identifying with these qualities in our partner can help make them our own.

This potential for identification is something that Roxanne feels is frustratingly absent in her decade-long relationship with her husband:

> Brad and I both feel like we're too similar. . .looking at each other is like we're looking into the mirror, maybe because we met when we were so young and developed along the same lines. . .We're good where we're strong together. . .but the way other couples support each other in the areas where the other one is weak, we don't do that. It's more the opposite where his weak points and mine get into kind of a vicious cycle. . . He feels insecure which makes me feel insecure which makes him feel lousy and it just gets worse. . .with Brad, it's so frustrating because I feel he has nothing to teach me. Which is his feeling about me too. We love each other to death, but it's the blind leading the blind.

The Partners' Psychological Development

Self-transcendence takes two. If at a certain point in a couple's relationship, one partner is capable of empathy and identification while the other is not, the possibilities for self-transcendence will be very limited. Recall how the birth of Ron and Joan's son became a wedge between them, rather than an opportunity to heighten their feeling of shared identity. Joan appeared to be capable of enlarging her sense of self to include her husband and her child, while Ron's psychological development had temporarily stalled in the cul-de-sac of refinding: his development lagged behind hers. Such discontinuities can trigger defensive collisions or collusions that must be resolved if the couple's potential for self-transcendence is to be realized.

Timing

Timing isn't everything, but it is significant. Whether the issue is intimacy, career, or family, each of us functions according to his or her own timetable. Our priorities concerning what we wish to do and when we wish to do it may or may not coincide with the priorities of our partner. Perhaps the most common conflict arises around the timing of family. Both partners may have the desire for children, but one partner may feel readier to begin a family than the other. Obviously, partners who are out of synch will have to contend with their differences. Barring a shared solution that genuinely takes both partners' needs and desires into account, joint activation of the capacity for self-transcendence is impossible.

Even when the fit between two partners is very good, there will be conflicts to resolve. Our vision of a shared future may duplicate our partner's, yet when it comes to living out the details there are usually significant differences that emerge. We may both want a child, for example, but find ourselves at loggerheads about how to parent once the child is born. If the sense of shared identity associated with self-transcendence is to persist through such conflicts, partners must continue to strengthen their ability to collaborate.

SELF-TRANSCENDENCE AND COLLABORATION

Collaboration is the way out of the collusions and collisions that either conceal or reveal the conflicts that come up between two separate human beings attempting to mingle their lives. Collaboration facilitates self-transcendence and self-transcendence facilitates collaboration.

"What about 'we'?" one woman said to her husband, with some exasperation. "You're not letting me in, you're not letting me help you. You say, 'I this' and 'I that.' What about 'we'?" Her question redirected her husband's attention to the overlap between them, the shared identity and sense of purpose that self-transcendence implies. Her question made collaboration possible. And in the wake of renewed collaboration (involving talk, tears, then making love), his experience of empathy and identification with her was dramatically intensified.

This couple's interaction reflects one of those upward spirals that are always a potential in love. Here, a reminder of self-transcendence encouraged collaboration that fostered heightened self-transcendence. No reliable formulas exist to help us respond to the endlessly variable crises and dilemmas we face in love, yet there is a clue in this interaction. More often than not, the path out of the labyrinth is found collectively, if it is found at all. Partners fare best when they rely on the collectively generated wisdom of the couple, rather than the individual approach of one partner or the other. The synergy in couples can be their saving grace.

Especially when partners have committed themselves to a shared future (through, say, the decision to raise children), their individual solutions to joint problems are no longer viable. The whole *is* greater than the sum of the parts; more important, however, the whole can't survive unless the parts mold to each other and mesh. This theme runs consistently through the accounts of partners who have been together contentedly for many years. Tolstoy said all happy families are alike; the happily coupled, too, are alike, at least in their agreement on the necessity for what a man in one of these couples called "mutual modification":

The only way a relationship lasts over the long haul is if you're willing to take on aspects of your partner.

You have to find a balance of what you can get out of not living completely within the idea you had for yourself of who you are. When you accept that both of you have a right to a life and that things don't always work out as you want, you grow together in ways you don't expect to.

Our relationship works when we don't stay too circumscribed in our views of ourselves...especially old ones...We don't stay too locked in our previous ideas about what we will or won't do, what we will or won't give in on...Especially when things are tough, when I feel like I've just about had it... Right then it's about "kissing the frog," instead of wishing the frog was a prince.... Giving up my feelings about how Doug's supposed to be or how "things" are supposed to be.

Unless Adelle and I are willing to be changed by each other, we don't make it as a couple...otherwise we're too attached to our own ideas about how things should be...and this means we can't deal with change...The couples we know either change each other or they break apart...It's mutual modification. That's the explanation for what people talk about, when they say husbands and wives start to resemble each other as time passes. I don't know about physically, but definitely personality-wise.

A couple's collaboration can be a way out of their distress, but not necessarily or exclusively on the terms of each partner as an individual. The capacity for self-transcendence bolsters this kind of collaboration through strengthening the feeling of "we." This feeling can enable us as individuals to experience our accommodation in the relationship less as a sacrifice that benefits our partner and more as a compromise that meets our shared needs as a couple.

SELF-APPRAISAL: THREE PROFILES

Irene: Self-Transcendence as a Resource

Divorced nearly ten years ago, Irene now feels she has found a soul mate in her second husband, although earlier in their relationship she wondered whether they were going to make it at all. Irene had lived alone with her son from her first marriage for more than six years before she met and married Dennis, an English professor at the university where she worked as a librarian. Dennis had a nine-year-old daughter from a previous marriage, and for a time the challenge of blending the two families seemed insurmountable. The children got along badly with each other. They seemed to have nothing in common at first, except their shared ability to provoke fights between their newlywed parents.

In this crucible, however, Irene was eventually able to forge a powerful bond with Dennis. Both of them had originally fallen deeply in love with the other, both were in their late forties, and both had a determination to make their relationship work. After a period of months, during which the children had become more and more miserable, and Irene and Dennis were unable to extricate themselves from their own angry conflicts, the couple joined a group for stepparents. This group was no panacea, but it confirmed their intuition that the most important precondition for a cohesive family was a cohesive relationship between the parents.

In spite of her frustration, Irene was able to empathize with her husband's struggle to balance his conflicting loyalties to his daughter and Irene's son, to his old family and his new one. She was able to feel that his struggle was very much like her own— and that, in fact, their separate efforts to balance family loyalties were more usefully and truly viewed as *their* struggle, rather than her struggle or his. Dennis was touched by Irene's empathy and her ability to take a step back from her anger. He had seen his ex-wife as vengeful and unforgiving, and it moved him that Irene could continue to care for him even if he didn't take her side at every opportunity. Irene, in turn, was moved when Dennis, seemingly reading her mind, began initiating a separate relationship with her son, teaching him football and taking him to games. Irene's conflicts with her husband didn't cease at this point, but the intermittent capacity of both partners to empathize and be moved by the needs of the other helped cement the bond that was growing between them.

Irene's previous marriage had suffered when the birth of her son played a role in interrupting her sexual relationship with her husband at the time. Dennis, on the other hand, had had no such problem, because he had always made sexuality a priority. Now, in their new marriage, his commitment to preserving sexual passion came up against Irene's inhibitions. As long as she could remember, Irene had felt sexually shy and somewhat repressed. In addition, the guilt she experienced toward her son now made it difficult for her to keep the bedroom door closed to him. Over time, Irene began to identify with her husband's greater freedom to enjoy and to preserve sexuality, even in the face of the children's demands. Through this identification, she became gradually more comfortable with both her own sexuality and her limit setting with her son.

Michael: Self-Transcendence That Is Compromised

Michael is a forceful yet incongruously soft-spoken attorney who has just turned fifty. Shelley, his wife, is a lively and articulate woman who manages the office of the firm that Michael began nearly twenty years ago. Together they have raised two sons, both of whom are now away at college. On the surface Michael and Shelley appear to have thoroughly interlaced their lives and created a shared identity as a couple. For some time, however, there has been a lack of reciprocity in their relationship that reflects Michael's problems with self-transcendence. Two years ago this lack of reciprocity led Shelley to threaten Michael with a separation.

When communicating about their shared experience, Shelley commonly talks about what "we" did, while Michael usually refers to what he did, or she did, as if together they'd actually done very little. This habit of speech of his strikes an especially discordant note when the two of them are side by side, talking with someone else. Almost as if Shelley weren't there, Michael typically fixes his gaze on the third party; then, recounting a shared family experience, he refers to Shelley as "her," rather than including his wife in the conversation by using the pronoun *you* or calling her by name. Meanwhile, she continues to talk in terms of "we."

For years Shelley privately upbraided her husband for what she calls this "verbal tic" of his. While she loved and admired him, and appreciated his devotion to her, she also complained about his inability to take her seriously and his rigid unwillingness to yield control. Not until her dissatisfaction threatened to jeopardize their marriage, however, did Michael really begin to question his role in their relationship.

He had a suspicion that his general style of being with people was outdated and, perhaps, problematic. He knew he derived a sense of security from playing what he saw as the conventional masculine role; at the same time, he was ashamed when the authoritarian aspects of this role were exposed in relation to his wife or sons. Michael felt torn. His guilt, his love for Shelley, and his fear of losing her all motivated him to "stretch" emotionally: he wanted to be able to accommodate and extend his empathy to her. Yet he felt trapped by habits that, in his words, were "bred into him." He came from a family with a long military tradition. And although he had rebelled against his father, an autocratic Marine colonel, it felt threatening for him to abandon family traits that seemed to have become part of his character.

Though it went against the grain, Michael agreed to Shelley's suggestion that they try and work through their difficulties with the help of a therapist. Eventually Michael was able to see that his irrational fear of losing control stood in the way of realizing his desires. Looking back on his marriage, he was clear that the periods he had enjoyed most intensely were the periods of greatest closeness with Shelley. This closeness usually came when he was able to *join* with her, either sexually or around the commitment they shared to their sons. Yet the same closeness also made him uneasy because it threatened his sense of control. Gradually Michael has developed more of an ability to pay attention to the closeness he wants, rather than the loss of control he fears. And with this shift has come a heightened capacity to experience and enjoy the feeling of "we" that he now shares, more and more comfortably, with his wife.

Jessica: Self-Transcendence as a Struggle

A highly creative television producer, Jessica has had two lengthy but disappointing marriages. Now in her mid-forties, Jessica projects an attitude of ironic amusement about romantic love. But when she talks about her own past relationships, she simply sounds bitter. Jessica now lives with a man who has recently said he is falling in love with her. She wishes she could continue to enjoy their relationship. But his love frightens her, more than she thinks it should. She wonders if her present fear can genuinely be justified by the betrayals she feels she's suffered in the past.

Jessica's first marriage, to her high school sweetheart, seemed full of promise for the first several years. But Rob wanted children, Jessica didn't, and their conflict gradually became more volatile and more corrosive. Jessica felt that Rob was threatened by her ambitions. She angrily interpreted his desire for children as a cover for his need to control her and keep her home. When a careless sexual encounter between the two of them left her pregnant, she arranged, against his wishes, to have an abortion. Several months later, Rob took steps to end the marriage, leaving Jessica feeling abandoned and enraged.

Like her first marriage, her second lasted for nearly seven years. Gavin was a music teacher and an aspiring composer with whom she began to live shortly after her separation. He was generous and nurturing, but a little too passive. Initially Jessica had felt relieved to be with a man who wasn't threatened by her strength and her aspirations. He appreciated her creativity and her commitment to her work, while Jessica felt satisfied to have joined her life to that of an artist. After several years, however, it became plain to her that he lacked the drive or talent to make a real career of his art. In addition she began to perceive him as more and more dependent: she experienced his needs as unwanted demands. She also found herself feeling critical of his sexuality: he was neither confident nor masterful enough for her to take him seriously in bed. When he became sexually withdrawn from her, she was briefly relieved but soon felt rejected. After discovering that he was having an affair, she became enraged. There was a brief, unsuccessful effort to reconcile; then Gavin left her. Once more she felt abandoned. She resolved never again to make herself so vulnerable.

Before long, however, Jessica's loneliness led to her present live-in arrangement, which she disparagingly refers to as a "relationship of convenience." Frank is an airline pilot in his late forties whose work keeps him away one week out of three. She describes him as aggressive and literate, passionate about flying and the theater. From Jessica's point of view, the relationship between them initially worked because their expectations were so low. But recently, when Frank said that he was falling in love with her, she found herself feeling threatened—as much by his affection as by the possibility of losing him if she couldn't respond in kind.

Jessica's three major relationships all reflect her difficulties with various aspects of self-transcendence. Empathy is particularly problematic for her. When Jessica becomes aware of the feelings or needs of someone she is close to, she feels threatened with the loss of her autonomy. Rob's needs and Gavin's were a threat to her, and so apparently are Frank's. Lacking a solid, separate sense of self, the experience of "we" is a dangerous one for her. And yet she is drawn to relationships because the incompleteness of her sense of self makes it difficult for her to be alone.

Passionate Love as a Journey of Transformation

> To love is good, too; love being
> difficult. For one human being to love
> another: that is perhaps the most
> difficult of all our tasks, the ultimate,
> the last test and proof, the work for
> which all other work is but preparation.
> —Rainer Maria Rilke

*L*ove is a journey that has the potential to transform us. Along the way, each of us is guided by our own inner map of the terrain of the heart. As a love relationship evolves and the journey proceeds, new experiences of intimacy can evoke our deepest wishes and fears and bring to the surface some of the least accessible aspects of our identity. In these intimate encounters, there is sometimes a troubling inconsistency between our current experience with our partner and the timeless imagery of our inner map. Love can indeed transform us, but not always without pain.

Erica (see Chapter One) describes having an ecstatic orgasm with her husband and finding herself overcome with...tears:

> When I feel Matt inside me, and we've both come, we're so close it almost feels like one person, like we're one person.

But I know he's going to pull away in a minute. . .we're going to be separate again. And all this stirs up the most intense feelings in me: love and gratitude. . .but also longing and pain because I know that this feeling of *completeness* can't last. . .it'll happen again, at least I hope so, but it'll never last. And memories of my mother get stirred up and folded into this whole thing somehow: not memories, feelings really, of being so close to her. . .and then not being close. . .Most of the time when I feel this way in bed I don't cry, I just push it away, it's too overwhelming. Even talking about it, I get tearful again.

Erica experiences tears of gratitude because her loving closeness to her husband is so good. But the very goodness of it brings her into contact with two internal images that lead to further tears. There is her image of the past oneness with her mother that she has lost but still longs for. There is also an idealized image of the merging she yearns for with her husband—and the disappointment that, even in this most intimate relationship of adulthood, the old oneness can never be completely restored. Her tears express her grief over the loss of both a perfect past (in which she felt one with her mother) and a perfect future (in which this oneness might be permanently revived). Evoked by a moment of communion with her husband, her tears of grief—however painful—are also healing. For it is only when we grieve our unfulfillable longings, and grow to accept them, that real fulfillment in love becomes possible.

Like Erica, we may find ourselves unexpectedly, and sometimes inexplicably, saddened by experiences of intense intimacy. Often such experiences have made possible a profound connection not only with our partner but also with the world of relationships *inside* us: the living images of ourselves and others that compose the inner map. Our sadness arises when the reality of these internal images is inconsistent with the external reality of our relationship. Erica's hope of perfect merging, for example, was inconsistent with the reality of her usual feelings of separateness from her husband, and this saddened her.

The image inside may be "better" than the image of our current relationship, or it may be "worse." But in either case, the inconsistency must be resolved. Usually this occurs in one of two ways. Either the map must be transformed to accommodate the current experience—or, through our defenses, we must find a way to bring our current experience into line with the imagery of the inner map.

When we can relinquish our attachment to a particular image, we transform the map and we transform ourselves. To let go of an internal image, however, we must be able to mourn its loss— for our emotional attachment to the image inside us can be as strong as our feeling for the relationship it represents. Listen to Sam (Chapter Three) describe the struggle between his wish to accept his girlfriend's love and his fear of losing (and grieving) an internal image of his parents:

> It's so easy for me to experience the relationship with Janie as dangerous, instead of just letting her love me. And at the same time, I know the danger's as close as my own mind. . . . it's not the real relationship with Janie that's dangerous. But I guess I'd rather see it that way. I'd rather play out the "Don't hurt me, I'll be real nice, then maybe you'll love me" story which is the one I played out with my parents, rather than just giving up on the hope of their loving me. . . It's embarrassing to admit it, but I still want to say to them, "Can't you please love me?" God, it's hard to give up that hope.

The fact that Sam's yearning to be loved is experienced in relation to parents who died long ago only underscores the key point here: It is not our *actual* relationships with our parents (or others) that we need to relinquish and mourn in order to love. Instead, it is the images inside us that *represent* those relationships we need to come to terms with, for these images have an emotional life of their own.

When Sam is loved by his girlfriend today, he confronts the contrast between past and present that makes his childhood image of being unloved by his parents all the more painful. The same contrast undermines the credibility of his old image as a guide to what he can expect from an intimate relationship. Now Sam is forced to struggle with two alternatives: he can mourn the old image or he can defend against mourning. If only he could tolerate his grief at not feeling loved by his parents, he could more easily allow himself to feel loved by his girlfriend. But the grief is apparently so threatening that he must protect himself by deciding that the "dangerous" present is no better than the past. By erasing the tension between past and present, he sidesteps the need to let go of the old image—and mourning is averted.

But as the psychoanalyst Mardi Horowitz has written, "Mourning is not heartbreak, it prevents the heart from being broken." Unless we grieve, and let go of certain aspects of the world within us, the development of our capacity to love is stalled. For the power of love to transform us, we must grieve both the problematic love of the past and our unrealizable hopes for ideal love in the present and future.

Refinding guarantees that those of us who fail to mourn the painful past will be condemned to repeat it. Mourning and letting go are inoculations against the compulsion to repeat. To free ourselves from the inhibiting influence of the past, we must experience our sadness over hurts and disappointments that can never be mended.

A common refuge from the painful past is the hope for a splendid future. When past love has been painful, it can generate images of idealized or even perfect love to comfort and compensate us. Unfortunately, these illusory images of perfection undermine our capacity to enjoy the actual comforts of real but imperfect love. Even when our expectations of love are so grandiose that they invariably lead to disappointment, they may be difficult to relinquish. For the more we feel our past has cheated us, the greater the compensation we feel entitled to in the future.

Love's endless task is to find a dynamic balance between our hopes, fantasies, and ideals on the one hand and the reality of what we can actually achieve in love on the other. Each time we let go of what love is not, we enable ourselves to experience a higher level of acceptance and fulfillment. Reconciling wishes and realities in this way is never a "one-time-only" event, however. In light of our changing needs and desires during the three stages of intimacy, we will recurrently confront our relationship's potentials and its limitations.

Becoming a couple, having children, or taking on shared projects that transcend the boundaries of the self can trigger a need to "rebalance the equation" between our inner fantasies and ideals and the actual reality of our experience. Sometimes this process is also triggered by the shock of unforeseen life events. An unexpected illness, an accident, or the death of a parent, may focus or intensify our appreciation of our partner. In such instances, our defenses melt away and we can realize the depth of our love and gratitude. No longer struggling with the past or future, we can allow ourselves to fully experience here-and-now all the passion and tenderness we feel for our partner. Episodes of crisis heighten our appreciation by thrusting us into the present moment, into external reality. These episodes temporarily weaken the hold on our hearts of our internal images and, in so doing, reveal the ongoing power of these images to inhibit our capacity to love.

The recognition that love can transform us—but only if we are willing to bear the pain of unfulfillable longing—is part of a specific attitude that helps make tender and passionate relationships possible. Along with an acceptance of mourning, this loving attitude includes compassion, flexibility, balance, perseverance, and the willingness to take risks. These are qualities to aspire to. Taken together, they make up a "realistic ideal" that can both orient and inspire us in our intimate relationships.

COMPASSION. Empathy and compassion are closely related. Both involve feeling *with* another person, but compassion adds to empathy the desire to succor or protect. Ideally, we have compassion for ourselves as well as for our partner. Seeing ourselves more clearly, and acquiring a more complex understanding of why we are who we are, compels a deeper compassion for our conflicts and consequent life choices. Having compassion does not distort what we see but rather enables a soothing acceptance of who we are and what we need to do. Similarly, compassion lets us accept the missteps and vulnerabilities of our partner with empathic understanding.

Compassion is also a crucial element in working through defensive collisions and collusions. As the details of a particular pattern of interpersonal defense come to light, compassion helps rein in the impulse to blame our partner or blame ourselves. When we are able to communicate our compassion for the feelings and point of view of our beloved, he or she may follow suit, setting the stage for healing and change. Without the direct and open expression of compassion, relationships can feel cool and distant, and the best of intentions may not be received as sincere.

FLEXIBILITY. Sexual flexibility is a way of both altering troublesome inhibitions and expanding sexual horizons. Beyond sexuality, flexibility is the freedom to experiment; it is an antidote to fixed roles in which, for example, one partner feels comfortable only as the caregiver, while the other can only be taken care of. To the extent that we're flexible, we can reverse roles and familiarize ourselves with both sides of the various interactions that are part of an intimate relationship. In this way, flexibility can enhance our empathy for our partner. It can also free us to explore alternative ways of behaving, to engage in trial-and-error learning to see what works. When our usual styles of self-protection result in problematic collusions or collisions, flexibility lets us try new modes of defense. Using "one leads, the other follows" to flexibly experiment with new behavior broadens our opportunities for learning and increases the likelihood of success in love.

BALANCE. Seeking an equilibrium between our needs and expectations and those of our partner serves us well in love. With an attitude of balance, we can expect that there will be times in which our wildest and best expectations will be met, and that there will also be times of great conflict, disappointment, and uncertainty. Without nullifying our experience of either emotional extreme, we can seek the middle ground, within ourselves and in the relationship. The capacity for integration is pivotal in developing an attitude of balance, which accepts that a lasting love involves compromise, and that not all compromises will immediately meet the conditions of parity. The empathy and identification at the heart of self-transcendence facilitate balance naturally by enabling us to put the needs of our partner, and of the relationship, on a par with our own.

Having distinct strengths in a few capacities can be empowering, but with an attitude of balance we also strive to develop those areas of ourselves in which we experience feelings of pain or inadequacy. Our awareness of our vulnerabilities prompts our efforts to grow. Sometimes we choose a partner whose strongest capacities are the very ones in which we feel weak—and our partner's example and encouragement stimulate our own development.[1]

Balance also entails a healthy skepticism about our own feelings and perceptions, in relation to those of our partner. We never assume that we are completely right or that our point of view is the only correct one. One of the most powerful ways in which intimate relationships enhance personal development is through our partner's ability to challenge our most basic assumptions. Our beloved can get under our skin, sensitizing us to aspects of ourselves from which we ordinarily hide. Without assuming that our partner's assessment of us is infallible, we're nonetheless willing to value and seriously consider what he or she has to say. This aspect of balance is crucial to the collaborations with our partner that resolve defensive collusions or collisions.

PERSEVERENCE. In love, perseverence furthers. Patience and persistence help us grapple with both our own and our partner's difficult feelings and needs as the journey of love unfolds. As psychotherapists, we have repeatedly seen those lovers who give up prematurely fail. This is not to imply that every love relationship should remain intact, but rather that too many disintegrate

---

1. The risk here is in choosing a partner mainly on the basis of what we feel we lack in ourselves. Over time, this sort of choice, though it arises out of admiration, can lead to envy and resentment.

because one or both partners are unwilling to persevere through the challenges and disappointments inherent in long-term romantic involvements. Perseverence helps us through the waning of idealization and the anxieties associated with painful refinding. With a persevering attitude, we can keep the bigger picture in mind, stretching our experience of time during a crisis. Without having to reach a decision or draw a conclusion "in the moment," we can step back from conflict, perhaps viewing it later from a fresh perspective. With perseverence, we're less likely to take our immediate experience of our partner at face value. We have the opportunity to learn that "trusting our feelings" can sometimes lead us to conclusions that are untrustworthy.

RISK-TAKING. To move beyond familiar and problematic styles of relating, we need the courage to take risks. Insight alone does not produce change: we must also be willing to initiate new modes of behaving and communicating. To bring passion and tenderness together in a lasting way requires the initiative to take risks during each of the three phases of intimacy.

Falling in love invites us to risk allowing another person to become deeply important to us. To the extent that idealization enables us to feel we have found our romantic ideal in our potential partner, the emotional stakes are very high. If our love is reciprocated fully, we feel that our hopes may be realized; if it is not, the impact not only on our hopes but also on our self-esteem may be devastating. To the extent that merging occurs, we also become more dependent upon our partner and more self-revealing. And with a healthy capacity for erotic involvement, we make our partner the focus of our sexual desire. When we fall in love, we take the risk—in the face of the uncertain future—of placing many of our deepest needs and aspirations in the cradle of the newly forming couple.

As we move into the second stage of intimacy, we struggle to come to terms with the relationship's shortcomings, as well as the emotional undercurrents we encounter as love deepens. Here it's necessary to take the risks sufficient to test the real potential of the relationship: the risks of grappling with our own flaws and our partner's now that the spell of idealization is broken—and the risks associated with refinding. To prevail through this phase of love, we must have the courage to explore all the dimensions of being a partner in this particular couple, while maintaining the freedom to end the relationship if it becomes too painfully problematic.

Perhaps the greatest initiative we take in love is that which marks the third stage of intimacy. When we're convinced that the love we're giving and receiving is real and reliable, we feel safe enough to risk those joint undertakings (such as child rearing) that require a lifelong commitment. Now we're willing to merge our lives in new ways. At this stage we must also ensure that the passions of love are not extinguished by the conventional routines of everyday living. To preserve sexual excitement and the special intimacy of the couple, it's essential to initiate shared experiences that aren't necessarily the norm, that are challenging, stimulating, and, yes, romantic.

RECONCILIATION: DISSOLVING OBSTACLES TO THE USE OF THE SIX CAPACITIES

When we cultivate an attitude that reflects the collection of qualities described above, the committed or marital relationship can be a powerful context for both deepening intimacy and transforming ourselves as individuals. Paradoxically, the conflicts between us as partners in love can provide the strongest impetus for this kind of growth. But our conflicts enable us to grow only if we are also able to reconcile. So long as our (overt or hidden) conflicts keep us estranged, they constrict our capacity to love. In contrast, once we reach some level of reconciliation, we love with a freer energy and a more open heart.

Ambivalence, unfulfilled longings, and incompatible desires are inevitably part of long-term relationships. Passionate love is not unconditional love. In the end, its future rests on the hard-won ability of two partners to forgive themselves and to forgive one another. Ultimately reconciliation enables Eros, the force of love that draws partners together, to prevail over aggression. As the psychoanalyst Otto Kernberg has written:

> Authentic forgiveness is an expression of a mature sense of morality, an acceptance of the pain that comes with the loss of illusions about self and other, faith in the possibility of recovery of trust, the possibility that love will be recreated and maintained alive in spite of and beyond its aggressive components.

When we are capable, again and again, of facing our conflicts with our partner and reconciling, we learn as individuals to trust more deeply. The tension and release of conflict and reconciliation keeps passion alive—and deepens our concern and appreciation for our partner and for the life we share. Reconciliation restores our freedom to make use of the six capacities and lets us make our way—sometimes stumbling, sometimes soaring—on love's journey.

BIBLIOGRAPHY

Barthes, Roland. 1978. *A Lover's Discourse*. New York: Hill and Wang.

Benjamin, Jessica. 1988. *The Bonds of Love*. New York: Pantheon Books.

Bergmann, Martin S. 1987. *The Anatomy of Loving*. New York: Columbia University Press.

Boszormenyi-Nagy, I., and Spark, G. 1973. *Invisible Loyalties*. New York: Harper and Row.

Boszormenyi-Nagy, I., and Framo, J., eds. 1965. *Intensive Family Therapy*. New York: Harper and Row.

Chodorow, Nancy. 1978. *The Reproduction of Mothering: Psychoanalysis and the Sociology of Gender*. Berkeley: University of California Press.

Eliot, T. S. 1980. "Four Quartets." In *The Complete Poems and Plays*. New York: Harcourt, Brace, Jovanovich.

Framo, J. L. 1980. Foreword to *Family Therapy: Combining Psychodynamic and Family Systems Approaches*, eds. J. K. Pearce and J. L. Friedman. New York: Grune & Stratton.

Freud, S. 1981. *The Standard Edition of the Complete Psychological Works*. Edited and translated by James Strachey. London: Hogarth Press; New York: W. W. Norton.

Gaylin, Willard, and Person, Ethel. 1988. *Passionate Attachments*. New York: The Free Press.

Goldbart, Stephen, and Wallin, David. 1990. "Mapping the Terrain of the Heart: Passion, Tenderness, and the Capacity to Love." *Tikkun*, 5 (2) (March/April 1990).

Greenson, Ralph. 1968. "Dis-identifying from Mother: Its Special Importance for the Boy." *International Journal of Psychoanalysis*, 49: 370–74.

Horowitz, Mardi J. 1990. "A Model of Mourning: Change in Schemas of Self and Other." *Journal of the American Psychoanalytic Association*, 38 (2): 297–324.

Huxley, Aldous. (1952) 1986. *The Devils of Loudun*. Reprint. New York: Carroll and Graf.

Kaplan, Helen Singer. 1974. *The New Sex Therapy*. New York: Brunner/ Mazel.

Kernberg, Otto. 1980. *Internal World and External Reality*. New York: Jason Aronson.

———. 1976. *Object Relations Theory and Clinical Psychoanalysis*. New York: Jason Aronson.

———. 1991. "Aggression and Love in the Relationship of the Couple." *Journal of the American Psychoanalytic Association*, 39 (1): 45–70.

———. 1993. "The Couple's Constructive and Destructive Superego Functions." *Journal of the American Psychoanalytic Association*, 41 (3): 653–77.

———. 1991. "Sadomasochism, Sexual Excitement, and Perversion." *Journal of the American Psychoanalytic Association*, 39 (2): 333–62.

Kohut, H. 1971. *The Analysis of the Self*. New York: International Universities Press.

———. 1977. *The Restoration of the Self*. New York: International Universities Press.

Lawrence, D. H. 1970. *Phoenix II: Uncollected, Unpublished, and Other Prose Works by D. H. Lawrence*. Edited by Warren Roberts and Harry T. Moore. New York: Viking.

Mahler, M.; Pine, F.; and Bergman, A. 1975. *The Psychological Birth of the Human Infant*. New York: Basic Books.

Minuchin, S. 1974. *Families and Family Therapy*. Cambridge: Harvard University Press.

Mood, John J. L. 1975. *Rilke on Love and Other Difficulties: Translations and Considerations of Rainer Maria Rilke*. New York: W. W. Norton.

Ortega y Gasset, J. 1957. *On Love*. Translated by Tony Talbot. New York: Meridian Books.

Person, Ethel S. 1988. *Dreams of Love and Fateful Encounters: The Power of Romantic Passion*. New York: W. W. Norton.

Rubin, Lillian. 1983. *Intimate Strangers*. New York: Harper and Row.

Schnarch, D. M. 1991. *Constructing the Sexual Crucible: An Integration of Sexual and Marital Therapy*. New York: W. W. Norton.

Shabad, P. 1993. "Repetition and Incomplete Mourning: The Intergenerational Transmission of Traumatic Themes." *Psychoanalytic Psychology.* 10 (1): 61–75.

Shelley, Percy Bysshe. 1951. "Epipsychidion." In *The Selected Poetry and Prose of Percy Bysshe Shelley.* New York: Modern Library.

Stoller, Robert. 1980. *Sexual Excitement.* New York: Simon and Schuster.

Welwood, John, ed. 1985. *Challenge of the Heart: Love, Sex, and Intimacy in Changing Times.* Boston: Shambhala Publications, Inc.

Winnicott, C.; Shepherd, R.; and Davis, M. 1989. *Psychoanalytic Explorations: D. W. Winnicott.* Cambridge: Harvard University Press.

Winnicott, D. W. 1965. *The Maturational Process and the Facilitating Environment.* New York: International Universities Press.

INDEX